FEMINISMS IN THE CINEMA

FEMINISMS IN THE CINEMA

edited by
Laura Pietropaolo
and
Ada Testaferri

Indiana University Press
Bloomington and Indianapolis

Manufactured in the United States of America

Library of Congress Cataloging-in-Publication Data

Feminisms in the cinema / edited by Laura Pietropaolo
and Ada Testaferri.
p.   cm.
Papers presented at a conference held Nov. 1990 at
York University and other papers.
Includes index.
ISBN 0-253-34500-6 (alk. paper). — ISBN 0-253-20928-5
(pbk. : alk. paper)
1. Feminism and motion pictures—Congresses.   2. Women
in motion pictures—Congresses.   3. Feminist film criticism—
Congresses.   I. Pietropaolo, Laura.   II. Testaferri, Ada.
PN1995.9.W6F455   1995
791.43'082—dc20
94-17548

1 2 3 4 5   00 99 98 97 96 95

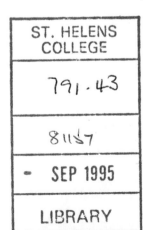

CONTENTS

Contents

ACKNOWLEDGMENTS

GIULIANA BRUNO, "Streetwalking around Plato's Cave," is reprinted from *Streetwalking on a Ruined Map*, © 1993 Princeton University Press.

Teresa de Lauretis, "On the Subject of Fantasy," is reprinted from *The Practice of Love: Lesbian Sexuality and Perverse Desire*, © 1994 Indiana University Press.

Judith Mayne, "A Parallax View of Lesbian Authorship," is reprinted from *Inside/Out*, edited by Diana Fuss, © 1991 Routledge, Chapman and Hall.

Laura Mulvey, "The Myth of Pandora: A Psychoanalytical Approach," is reprinted from *Sexuality and Space*, edited by Beatriz Colomina, © 1992 School of Architecture, Princeton University.

B. Ruby Rich, "An/Other View of New Latin American Cinema," has appeared in "Iris," No. 13, Summer 1991, © B. Ruby Rich.

Trinh T. Minh-ha, "'Who Is Speaking?' Of Nation, Community and First Person Interviews," is reprinted from *Framer Framed*, 1993, Routledge, Chapman and Hall, Trinh T. Minh-ha.

We would like to thank Telefilm Canada; the National Film Board of Canada; York University's Film Library; Dean Tom Traves, Faculty of Arts, York University; the Social Sciences and Humanities Research Council of Canada; and the Secretary of State, Multiculturalism for their support. Finally, our special thanks go to the following individuals who helped with the preparation of this text: Terry L. Cagle, Joan Catapano, Jack Ford, Richard Kidder, and Enrico Vicentini.

INTRODUCTION

Ada Testaferri

Fᴇᴍɪɴɪꜱᴍꜱ ɪɴ ᴛʜᴇ Cɪɴᴇᴍᴀ gathers a selection of papers read at the homonymous conference held at York University in November 1990 and a number of other articles commissioned by the editors for the purpose of forming a volume where the principal concern of each writer is the presentation of a position of marginality. While working against the dominance of mainstream discourses and phallocentric culture has been for a long time the grounding of contemporary feminism, in more recent years marginality has assumed a sociopolitical role within the framework of feminism in general and has become a political strategy to dismantle and challenge possible nuclei of established power within feminist thought itself.

Yet to present a comprehensive idea of the many differences within contemporary feminism would indeed be impossible. Nor is this the purpose of the present volume. What the editors intend to do here, by using "feminisms" in the plural, is rather to revisit some of the crucial questions traditionally raised by feminist research, and to propose them again from the perspective of simultaneity within different cultural and sociopolitical positions.

In more than one way the essays published here intersect each other, even though each writer was given total freedom in choosing her topic. Therefore, this volume presents a certain unity in the cross-referentiality of the issues discussed in spite of the different theoretical approaches and the diversified cultural background of the authors.

Besides comparing heterogeneous sociocultural backgrounds of writers from different countries and ethnicities, the editors intend to establish and measure the terms of mutual influence of feminist filmmakers and feminist theorists. At the conference this complementary juxtaposition of film theory and filmmaking was made evident especially through the screening of a number of feminist avant-garde films and of art cinema in general.

Cinema is an art form which more than any other crosses disciplinary boundaries and ties together the rather exclusive tendencies of creative discourses, such as art and philosophy, and the more inclusive tendencies of large technological phenomena, such as contemporary mass media and sociopolitical discourse. Furthermore, the notorious multidisciplinary nature of cinema and its simultaneous and pluralistic methods of distribution ensure its impact on large strata of the population and in fact its popularity. To study, therefore, the interaction between feminist film theorists and feminist filmmakers means to investigate the extent to which feminist thought penetrates and directly affects female as well as male social behavior and day-to-day reality.

During the conference a close dialogue was established between theorists and filmmakers, and, as can be seen in the present volume, some of the contributors indeed wear two hats, as they are at once directors and scholars.

Although the conference was not structured around given topics and was organized loosely around sections of formal readings of papers, round-table discussions, and film screenings, the editors of *Feminisms in the Cinema* thought it practical to gather the various articles which appear in the volume under a few general headings. These should not be taken as rigid categories, but should be seen rather as a formal device to highlight specific issues. As a matter of fact, it will be immediately apparent that many of the essays show a tendency to overlap. In most cases this is due to the nature of the problems discussed, which, although possibly requiring different solutions in accordance with the sociocultural position of the authors, reveal at the same time a clear path of connections. These link one topic to another and even generate, through the discussion of specific issues, the need to explore adjacent or derivative topics. Rather than a linear overview of past and present feminist research governed by the signs of a chronological as well as an epistemological sense of progression, *Feminisms in the Cinema* intends to further the knowledge of feminist phenomena by creating clusters of thought gathered around crucial nuclei of research and working from different viewpoints to uncover new ground and fill in the areas left out, or not sufficiently explored, by mainstream feminist research. This process of rethinking traditional issues by constantly shifting the position of the thinker suggests a progressive and multilateral expansion of the issues under consideration. Rather than formulating conclusive and all-comprising theories, contemporary feminisms point to the fact that no theory can be all-embracing and therefore all-conclusive. Even though our Einsteinian era, dominated as it is by the law of relativity, has generated the notion that knowledge can be neither absolute nor central, the characteristic of self-fragmentation and of the fragmentation of its field of investigation is specifically proper to contemporary feminism. While this is also a trait of postmodern critical methodologies, feminist thought pushes even further the deconstructive model of investigation by establishing a process of pertinent and constant questioning, not only of intercultural issues but also of its own conceptualization. And it does so, on the one hand, by promoting an intracultural investigation which allows an ever more ample knowledge of its own issues and, on the other hand, by restating that knowledge is always relative to and inscribed into well-defined sociocultural and historical limitations. While some people might be dissatisfied with an absence of conclusions, feminism's consistent questioning has given in fact many answers. Moreover, its continuous questioning of the validity of its own theorizing and its own practices makes contemporary feminism one of the most exciting phenomena of our times.

Feminisms in the Cinema is divided into four parts:

1. Modes of Identification and Representation;
2. The Role of Fantasy in Lesbian Representation and Spectatorship;
3. Inscribing Woman in Socio-Historical Contexts; and
4. Feminist Film Readings: Personal Politics/Social Politics.

Together with the demands for equal pay and for the equal rights to vote, the question of representation has been one of the longest fights sustained by feminists. Indeed, socioeconomic and political equity between genders is, at large, connected and interdependent with issues of representation.

Since the mid-seventies, Laura Mulvey has dealt with these issues and, more specifically, with the way women have been represented in traditional Hollywood cinema, where women's images are constructed by the male gaze as pleasurable spectacle. But for many years now, women, and more specifically feminists, have entered the world of cinema as subjects, that is to say, as producers of images.

While it is still reasonable to mistrust representation in general because it implicitly signifies the authoritative look of an active subject upon a possible object, one should welcome the works of women filmmakers, especially when they perform the reflexive act of looking at themselves, an act of representation which legitimately collapses the distance between subject and object.

In any other form, representation as such—that is, representation by others—must still be resisted at any cost as an act of violation directed toward a single person, as well as a specific group, or a race, or an entire sex. Yet most theories and discourses are necessarily linked with modes of representation. While representation should be resisted, it seems impossible to avoid it totally in the praxis of discourse.

In the seventies feminists fought representation with a sound political strategy; that is, they entered male ideologies and performed a series of acts of appropriation. In so doing, those feminists were able to unhinge dominant discourses and their power. This technique is still valid today as a device for the dismantling of the strongholds of any dominant discourse. With this in mind, *Feminisms in the Cinema* begins part I: "Modes of Identification and Representation." Laura Mulvey's article, "The Myth of Pandora: A Psychoanalytical Approach," is a classic statement about myth deconstruction and appropriation. In her investigation of the myth of Pandora, Laura Mulvey traces the topics of ambiguity connected to the images of the feminine from its Greco-Christian sources, through centuries of art and literature, up to modern cinema. Within the parameters of semiotics and psychoanalysis, Mulvey deconstructs the myth and proposes a feminist reading of Pandora and her box. The ambivalent signification of Pandora's box, a metonymic container of the feminine and, more specifically, a symbol of female genitalia, is but one of the myth's referents. Mulvey, in fact, points out that the container must be linked to the question of female curiosity. But even woman's cognitive capabilities and her desire for knowledge have had a long tradition of negative representations deriving from a series of cultural fetishistic displacements. In her reading of the myth, Mulvey transforms its negative connotations into positive and liberating forces. The act of transgression implicit in female curiosity has informed a male-centered semiotic system that has traditionally associated the female body with images of castration and death. But Mulvey, by underlining in the myth of Pandora woman's courage to look even into the forbidden, forges a new system of signs in which the female gaze is associated with an act of self-revelation and self-knowledge, an act constitutive of the subject.

Laura Mulvey's essay therefore opens up and indicates the way to reinterpret mythical discourse from a female point of view and, in so doing, points to "difference" as a matrix for the gendered discourses of our time. What is marginal here is female discourse at large, which in fact, in the case of the myth of Pandora, was, in its specificity of female discourse, simply not existent. Mulvey's article not only provides a defense against the distorted image of woman in the myth of Pandora but also constitutes a creative act generating a new myth. More important, it claims for women the right of self-representation. Appropriately, the two articles which follow—"Locating the Displaced View" and "Voices of the Grandmothers"—

deal with this right to self-representation and simultaneously with the problem of identification.

Midi Onodera's article is a brief account of her growth both as a person and as an artist. An Asian woman and a lesbian, she grew up in a middle-class neighborhood where she experienced discrimination mainly on account of her lesbianism. She describes her latest film, *The Displaced View*, as a search for her Japanese Canadian identity. Communication is a recurring theme in Midi Onodera's work, and in this film language functions as a means of connecting one Japanese generation to another as well as a means of separation from English-speaking audiences. In this way, Onodera claims her right to difference and identification in a cultural context dominated by a white majority.

Similarly, Métis filmmaker Christine Welsh discusses in her article her almost lifelong search for her own origins. Like Onodera, she grew up in a white, middle-class context and was made to learn, even within her family, to deny and repress her difference. Her recent work, *Women in the Shadows*, narrates her search for identity which eventually occurred through contacts with her female ancestors. In reconstructing their past, Welsh also gives an account of Native and Métis women's conditions in colonized Canada.

Both articles are representative of a pernicious process of marginalization, where the marginalized subjects are forced by the dominant culture to adopt a self-repressive pattern and even internalize their own reality. At first, identification with a minority is felt as a negative and undesirable feature. Interestingly enough, both Onodera and Welsh belong to middle-class families. In their case, class distinction worked at once as an apparently positive element of integration with the white, middle-class majority, and as an obvious instrument of repression through assimilation. Both were able ultimately to resist assimilation. These two examples point out, however, that class and social differences play an extremely important role in representation, a role that is definitely negative because of its presumption to liberalism and inclusion while, in fact, the cost of such inclusion is the partial elimination and indeed the denial of difference. This, simply stated, is the humanitarian liberalism that characterizes Western culture in general: "We are all equal, as long as you act like me."

Furthermore, the two articles show how the notion of margin is not finite, since the processes of marginalization can reproduce themselves even within already marginalized individuals. And so we ask: Is a Métis woman marginal to a white male? Is she marginal with respect to a white and/or Native woman? Is a lesbian identity more oppressed than the identity of a woman of color? The question is how to claim an identity in a society that creates a hierarchy of oppression.

Finally, the difficulties of representation, self-representation, and identification as an objective goal of the documentary genre are the topics of the interview-article by filmmaker and theoretician Trinh T. Minh-ha, who discusses her film *Surname Viet Given Name Nam*, a work that documents the condition of Vietnamese women both in Viet Nam and in the United States and which questions some basic premises of feminist speculation.

Traditional notions related to the constitution of the subject and the limits of its construction are rigorously examined by Trinh T. Minh-ha, whose film is precisely a denunciation of the criterion of objectivity supposedly proper to the documentary genre. She clearly demonstrates the fiction and therefore the preconstitution of the interviewed subject, of the interviewer, and of the director. The interviewed subject, she points out, is always conscious of its "representability" which is linked to a sense of identification intended as identification with a certain culture. In the specific case of the Vietnamese women interviewed in her film, this issue is indeed very problematic and in contrast with the general homogenous picture we have been given of Vietnamese culture. Through a series of temporal and spatial dislocations, Trinh T. Minh-ha's film focuses on the "multiple strategies of cultural identification," a complex pluralistic phenomenon which cannot be taken as a simplistic binary process; i.e., polarized and polarizing. The question of female identity is presented, rather, as a process of inclusions and exclusions, as a continuous dialogue with the "other," operated externally and internally.

The multi-voiced discussion of Trinh T. Minh-ha's film brings to the open the many constraints which characterize representation. Ultimately, even more than other texts examined here, the film points to the effect of representation on the female subjects, represented by stressing their expectations vis-à-vis their own sense of self, their own culture in general, the viewpoint of the film director, and, finally, the expectations of a given spectatorship. We can conclude, therefore, that the process of representation is itself elusive, and even that self-representation can be an illusory pursuit.

In "The Role of Fantasy in Lesbian Representation and Spectatorship," some of the issues discussed in part I are taken up again but are viewed more specifically from the marginalized position of the lesbian woman.

Teresa de Lauretis and Patricia White deal with the subject's identification of the lesbian spectator, a topic that has generally not received much attention because the assumption of many scholars who treat problems of spectatorship is that the main factor in the spectator's identification with the fictional character(s) of the film is gender.

In "On the Subject of Fantasy," Teresa de Lauretis extends the term "subject" beyond the traditional definitions given by psychoanalysis and feminist theory, because she says it implies necessarily also a social dimension. The "social subject" comprises various forms of sociocultural discourse, their practices and their modalities of representation. The relationship between subject and filmic fantasy is the basis upon which de Lauretis re-theorizes the "subject" matter. Through a reexamination of key texts by Freud, Laplanche and Pontalis, Jean Rivière, and the most recent neo-Freudian feminist theorists, de Lauretis demonstrates the fallacy behind the belief that every spectator can identify with any screen character. To prove the point, she analyzes two extremely subjective readings— one by E. Cowie, one by S. Cavell—of the same text, *Now Voyager* (1942). De Lauretis argues, moreover, that certain ambiguities in Cowie's article have generated a series of theoretical misconceptions.

Although it is pertinent to speak of a certain homology between the psychoanalytic subject of fantasy and the subject of the film's fantasy, one cannot ignore their intrinsic difference. It is necessary therefore to consider their "location," which is different in the analytic situation and in the movie theater. In discussing other theories on the topic, de Lauretis maintains that it is absolutely impossible to assert that any film fantasy refers to any single spectator, just as it is not true that any film can construct its spectator as the subject of the film fantasy. Only a dangerous banalization of differences can result from undiscriminated analogies between film fantasy, subject fantasy, and spectatorship. And by banalizing difference, whether racial, homosexual, or lesbian, modern feminist spectator theorists run the risk of aligning themselves with dominant thought.

Patricia White is also interested in studying the relationship between film fantasy and spectatorship. Her approach to *Nocturne* by director Joy Chamberlain combines feminist theory, film theory, and psychoanalysis. In her article she presents *Nocturne* as a case study of lesbian self-representation and lesbian spectator identification. Her accurate and sensitive reading of the film makes clear an important point in spectator theory as well as in feminist theory in general: lesbian desire exists and it cannot be either desexualized or misrepresented.

Both essays are important because they inscribe the lesbian viewer in cinematic and theoretical discourses not simply as an interpretant performing a function similar to the interpretant of the literary triad—text, writer, and reader—but rather as a shaper of identification at a deeper level. It is therefore the lesbian gaze that determines the subject's position of the lesbian viewer. Furthermore, as desire in any type of discourse is the mark of the subject, by asserting lesbian desire, the culturally invisible position of the lesbian woman acquires evidence. Indeed, her different sexual orientation reveals her in a subject position even though this position is inscribed in a marginalizing culture.

Monika Treut's article, "Female Misbehavior," does not concern itself specifically with issues of spectatorship. It seems appropriate to include it in part II because its author stresses the importance of fantasy in masochistic performances. Monika Treut's contribution is articulated in two parts: the first is a discussion of sadomasochistic performance in terms of the liberating force of its practices; the second is a scathing commentary on the myth of romantic love which has fostered and continues to foster the desexualization of the body—especially the female body—and the idealization of a complacent system which misrepresents the nature of love and sex while favoring oppression and repression.

Staging sadomasochistic performances and their effect on real life, as in the case of pornography, is a debated topic of today's society and of feminist groups. Sadomasochist performances and ritualizations, characterized, for example, by a certain fascination with leather items, have been for a long time interwoven with homosexual stylization.

Monika Treut's article is not only a clarification on this debated topic but also a defense of fantasy and performance as cathartic practices. Furthermore, in dealing with sadomasochistic lesbians, Treut points to the self-awareness of these women, often a marginalized minority within lesbian groups, and juxtaposes it to the objectification and loss of self-awareness which women, and more specifically heterosexual women, withstand in the gendered representation of phallocentric discourses.

Part III, "Inscribing Woman in Socio-Historical Contexts," consists of three articles very different in their approach.

Since the majority of the articles in this volume address issues of "modern" feminism, the editors thought of including two papers which deal with the pioneering work of two women filmmakers. Kay Armatage presents Nell Shipman, born in British Columbia in 1892, while Giuliana Bruno writes on Elvira Notari (Naples, 1875), the first woman to direct films in Italy, and on the concept of spectatorship at the beginning of this century.

Kay Armatage rightly notes that "dominant critical methodologies grounded in feminist film theory" would not be appropriate to assess Nell

Shipman's work. She suggests therefore an approach which combines historical research and modern theoretical practices. The term *heroic femininity* for Nell Shipman seems indeed appropriate not only to define her female characters often fighting against the inclemency of weather and nature but also to describe her life as an independent and isolated filmmaker and producer.

Giuliana Bruno's article presents a fascinating picture of Notari's "urban cinema" and of the city of Naples. The reality of the city becomes a text which Bruno juxtaposes to Notari's films—and to silent film in general. Against the background of the recently industrialized city, she theorizes the pleasure of film watching as a parallel to the pleasure of "streetwalking." In theorizing female spectatorship she also focuses on the pleasure of the *flâneuse*—"streetwalker"—thus recovering the latter term, traditionally associated with the oppression of women, to signify freedom.

In setting an archaeological background to women's filmmaking, the editors' choice fell on Canada and Italy for personal reasons, the two places being respectively the country of choice and the country of birth for both. Besides being in part motivated by these sentimental affiliations, however, both articles point at once to some of the difficulties encountered and yet overcome by women directors during the years of silent cinema.

In some respects, the early years of the film industry were favorable to women directors, since the industry had not immediately shown its capital gains. As soon as large profits could be earned, however, women directors encountered an ever-increasing number of difficulties on all fronts. After the big feminist wave at the beginning of the century, women's role in film changed drastically and women were relegated mainly to the role of actresses by male Hollywood filmmakers.

The third article included in part III deals with Latin American cinema since it has attracted the attention of many critics both in the United States and in Europe. But, as Ruby Rich notes in her article, Latin American films have often been reduced by these critics to mere stereotypical products. In an attempt to correct this, she gives a thorough account of the changes that have characterized the recent history of many Latin American countries in order to point out how they have affected their film industries, both as socioeconomic structures and as creative forces. Moreover, she contextualizes the work of women filmmakers in the political reality it generates and draws comparisons between their work and work produced by men. Latin American cinema of the 1980s is characterized, especially thanks to women directors, by "the breaking of taboo and prohibition [and] the freeing of the imagination and fantasy." These, Ruby Rich proposes, should be the new parameters for a different appreciation of the evolution of Latin American cinema.

This last article allows a comparison with the other two, a comparison which embraces different cultures and times. The role of women filmmakers in all three cases constitutes a complex reality comprising elements of originality and of isolated struggle, on the one hand, and, on the other hand, defined and ever determined by socioeconomic factors. Entering the world of cinema as director, a woman filmmaker defines and asserts her own subjectivity not only as an aesthetic operator but also as a sociopolitical entity, at all times and in all cases.

Finally, we give two examples of feminist film readings in part IV. Here too we have chosen issues of marginality. The position of lesbianism and its definitions in contemporary feminist works on the female subject is the topic of Judith Mayne's article. She too, like de Lauretis and White, denounces the general uneasiness on the part of feminist theorists in dealing with lesbianism. Her article reviews a large corpus of film materials as well as theoretical texts which are concerned with the definition of lesbian authorship.

Part of her article centers on a reading of Midi Onodera's *Ten Cents a Dance (Parallax)*, and she argues that the film addresses lesbian sexuality in a novel manner by suggesting at once its difference as well as its similarity to other expressions of sexual desire. In so doing, Judith Mayne's reading finds connection with the article written by Midi Onodera herself and also with similar issues raised from different perspectives by de Lauretis, White, and Treut.

Difference in sexual orientation is presented by all these authors as a component of our social and biological reality. Discrimination against different sexual orientations is not discussed here as an occasion to claim victimization, but it is properly politicized to show the dynamics of power and its strategies of exclusion and misrepresentation. The personal choice, therefore, in sexual preference becomes a political statement because, as we all know too well, the personal is political.

The concluding essay in this volume, Marguerite Waller's "Liliana Cavani's *Portiere di notte*," points to the power struggle among socially defined groups and to their politicization.

Waller sees a clear connection between anti-Semitism and anti-feminism. *The Night Porter* for Waller is essentially a powerful comment on history and on one's own responsibilities in history. She argues that if we consider history a binary, linear construct, where actions are either good or bad, we conclude easily and dangerously that the Holocaust is the "unthinkable other." But *The Night Porter* disrupts these polarities and involves us in the phenomenon which continues to manifest itself in other guises.

It is perhaps Waller's article that more obviously denounces the dangers of a polarized vision of reality. In a pluralistic vision of reality, where differences are respected and represented, power and its instrumentalization through sociopolitical and economic discourses is, thus, by necessity, decentralized. Self-representation must consequently become a political device to dismantle the power of dominant discourse, whether it is based on gender, race, or socioeconomic and sexual orientations.

As editors of *Feminisms in the Cinema*, we have selected the articles for this volume with this optimistic, but not utopian, premise in mind. Our hope is to contribute to studies in feminist theory and in feminist cinema which share in our conviction. It is also our hope that marginalized groups continue the exploration of their own sense of identity as well as the politicization of their reality through self-representation.

I.

MODES OF IDENTIFICATION
AND REPRESENTATION

I

THE MYTH OF PANDORA
A Psychoanalytical Approach

Laura Mulvey

PANDORA, in the Greek myth, was a beautiful woman, manufactured by the gods to seduce and bring harm to man. She was sent to earth with a box that secretly contained all the evils of the world. The box and the forbidden nature of its contents excited her curiosity and she opened it. So evil escaped into the world and woman brought misery to man. Only hope remained.

I am using the myth of Pandora as a starting point in this chapter in two different ways. First, I want to discuss Pandora as an icon of the feminine whose attributes demonstrate how easily images and expressions having to do with space come to inhabit or colonize female iconography. I first analyze the myth in order to extract its topographies: the space, the surface exterior and secret interior, of both the female mythological figure and the box. Second, there is the question of curiosity. Pandora's curiosity has always had a special appeal for feminists as an early example of women's (transgressive) desire to know. I am attempting to appropriate the idea of feminine curiosity and reformulate it into a feminist drive to investigate, intellectually and theoretically, myths and images of women. These myths and images have frequently, in the history of patriarchal culture, materialized into a polarization between a visible and seductive surface and a secret and dangerous essence. This topography privileges the visible surface of beauty, while projecting onto it the instability of masquerade. Beauty can assume the appearance of a veil. A feminist analysis of this "topographical syndrome" must focus on its duality, and on its investment in sight, what is seen and what might be unveiled. This process also involves questioning metaphors of understanding that derive from sight and then discovering others that derive from decoding. Pandora, from a feminist perspective, has to be conceived as a puzzle or riddle in which the spatial division is part of a cipher. If the metaphor of unveiling a concealed truth is applied to the Pandora myth, it necessarily stays stuck within the spatial terms of the myth. It is essential for feminists to analyze through metaphors of understanding as "deciphering" rather than metaphors of understanding as "seeing."

This (female) drive to investigate is directed at a culture in which woman has not, traditionally, been the possessor of knowledge and which has, traditionally, tended to consider femininity as an enigma. In this gap the image of woman acquires a special value as a sign. Metaphorical, allegorical, and abstract concepts find a vehicle for expression, as, for instance, in the figure of Justice with her scales or the girl on a bottle of olive oil that denotes a first, or virgin, pressing. In this sense the image of woman has become conventionally accepted as very often meaning something other than herself.[1] In semiotic terms, the signifier supports a symbolic as well as a literal signified and the two terms come to inflect and inform each other. Feminist theory has drawn attention to the way in which images of women have also assumed another special visibility in a collective mythology, visual vocabulary, and iconography of sexuality. These images cannot be decoded simply through a knowledge of emblems and symbols. As they bear witness to a difficulty of sexuality and sexual difference, they form at the site of repression where "Something" that cannot find conscious articulation is displaced onto "Something else." It is here that feminists have turned to psychoanalytic and semiotic theory first and foremost as implements for this task of deciphering and decoding images of women that disguise other meanings, most particularly the censored discourse of sexuality. In the course of this chapter, I want to try to argue for the efficacy of these theories and demonstrate the influence they have had on the development of my thought and my approach to feminist aesthetics. I will return to these issues in the second part of the chapter.

Pandora's Creation: Beauty, Artifice, and Danger

The myth of Pandora first appears in Greek mythology, in Hesiod's *Works and Days* (he returns to it later in the *Theogony*) as an account of the first woman. Prometheus tricked Zeus and stole fire and gave it to man. Zeus was determined to have his revenge, and answered one deception with another. He said, "I will give men as the price of fire an evil thing in which they may all be glad of heart while they embrace their own destruction." He told Hephaestus to mix earth with water and put in it the voice and strength of the human kind and "fashion a sweet and lovely maiden shape, like to the immortal goddesses in face." Aphrodite, the goddess of love, gave her the power to seduce putting "grace upon her head." Hermes gave her "a shameless mind and deceitful nature, lies and crafty words," while the Divine Graces gave her "gold necklaces and crowned her head with spring flowers." Pallas Athena girded and clothed her with a silver raiment, an embroidered veil, and a crown of gold with much curious work. Zeus then told Hermes to take Pandora to earth, as a snare and a plague to men, to seduce Prometheus' brother, Epimetheus, as Prometheus himself was too cunning and would see through the trick. When Epimetheus saw her, he forgot Prometheus' warning to reject any gift from Zeus but to send it back for fear it would bring harm to man. "He took the gift, and afterwards, when the evil thing was already his, he understood. Previously men lived on earth free from ills and hard toil and sickness. But the woman took off the great lid of the jar and scattered all these and caused sorrow and mischief to man." Pandora was an artifact, crafted by Hephaestus as a living trick, and all the gods contributed to creating her extraordinary beauty. Hesiod describes her as "a steel trap from which there is no escape."

In *Monuments and Maidens*, Marina Warner describes Pandora in the following manner:

> a most subtle, complex and revealing symbol of the feminine, of its contradictory compulsion, peril and loveliness . . . artefact and artifice herself. Pandora installs the woman as the eidolon in the frame of human culture, equipped by her unnatural nature to delight and to deceive. . . . Female forms are associated from the very start with beauty and artistic adornment and its contradictory and often dangerous consequences. . . . These mythological principles have assisted the projection of immaterial concepts onto the female form, in both rhetoric and iconography. Men act as individuals, and women bear the burden of their dreams. (214)

The story of Pandora's creation, and the story of the purpose behind her creation, also install her as a mythic origin of a spatial or topographical dimension to this phantasmagoric representation of female seductiveness and deceit. There is, first of all, a dislocation between Pandora's appearance and her meaning. She is a Trojan horse, a lure and a trap, a trompe l'oeil. Her appearance dissembles her essence. The topography is one of binary opposition, a split between an inside and an outside, between seductive surface and dangerous depth. Out of this antinomy emerges the iconography of femininity as a divided space, with the "surface" often being realized through the idea of beauty as a mask that disguises a dangerous nature. The logic binary opposition flourishes, when difficult material and repressed ideas that threaten consciousness need to find an assimilable mythic form. Gaston Bachelard comments in *The Poetics of Space*:

> Outside and inside form a dialectics of division, the obvious geometry of which blinds us as soon as we bring it into play in the metaphorical domains. It has the sharpness of the dialectics of yes and no, which decides everything. Unless one is careful, it is made into the basis of all thought of the positive and negative. (211)

The antinomy between outside and inside, surface and secret, is the source of a series of images of femininity as artifice. Artifice, appearance, cosmetic, made up. This phantasmatic topography has haunted representations of femininity across the ages, not consistently manifest, but persisting as a strong intermittent strand in our cultural traditions. As a manufacture, Pandora is a prototype for the mechanical female, androids we might say today, such as Olympia in Hoffman's story *The Sandman*, the False Maria in *Metropolis*, Hadaly in Villiers d'Isle d'Adam's *The Eve of the Future*, all of whom personify the fantasy of female beauty as artifice. As an enchantress who deceives, Pandora is also a prototype for the *femme fatale*. A seductive appearance that is appealing and charming to man generates its polar opposite, an interior that is harmful and dangerous to man. The spatial configuration that characterizes Pandora is also extended to the box. So two topographies make up the mystery and danger in the myth, that of the woman and that of the box. And both are patterned around an inside and an outside, a "dialectics of division," as Bachelard puts it.

The Box: Sexual Metaphor and Its "Poetics of Space"

In classical mythology, Pandora had with her an iconographical attribute, a large jar, which contained all the evils of the world. In their book *Pandora's Box*, Dora and Irwin Panofsky have shown how, during the Renaissance, the jar shrank into another version of the attribute, a small box that Pandora generally carried in her hand. The jar and the box are both enclosed spaces; they are different but interchangeable containers; both, in this story, carry a forbidden secret locked away; and both are subject to "the dialectics of inside and outside." But when the container shrinks, from jar size, the approximate size of Pandora herself, to the small box, an extension of meaning takes place, a sexualization of the resonances associated with the box. The box, unlike the jar, generates a metaphoric relationship to the female genitals. These motifs suggest a metaphoric representation of myths associated with the female body and extend the image of concealment, the container and secrecy. The motif of secrecy that is associated with the female body is discussed by Ludmilla Jordanova in the following terms:

> Veiling implies secrecy. Women's bodies, and, by extension, female attributes, cannot be treated as fully public, something dangerous might happen, secrets be let out, if they were open to view. Yet in presenting something as inaccessible and dangerous, an invitation to know and to possess is extended. The secrecy associated with female bodies is sexual and linked to the multiple associations between women and privacy. (92)

And she continues later with this theme, saying "in the Pandora story secrecy is reified as a box." The metonymy that links the space of a box to the female body with connotations of secrecy and sexuality suggested by Ludmilla Jordanova reminded me of the following exchange between Freud and Dora, whose case history he discussed in *Studies in Hysteria*. They are analyzing Dora's "first dream":

> Does nothing occur to you in connection with the jewel-case? So far you have only talked about jewelry and said nothing about the case.
> Yes, Herr K. had made me a present of an expensive jewel-case a little time before.
> Then a return present would have been very appropriate. Perhaps you do not know that "jewel-case" ["Schmuckkastchen"] is a favorite expression for the same thing that you alluded to not so long ago by means of the reticule you were wearing—for the female genitals, I mean.
> I knew you would say that. (69)

The metaphor referred to by Freud is, as it were, confirmed by its general use. However, the motif of the female body as container may also refer to the womb, the enclosing space inside the mother's body that provides an instant source of connotation and a "poetics of space" quite usual in culture (Mills). The womb is, obviously, not subject to the same taboos as the female genitalia, unmentionable except in vulgar speech, where a whole range of metaphoric terms exist as substitutes, either erotic or derogatory. In Freud's example, the jewel case, although strictly speaking a metaphor for the female genitals, carries with it connotations of space and the "dialectics of inside and outside"; the jewel case, too, is a container and can therefore reiterate between Pandora's box and female sexuality.[2]

Iconographically, the figure of a woman can be identified as Pandora by the presence of her box, and a box can gain mystery and allure by association with Pandora. Iconographical associations are usually formed by juxtaposing characters with the most significant object associated with their figure or their story. We can identify Hercules by his club or St. Catherine by her wheel only through awareness of cultural convention and familiarity with the relevant details of the story. This is also true, on one level, of Pandora and her box. However, her attribute has an added significance, taking it beyond the realm of iconography and introducing the psychoanalytic concept of displacement. The box repeats the topography of Pandora herself: her exterior mask of beauty concealing an interior of combined mystery and danger. The box, then, can be interpreted as a displacement of Pandora's seductive danger onto an emblem of female sexuality described, in the myth, as the source of all the evils of the world.

The mask and the box: each conceal a secret that is dangerous to man. The Panofskys record two examples of Pandora iconography in which the sexual significance of the box is made explicit. One, an engraving by Abraham van Diepenbeek dating from the mid-seventeenth century, shows Pandora "holding the fateful pyxis as a fig-leaf," and the accompanying contemporary text by Michel de Marolles points out that Pandora is "holding her box in her right hand, lowered to that part, which she covers, from which has flowed so many of the miseries and anxieties that afflict man, as though the artist wished to show that there is always something bitter in the midst of a fountain of pleasure and that the thorn pricks among the flowers" (77). The second is a drawing by Paul Klee, dating from 1936, *Die Busche der Pandora als Stilleben*, "representing the ominous receptacle . . . as a kantharis-shaped vase containing some flowers but emitting evil vapours from an opening clearly suggestive of the female genitals" (133). Thus the sexualized image becomes tinged with repulsion and disgust.

Curiosity: Where the Woman Looks

Pandora is now better known for her curiosity than for her opinions as artifact and lure. Although she was forbidden to open the box and warned of the danger it contained, she gave way to her curiosity and released all the evils into the world. Only hope remained. In Nathaniel Hawthorne's version of the myth, told for children in *Tanglewood Tales*, Pandora's story is a warning of the dangers of curiosity. And this theme also links her story to Eve, the first woman of Christian mythology, who persuaded Adam to eat the apple of knowledge. The Panofskys point out that this parallel was noted by late-medieval mythographers wanting to use classical precedent to corroborate the Christian story of the fall of man. Although Eve's story highlights the knowledge theme, the epistomophelia, as it were, inherent in the drive of curiosity, the myth associates female curiosity with forbidden fruit rather than with forbidden space. The motif of space and curiosity can be found again symptomatically in the fairy story "Bluebeard." The story is about his last wife, a young girl who is given the free run of his vast palace with the exception of one room which her husband forbids her to enter. Its little key begins to excite her curiosity until she ignores the luxury all around her and thinks of nothing else. Then, one day, when she thinks her husband is away, she opens the door and finds the bodies of all his former wives still bleeding magically from terrible wounds and tortures. Her husband sees the blood stain that cannot be removed from the key and tells her that the punishment for breaking his prohibition, for curiosity, is death alongside his former wives, who he explains had also been irresistibly drawn to the little room. Angela Carter retells this story in *The Bloody Chamber*, and compares the room with Pandora's box and the heroine with Eve.

Curiosity set up a configuration of space through its association with investigation. Curiosity in its desire to see is directed toward secret, concealed spaces and carries with it the connotations of transgression and danger. In her article "The Woman's Film: Possession and Address," Mary Ann Doane discusses the woman's look of paranoia in the films with a female investigative protagonist set in a home suddenly invested with the uncanny. She says:

> One could formulate a veritable topography of spaces within the home along the axis of this perverted specularization. . . . Many of these films are marked by the existence of a room to which the woman is barred access. *Gaslight*—the attic; *Dragonwyck*—a tower room. In *Rebecca* it is both the boathouse and Rebecca's bedroom, ultimately approached by the female protagonist with a characteristically Hitchcockian moving point of view shot towards the closed door. . . . Dramas of seeing that becomes invested with horror within the context of the home [whose] narrative structures produce an insistence upon situating the woman as agent of the gaze, an investigator in charge of the epistemological trajectory of the text, as the one for whom the "secret behind the door" is really at stake. (71)

It is significant that the woman's look is so strongly associated with enclosed, secret, and forbidden space. I was first struck with the female gaze of curiosity and investigation in Hitchcock's 1947 film *Notorious*, in which a female protagonist is sent as an undercover agent to investigate a house, redolent of uncanniness. She, only temporarily, becomes the investigative force, empowered with an active look, that carries the narrative forward in the desire to penetrate the mystery or enigma. She, who has been established at the opening of the film as object of the gaze, as enigma, and probably dangerous, then conceals its power behind her "cosmetic" mask. And her mask of seductiveness is echoed in the topography of the house, its closed doors and locked cupboards potentially containing a secret, dangerous to man, order, and the Law, that her own structure of concealment replicates. There is a displacement here, reminiscent of the displacement in the Pandora myth, between the dialectics of division figured through the woman and the secret spaces of the house; an investigator of these spaces, she also generates the figuration of "curiosity."

My interest in the Pandora myth stemmed originally from a wish to consider the aesthetics of curiosity. Curiosity describes the desire to know something that is concealed so strongly that it is experienced as a drive, leading to the transgression of a prohibition. The desire to see may be connected with the desire to know—but it may not lead to enlightenment. This is where the contribution of theory is truly important. Theory, as a means of decoding signifiers and symptoms, provides an instrument for seeing with the mind, seeing through the mask of visibility, not to something concealed, literally behind it, but "seeing through" in the sense of grasping the nature of a masquerade and understanding its significance. It is because of the persistence of the Pandora phenomenon that feminists reacted against the visual and were drawn to theories of decoding. The influence of this approach can be seen, for instance, in the development of feminist film theory. Drawing in particular on the Hollywood cinema of the studio system, feminists argued that the image of woman said little or nothing about women but should be taken as symptomatic of phallocentric desires and anxieties projected onto an image of femininity. The images that had circulated as signifiers of sexuality could be traced to their source in the male psyche, and the signifiers of the anxieties installed in the patriarchal psyche could begin to be decoded. Curiosity as a desire to know may also be linked to pleasure, but a pleasure that again displaces the visual. Just as feminist aesthetic theory stems from the decoding of signifiers, symptoms, and iconographies, so there is a pleasure in riddle- or puzzle-solving. And then, feminist critics have frequently commented on Freud's characterization of femininity as a riddle, and the representation of femininity as a mask restates, as it were, this concept of the mysterious, the secret, the something hidden.

Pandora combines the iconography of mystery with a narrative of curiosity. If, as I suggested earlier, the box is a displaced representation of female sexuality as mystery and threat, Pandora's curiosity about its contents may be interpreted as a curiosity about the enigma that she personifies. And curiosity about her own division into an inside/outside topography. And her desire to see inside the box can be *re-represented* as a self-reflexive desire to investigate the enigma of femininity itself, literally figured as reified and alienated into a displaced space. The point, then, is to recast the figure of Pandora, her action and its fearful consequences, in such a way that the literal topography of her structure can shift from the register of the visual into the register of the theoretical. Pandora, caught in the myth, cannot make this step, but feminist theorists, seeking to translate the iconographies of the feminine to reveal their origins, can take her curiosity and transform it into a seeing with the mind.

To sum up, there are three "cliché" motifs, elements of myth, that are central to the Pandora's iconography:

   1. Femininity as enigma.

   2. Female curiosity as transgressive and dangerous.

   3. The spatial or topographical figuration of the female body as an inside and outside.

And I would like to try to reformulate them, to illuminate the tautology, as follows:

   1. Pandora's curiosity acts out a transgressive desire to see inside her own surface or exterior, into the inside of the female body metaphorically represented by the box and its attendant horrors.

   2. *Feminist* curiosity has to pick up Pandora's look and transform the topography of the feminine through theoretical investigation, with the aim of understanding and decoding this duality that haunts the female body in patriarchal representation. From where does it emanate? Of what is it a symptom? Is it possible to follow through the chain of displacements that shift meanings from one signifier to another? How do the signifiers link together?

Curiosity and Feminist Psychoanalytic Theory

Roughly speaking, there are two aspects of Freudian psychoanalytic theory that have been taken up by feminists. The first is methodological. It has to do with the ways in which Freud theorized repression, the structure of the unconscious, and the ways in which it operates. Second, there is the question of content, of what it is that the human psyche represses in the course of both its structural development and its individual experience. Freud saw sexuality (and the constitution of sexual difference) as a—if not *the*—major force facing the human psyche with difficult, irreconcilable demands, in conflict with culture and thus open to repression. Feminists, trying to understand how femininity is socially constituted and subject to historical and cultural change, found common ground with the emphasis that Freud put on the contingent nature of sexual difference. And feminists picked up the vocabulary and the theory that Freud had evolved in order to identify symptoms emanating from the unconscious, in order to identify symptoms emanating from the social fantasies that characterize patriarchal culture.

I found it impossible to begin to untangle the significance of the "dialectics of inside and outside" that permeates this particular iconography of a female figure without having recourse to psychoanalytic theory. I began to see parallels between Pandora's story, feminist theory, and the influence that psychoanalysis has had on feminist theory, and these parallels bore out the fact that the alliance between feminism and psychoanalysis is neither accidental nor arbitrary. Once the metaphors of concealment, such as "masked" or "veiled," which reinforce the division between inside and outside, can be stripped of their literal, plausible validity, then this topography itself may be interpreted as a psychoanalytic symptom that needs to be deciphered. Its formal structure is an intrinsic part of the symptom. A symptom, like a cipher, may be decoded by the right key, in this case psychoanalysis; the unconscious always tries to hide the key to its code.

A symptom, as a manifestation of the psyche's attempt to conceal an unconscious wish from the conscious mind, may also be understood to have a spatial structure, a surface appearance, and a hidden, secret, and dangerous meaning. Freud used archaeological metaphors to convey the repression of memories and their preservation by the unconscious, for instance, an antiquity concealed in a tomb or, say, the ruins of Pompei, preserved like fossils, buried by time. Here the passing of time and the process of repression mesh together to suggest images of surface and lost depth. But just as an archaeological find need not make sense if it is recovered outside its own cultural and historical context, so the stuff of the unconscious also has to be "decoded" rather than simply "dug up." In the *Interpretation of Dreams*, Freud describes the materializations of the unconscious, due to their extreme distortion, as comparable to a hieroglyphic language or a rebus.

Following Freud's imagery, the topographies in the Pandora myth, the mask of femininity and the secret space of the box, must be understood as two parts of a rebus. In Freudian theory, the only means of deciphering the "hieroglyphic" language, the rebus of the unconscious, of cracking its cipher, is by analyzing the primary processes, that is, condensation and displacement. They are the mechanisms the unconscious uses to disguise its thought, either by concealing one repressed idea in the guise of another or by transferring the affect of one idea to another that is apparently unconnected but secretly linked. Condensation and displacement are, as it were, the cipher, and the various practices of psychoanalysis supply the key. Psychoanalysis follows these clues, like threads into the labyrinth of the mind, and shows how, in the language of the unconscious, ideas assume these disguises to evade the censorship imposed by the conscious mind, and how drives, or primal fantasies, that evade conscious articulation struggle to find some visible means of expression. In such circumstances the signifier is bound to be at several removes from its signified. Furthermore, following Lacan, the two can never hope to be reunited into coherent and transparent meaning. But while there may always be a *beyond* to our understanding and while analysis is doomed to be interminable, feminist theory can still work to decipher and decode the symptoms that erupt as signifiers of fantasies invested in the image of the female body.

In the myth of Pandora, the Freudian primary processes—that is, displacement and condensation—are not only clearly at work but actually disguise their workings in her topographic structure. The elements in her myth set in motion a series of "cultural" displacements: the initial connotation of enclosed space as feminine space (the womb, the house) slides into the idea that an enclosed space may well be secret. The Mona Lisa or the Sphinx are emblematic of this mysterious and unknowable feminine enigma. As incomprehensibility generates anxiety, the space of enigma slides into the disguising surface of dissembled threat, and the fascination of the "femme fatale," for instance, comes to be tarred with the brush of deceptive masquerade. Nowadays accoutrements of feminine fascination are associated with artifice (makeup, cosmetics, constructed allure), and Pandora's ancient, pre-consumer-society origins as an artificial construction highlight the deep-rooted linkage between feminine seduction, artifice, and deception. The topography of an exterior and an interior connects all these figurations into a structural homology so that the slippage of one set of images and connotations onto the next, and then onto the next, seems both natural and logical. The problem is this: the significance of the slippage from idea to idea, and the dependence of one connotation on its condensation with another, is overwhelmed by the recurrent image of masquerade, so that the myth implies that the source of the mystery may be "unveiled" and revealed "inside" the figure itself. While the seductive woman encapsulates a surface/secret split, she becomes a figure for the potential revelation of a hidden truth, and this metaphor then erases the metonymies that have enabled it to come into being. So the topography, by suggesting that meaning lies concealed behind a disguise, disguises the processes of displacement.

Freudian theory can point toward the way that the female body functions as a signifier of sexual difference, and it provides concepts that allow a first step to be taken toward an explanation for the topography of the feminine. And it is at this point, on the vexed issue of castration, that Freud's ideas are both useful and problematic for feminist theory. In terms of castration anxiety, the female body's topography has to present a facade of fascination and surface that distracts the male psyche from the wound concealed beneath, creating an inside and outside of binary opposition. While the mask attracts and holds the gaze, anxiety produces a dread of what might be secretly hidden. This structure, of belief in the female phantasmagoria, followed by deception and disgust, is close to the structure of fetishism. As a signifier, par excellence, the female body can become a channel for the processes of condensation and displacement as a repressed idea conjures up images to "latch" on to, that both disavow and represent the source of anxiety. In this sense, any process of disavowal can be organized around the female figure's seductive surface and hidden otherness.

Barbara Spackman, in her book *Decadent Genealogies*, uses the figure of Pandora in her discussion of D'Annunzio's aesthetics to analyze the unveiling of the woman's body as a gesture of fascinated repulsion. It is a gesture that reveals the sight of the woman's body as the sight of her wound and the sight of Medusa. Within this aesthetic, masculine desire is caught in an oscillation between erotic obsession with the female body and fear of the castration that it signifies. In her paper "Inter musam et ursam moritur" she also discusses this topography of the feminine:

> The grotesque female body is not a product of inversion . . . it belongs to the topos of enchantress-turned-hag, a topos that opposes the beautiful enchantress (woman as lie) to the toothless old hag hidden beneath her artifice (woman as truth). From Dante's "femmina balba" in *Purgatorio* 19, to Ariosto's Alcina and Machiavelli's *lavandaia* . . . this topos effects a transfer through displacement: the *bocca sdentata* of the hag stands for the "other mouth" the *vagina dentata*. As a figure for truth, the toothless mouth and the stench it exhales are so much part of the Western tradition that it is such a figure that Nietzsche will overturn in the "Preface" to *The Gay Science* in order to critique the hermeneutic model that would find essence behind appearance. Refiguring woman is tantamount to refiguring truth, and to side with either the enchantress or the hag is to remain solidly within that tradition.

Pandora's body is artifice par excellence, "cosmetic" with all the word's resonance and connotation, and the association between the female body with either castration, the wound, or a more profound horror is displaced onto the box. These reverberations between Pandora and her box are set in motion in the first place of contiguity (in the juxtaposition of the figure to its iconographic attribute) but also by the structural similarity between two containing, enclosed spaces, their "dialectics of inside and outside." It is the process of displacement, and its close associate metonymy, that allows us to read the myth of feminine topography as a symptom to be deciphered. It is this displacement that transforms Pandora's gesture of looking into the forbidden space, the literal figuration of curiosity as looking in, into a figure for epistomophelia, a desire to uncover the secret of the very figuration she represents. Displacement resists the fixation of the look, obsessed with its own symptom; it transforms the drive of curiosity from the desire to see into the desire to know.

I now want to pursue some of these points through a discussion of the cinema, using ideas developed by feminist aesthetics and criticism. The cinema has invested deeply in the concept of feminine seductiveness as a surface that conceals. That is to say the codes and conventions of Hollywood cinema refined the representation of femininity, heightened by the star system, to the point where the spectator's entrancement with the effects of the cinema itself became almost indistinguishable from the draw exerted by an eroticized image of woman. It is as though the scopophilic draw of the cinema, the flickering shadows, and the contrasts between light and dark achieve an anthropomorphic realization in and around the female form. Framing, makeup, and lighting stylized the female star, inflecting the tendency of representations of female sexuality to slip into "to-be-looked-at-ness"—to produce the ultimate screen spectacle. The luminous surface of the screen reinforces the sense of surface radiated by the mask of femininity, flattening the image, so that its usual transparency, its simulation of a window on the world, becomes opaque. In its most perfect form—for instance, Marlene Dietrich's mask-like appearance in her films with Joseph von Sternberg—the figure of the woman on the screen is stylized to the point of artificiality, so that makeup and lighting combine to etch exquisite features onto a blank surface.

Psychoanalytic film theory has argued that the woman "fronts" for the cinematic machine, giving suspension of disbelief the added backing of the fascinating female form, attracting the gaze and suppressing inquiry of knowledge of the machine's functioning. Annette Michelson, in her article

"On the Eve of the Future," locates a fantasy premonition of the cinema in this story. Edison manufactures the perfect woman for his male friend, to substitute for the beautiful but imperfect girl he loves:

> The female body then comes into focus as the very site of the cinema's invention, and we may, in an effect of stereoscopic vision, see the philosophical toy we know as the cinema marked in the very moment of its invention by the inscription of desire. (20)

And she then invokes the familiar murmur of fetishistic avowal, equally: "I know, but all the same. . . . "

In a similar vein, Jacqueline Rose, in her article "Woman as Symptom," writes:

> It is a particular logic of desire that is produced and reproduced by the cinema machine. A logic truth which cinema as an apparatus tries to close itself off as a system of representation, but constantly comes up against the vanishing point of that system where it fails to integrate itself and then has to refuse the moment of difference or trouble by trying to run away from it or by binding it back into the logic or perfection of the film system itself. . . . And insofar as the system closes over that moment of difference and impossibility, what gets set up in its place is essentially an image of the woman. (219)

Stephen Heath has said:

> Cinema has played to the maximum the masquerade, the signs of this exchange, femininity, has ceaselessly reproduced its social currency. From genre to genre, from film to film, the same economy: the woman in image, the totalising of her body, her, into unity, the sum of the gaze, the imaginary of her, then, as that perfect match, perfect image. . . . (187)

My interest in the Pandora myth, as I said earlier, stemmed originally from a wish to consider the aesthetics of curiosity, a wish that stemmed in turn from my interest in giving greater complexity to the argument in my article "Visual Pleasure and Narrative Cinema." I thought that an active, investigative look, but one that was also associated with the feminine, could suggest a way out of the rather too neat binary opposition: masculine look as active and voyeuristic in polarization with femininity as spectacle, passive and exhibitionist. In my earlier article I used examples from Hitchcock to argue my point, and he again can illustrate the dualism of the female body.

In *Notorious* Ingrid Bergman is dispatched to investigate a house of spies, once again an enclosed space and one redolent of uncanniness. The uncanniness is confirmed, and personified, by the Hitchcockian figure of "Mother." The *Notorious* house and Mother prefigure the cinema's most uncanny house ever, the Bates house in *Psycho*. In both films Hitchcock uses the characteristic camera movement, which Mary Ann Doane mentions, to represent the way that the house and its internal spaces draw the heroine into its interior with the physical force of her curiosity. Hitchcock's mise-en-scène suggests that the gradual movement of the heroine toward and into the house is a movement leading to a confrontation between the body of the young woman, alluring and cosmetic, and the mother's body, redolent (especially, of course, in *Psycho*) of disintegration, decay, and death. The mask of feminine beauty then takes on another level of disavowal, that is, the specific, psychoanalytic problem of the mother's body.

Hitchcock provides a symptomatic example of the problem of the mother's body as an abyss or morass; it is a defetishized body, deprived of the fetish's semiotic, reduced to being the "unspeakable" other of the mask and devoid of significance. This motif is close to the Kristevan concept of the abject, that is, the disgust aroused in the human psyche by lifeless, inanimate bodily matter, bodily wastes, and the dead body itself. For Kristeva, abjection is closely associated with separation from the mother's body. The small child, of both sexes, in the process of establishing autonomous subjectivity, has to establish an autonomous "clean and proper body." While previously the child found pleasure in its bodily wastes and the satisfying undifferentiation between its body and that of its mother, when it needs to define boundaries and separations, feelings of disgust come into play. Barbara Creed argues the "monstrous feminine" in horror movies represents an archaic mother:

> within patriarchal signifying practices, particularly the horror film, she is reconstructed and represented as a negative figure, one associated with the dread of the generative mother seen only in the abyss, the monstrous vagina, the origin of all life threatening to reabsorb what it once birthed. . . . In horror films such as *Alien*, we are given the representation of the female genitals as uncanny—horrific objects of dread and fascination.

And she points out that there is also a series of displacements between different aspects of the maternal figure:

> Clearly it is difficult to separate out completely the figure of the archaic mother . . . from other aspects of the maternal figure—the maternal authority of Kristeva's semiotic, the mother of Lacan's imaginary, the phallic woman, the castrated woman. . . . At times the horrific nature of the monstrous-feminine is dependent on the merging together of all the aspects of the maternal figure into one—the horrifying image of woman as archaic mother, phallic woman and castrated body represented in a single figure. (134)

The Pandora myth and the examples of Hitchcock's heroines who investigate the uncanny house suggest that, although both sexes are subject to abjection, it is the heroine rather than the hero who can explore and analyze the phenomenon with greater equanimity. It is the female body that has come, not exclusively but predominantly, to represent the shudder aroused by liquidity and decay.

If Pandora's gesture may be interpreted as a self-reflexive look at a misogynist fantasy of femininity, the box represents the association between the feminine and horror or evil. I have argued that psychoanalytic theory provides a reading of the origin of this association, both through the image of castration and through a condensation between the body of the mother and death. Although Pandora has been used for so long as an allegory of releasing trouble into the world, from a feminist point of view her look of curiosity represents a willingness, on the part of women, to investigate those aspects of the feminine that are, symptomatically, repressed under the regime of fetishism. Feminist theory must then decode, articulate, and analyze these symptoms in order to transform the look of curiosity, the desire to know, into understanding so that the status of the female body as signifier can be challenged and transformed.

While curiosity is a compulsive desire to see and to know, to investigate what is secret and reveal the contents of a concealed space, fetishism is born out of a refusal to see, a refusal to know, and a refusal to accept the difference that the female body symbolizes. Out of this series of turnings away, of covering over, not the eyes but understanding, of looking fixedly at any object that holds the gaze, female sexuality is bound to remain a mystery, condemned to return as a symbol of anxiety while overvalued and idealized in imagery. Hollywood cinema has built its appeal and promoted its fascination by emphasizing the erotic allure of the female star concentrated in a highly stylized and artificial presentation of femininity. The masquerade is exaggerated by the glossy finish of the cinematic medium, comparable to the surface gloss of fetishism. The myth of Pandora and the box are similarly imbricated with the structure of fetishism. But Pandora opens the box containing everything that fetishism disavows. The box is, in this sense, a fetish that fails.

Notes

1. Marina Warner has demonstrated the role played by feminine figurations in allegory. She says: "Allegory means other speech (alia oratio) . . . it signifies an open de-

clamatory speech which contains another layer of meaning. It thus possesses a double intention: to tell something that conveys one thing but which also conveys something else." Marina Warner: *Monuments and Maidens* (London: Picador 1985), p. xix.

2. See Jane Mills, *Womanwords*. Mills points out, across various definitions, the persistence of "container" words as evocative of the female genitals, or woman more generally. The word *vagina*, for instance, is Latin for a sheath or scabbard (244). Her entry for *hole* includes the following: " . . . a hollow place or cavity. By the C16th, having acquired many meanings, including that of the orifice of any part of the body (1340), a secret hiding place (C14th), and a secret room in which an unlawful occupation is pursued (1483), hole became slang for vagina" (118). And "Vessel, originating in the Late Latin vascellum, meaning a small vase or urn and a ship, is yet another example of a word which describes woman as a container. Vessel denoted: a household utensil; . . . any article designed to serve as a receptacle for liquid; and a womb" (246). She also traces *pussy* to "Old Norse puss, meaning a pocket or pouch" (200).

Works Cited

Creed, Barbara. "Alien and the Monstrous Feminine," in Annette Kuhn, ed., *Alien Zone*. London: Verso, 1990.

Doane, Mary Ann. "The Woman's Film: Possession and Address," in M. A. Doane, P. Mellancamp, and L. Williams, eds., *Revision*. Los Angeles: American Film Institute, 1985.

Freud, Sigmund. *The Standard Edition of the Complete Psychological Works of Sigmund Freud*. Vol. VII. London: Hogarth Press, 1955.

Heath, Stephen. *Questions of Cinema*. London: Macmillan, 1981.

Jordanova, Ludmilla. *Sexual Visions*. London: Harvester Press, 1989.

Kristeva, Julia. *The Powers of Horror*. New York: Columbia University Press, 1982.

Michelson, Annette. "On the Eve of the Future: The Reasonable Facsimile and the Philosophical Toy." *October* 29 (1984).

Mills, Jane. *Woman Words*. London: Virago, 1991.

Panofsky, Dora, and Irwin, eds. *The Changing Aspects of a Mythical Symbol*. London: Routledge and Kegan Paul, 1956.

Rose, Jacquelin. *Sexuality in the Field of Vision*. London: Verso, 1986.

Spackman, Barbara. "Inter musam et ursam moritur," in Marilyn Migiel and Juliana Schiesari, eds., *Refiguring Woman: Gender Studies and the Italian Renaissance*. Ithaca: Cornell University Press, 1991.

Warner, Marina. *Monuments and Maidens*. London: Picador, 1985.

2

LOCATING THE DISPLACED VIEW

Midi Onodera

Anyone who has ever tried to make a film can agree that even an unsuccessful film is difficult to produce. Filmmaking, working with the visual language of film, combines the emotion, eloquence, and power of art with the visual and technical imagination. Film is not an original medium. It is an accumulated palette of painting, sculpture, photography, dance, music, language, and story telling.

I went to the Ontario College of Art in the early 1980s and concentrated on photography, film history, painting, and sculpture. In my last years at the college I was enrolled in full-time independent study, which meant that I could access equipment from the school and had two mandatory critiques a year. During my last critique, my painting instructor and head of the experimental arts department told me that I was going against the traditions of painting by writing on the canvas and telling stories. He was extremely discouraging about my future as a painter. But what I realized at that point in my development was that film combined all of the elements I wanted to explore through painting. It was the best thing that could have ever happened to me.

But just because I have chosen to express myself through film and not through traditional art practices, it does not mean that I can ignore the structures of the form.

I approach film much as I did a blank canvas. In my early films I concentrated on learning how to control and manipulate the technical properties of the medium. I played with grain, texture, composition, and light and shadow. I experimented with twenty-four static images per second which projected the illusion of movement. And I looked between the frames for my stories.

But beyond these concerns, for me the ultimate power of film rested and rests in its potential to directly reflect the social morals and climate of our time. Through film, I could accommodate both my desire to entertain and my need to explore the world through my vision.

Mainstream film production is geared toward reflecting our collective feelings, touching a common audience element. For instance, in the early seventies, the nuclear family was threatened by free-love hippies, Vietnam, and the excursions into psychedelic drugs. We struggled with our gender and racial differences, the feminist movement pierced the lives of women, and, for better or for worse, immigration continued to expand the cultural mosaic of North America. As the changes continued to complicate our once seemingly homogeneous society, we began to feel vulnerable. Our neighbors were no longer just like us. They were no longer white, middle-class moms and dads who invited us to swinging cocktail parties, but were psychotic killers who forced their way into our homes and threatened us with illegal firearms and, god forbid, our own kitchen knives. Our safe existence was in jeopardy and films such as *Dirty Harry, Death Wish* (parts 1, 2, and 3), *Black Christmas*, and *Play Misty for Me* fed off our insecurities. No one was safe anymore. We were all potential victims and killers.

Just as mainstream film can in some ways be seen as a social barometer which addresses our collective concerns, the independent art film reflects the views of an individual. In Canada, independent film rests on a solid base of documentary work dominated by the National Film Board of Canada and on the idea of *auteur* filmmaking. We look at films not by their content alone but more by how we connect these films to a body of work. They are David Cronenberg signatures, Atom Egoyan obsessions, Sandy Wilson preoccupations, and Ann Wheeler musings. Perhaps we have never gotten over the fact that the director can be the cameraperson, the grip, the gaffer, the craft service person, and even sometimes the actor. Or perhaps, in our effort to preserve our identity as Canadians, we are subconsciously and consciously anti-Hollywood.

But I would be fooling myself if I said that I was immune to the influences of mainstream television and film, music, or literary trends. I am affected and influenced by a number of sources: popular culture, the sociopolitical climate of the country, my concerns as a feminist, as a Japanese-Canadian woman, and as a lesbian.

As a filmmaker I am affected by the language of film, the history of cinema and representation, and the desire to communicate my ideas to a film audience. And in order to bring all of these elements together into a coherent vision I juggle both the cinematic and the personal.

Over the years I have found that I need to approach each project with two basic desires. My cinematic concern focuses on the interplay of my chosen content or story with the implementation of film form and language. My personal challenge as an artist is to discover something about myself through the filmmaking process.

A few months ago I had the opportunity to direct an artist's profile on David Cronenberg for the Toronto Arts Awards. David talked about his perceptions of filmmaking. He said:

> I think a good filmmaker, like a good race car driver, must be slightly psychopathic in the sense that his threshold of danger and fear is higher than the norm, and that allows him to push himself a little further than most people would go into areas and arenas that are scary, that are fraught with danger. And I do think that any art, when done properly, is quite dangerous. It's dangerous to the artist. Whether or not it may be dangerous to society is another, enormous question.

Maybe it is dangerous. But, for whatever reason, it seems that we have erected shrines around the personal voice. This of course has both positive and negative effects. On the plus side, we are fortunate that there is a substantial amount of arm's-length government funding for films by artists. The Canada Council has long been supportive of many exciting works across the country. Ontario is the most privileged province in this country for supporting the arts. Not only do we reap the benefits of the Ontario Arts Council, but there is also the Ontario Film Development Corporation and, in Toronto, the Toronto Arts Council. However, as we all know, art funding is an endangered species.

On the negative side, personal voices are difficult to dispute and sometimes difficult to understand. There is sometimes very little room for constructive, informed criticism and analysis. In some cases, we have become so sensitive to hearing the voices of others and isolating them into categories that there is little room for crossover and exchange of ideas and work.

For example, although my film background is clearly influenced by experimental film production, ever since *The Displaced View*, some audiences now view me as a documentarian. I am constantly being asked when I moved into the mainstream or when I gave up experimental film. I don't consider my work to be mainstream and I am not a documentary filmmaker. I remain committed to independent film production. I need to view my involvement with film as a process of learning, experimenting, and discovering.

The Displaced View, produced in 1988, marked a point of personal growth for me, both artistically and politically. In terms of my political development, it was one of the first times I consciously acknowledged myself as a person of color. Racial identity had played a minor role in my life up until this point. Our family was a very small minority in an all-white, mainly Jewish neighborhood, and my connection with the Japanese-Canadian community was minimal. Unlike my grandparents and parents, I have never been overtly denied access to anything because I am Japanese-Canadian. It was, however, the discrimination I faced as a lesbian that allowed me some insight into the struggle for racial identity.

Cinematically, *The Displaced View* tackles the notion of the documentary as truth. The construction of the film is documentary based, insofar as nonactors perform in stories which are based on authentic oral history—the cultural and familial links between three generations of Japanese-Canadian women. However, the stories are reconstructed and reassembled through a script, and the creation of a fictional family is used as the vehicle by which the audience reads the story. The three generations of women are represented on screen by my grandmother, my mother, and myself. Although elements of our personal relationships are revealed, they are interwoven with the individual histories of other families. *The Displaced View* uses the perceived personal voice as a narrative ploy to direct the viewer.

Furthermore, the film references the art of Japanese brush painting. Again, approaching film as a blank canvas, I use the vertical Japanese script not only as a visual device but also as a communication vehicle for my Japanese-speaking viewers. It was important to me that the film acknowledge the Issei (first-generation Japanese-Canadian) audience members from the position of language. Although most Issei have been in this country for over three-quarters of their lives, most remain fluent in Japanese and do not possess a comprehensive grasp of the English language. My grandmother, who recently celebrated her 100th birthday, speaks a unique combination of Japanese from the Meiji period (1868–1912) and English. She came to Canada over eighty years ago, and so her Japanese reflects the Japan of that era but is combined with various English words for which there is no Japanese translation.

The motivation behind leaving untranslated the spoken Japanese in the film stems from my desire to place an English-speaking audience in a similar position as myself. I wanted to reinforce the language difficulties between myself as a Sansei (third-generation Japanese-Canadian) who does not speak Japanese and my grandmother's generation.

With the release of *The Displaced View*, my work was suddenly accepted into the Asian Canadian and American markets. Although I had produced several short films before this, *The Displaced View* secured my position as a "producer of color." Suddenly, my work was reflecting the multicultural mosaic, and I found myself sitting on race and representation panels and attending conferences and film festivals as a "producer of color." Suddenly, the fact that I am of Asian descent took front seat to my work. I started to become aware of the fact that I was sometimes the only "visible minority" on a panel. And I found audiences wanting me to speak for all "producers of color."

I am not new to this business of labeling and categorizing work and producers. Before *The Displaced View*, I produced *Ten Cents A Dance (Parallax)*. In late 1984, I began production on this film with a small grant of $2,000 from the Ontario Arts Council. The project was originally presented as a vehicle to illustrate the difficulties of communication in relationships. However, over the course of developing the film, I realized that the concept of misinterpretation and misunderstanding was obviously the most prevalent in sexual encounters, more specifically "one night stands."

The idea of including "parallax" came from my desire to begin to integrate cinematic elements with the subject of the work. The split-screen device employed by the film is meant both to comment on the technical mechanism of film and to highlight the shift in meaning or double interpretation sometimes associated with communication between two people. "Parallax error" is a photographic term meaning the apparent shift in the position of an object from which it is viewed.

The film was shot with two 16mm cameras simultaneously over a period of three weekends. The ratio was 1:1 and it was shot in the order in which it is presented in the final version. After stock and lab costs, the bulk of my almost nonexistent budget went into providing food and drink for my cast and crew. I couldn't afford to pay anyone for their involvement and relied on my friends' generosity.

Each section was scripted under my supervision, but the artists involved were allowed almost free rein with regard to the form and specific content of the script. The first scene is a negotiation of a sexual encounter between a lesbian and a straight woman. In this scene I wanted to concentrate on the unspoken tension between two women who tossed aside political concerns in favor of pursuing their mutual sexual attraction.

The second scene was inspired by concerns within the Toronto gay community at that time: specifically, public washroom sex and police raids on certain "known" public washrooms. In Toronto, St. Catharine's, London, Orillia, and other cities, men, regardless of their sexual orientation, were being arrested for acts of gross indecency. Some of their names were splashed onto the front pages of *The Globe and Mail*. Their lives and the lives of their families would never be the same.

The third scene was developed from an actual conversation with a woman from a phone sex service. At that time, the only phone sex services were in the states and they had yet to break into the Canadian market. Not only did I want to explore sexual encounters and the difficulties of communication, but I wanted to concentrate on encounters which fell across the lines of gender and sexual orientation.

Like *The Displaced View, Ten Cents A Dance (Parallax)* was the first film which brought me face to face with the reality of producing work which directly addressed issues of a specific community. The reaction to both of these films has been very interesting. Although *Ten Cents A Dance (Parallax)* has recently begun to receive critical attention, when it was released in 1985–86, some members of the lesbian and gay communities were very disturbed by it.

At the 1986 San Francisco Lesbian and Gay Film Festival, the film was screened in a program of lesbian shorts. Although the audience, who were mostly lesbians, enjoyed the first scene between the two women, there was a "near riot" when the second scene of two men having sex in a washroom came on. After the festival, there was a heated debate within the San Francisco lesbian community. Some women felt that as a lesbian I could not and should not represent gay men. They accused me of promoting unsafe sex since the men did not wear condoms, and they were outraged that I did not solely concentrate on lesbian issues. Just as I did not intend *The Displaced View* to be seen as my "ethnic film," I was surprised when *Ten Cents A Dance (Parallax)* turned into my "gay statement."

These films, and the rest of my work, are informed by my perspective as a lesbian, as a woman of color, as a feminist, and as a Canadian. However, any work is not dictated by any of these positions.

Having said that, I want to return to the idea that personal films are sometimes above criticism and dispute. Specifically, over the last few years, there has been an increased number of debates surrounding appropriation of racial issues and identity and the lack of critical and theoretical work produced by and about filmmakers of color. Again, because of my involvement with the lesbian and gay film circuit, I can draw a number of parallels between these vastly different communities.

In our eagerness to address the historic neglect of works by people of color, we as consumers sometimes forget to position our work in the context of film language and history. We are sometimes too quick to support work, not because of its creative and innovative approach, but because it was produced by a person of color. Sometimes white critics and theorists do not engage with work by producers of color because they feel unqualified to critique the work. And when they do tackle community-based artwork, they approach it through traditional art criticism and theoretical analysis. The standards which art historians, theorists, and critics use to judge "creative excellence" are for the most part Euro-American-based and do not reflect the concerns of community-based art production.

The interjection of racial concerns into a film or an artwork seems to set everyone off in all directions. Whether it is within the larger independent film community or specifically the lesbian and gay community, racial difference strikes a powerful nerve in all of us. As a person of color, I can feel rage and frustration at the racism prevalent in our society.

I am committed to the fight for job equity in the arts in the film industry at the level of administration. However, at the creative and critical level, there is no such thing as equity. I have difficulties with supporting work simply because it is produced by a person of color or a lesbian or a gay man. I would strongly argue that simply "being a person of color" or simply "being gay" does not guarantee that the artist's work will be entertaining, politically motivated, or creatively outstanding. When dealing with work by producers of color or producers who come from a different experience and place, it is difficult to immediately contextualize the work with the construction of their community's identity and concerns. It seems that sometimes we as consumers take the simple route of validating the artists and their voice first and the work second.

I do not believe that white critics and theorists should shy away from examining works by producers of color. However, their opinions and analyses stem from a white perspective and sometimes they are uninformed about the issues themselves. This problem is also prevalent in critical analyses by straight critics and theorists of work produced by lesbians and gay men. Critical writing by anyone outside the specific producing community gives us one perspective. It can be an indication of the dominant, white, heterosexual codes. Analyses from within the specific community, on the other hand, can have an inside perspective. However, just because a critic is a member of a specific community doesn't mean that she or he has the critical grounding to contextualize and deconstruct the work and issues presented.

As this country becomes more and more aware of its multicultural reality, voices and concerns of "the other" struggle to be heard. Here, innovation and experimentation are the keys to the development of artistic and political clout for "people of color," lesbians, and gay men. Therefore, in order to encourage and engage with work produced outside a heterosexual and European standard, I feel that it is imperative to support the growth of an alternative discourse around these creative and theoretical issues.

I don't want the film or art market to dictate my stories. Nor do I want my community to limit the content and execution of my films. I don't believe that only women can write stories about women. Nor do I believe that people of color should create work only about people within their own communities. However, I personally feel that it is necessary that I take responsible steps when dealing with characters or issues outside my experience. I am currently working on my first feature-length film, which deals with the issue of gender identity. For the last two years, I have done extensive research in various transsexual communities in Canada and the U.S. It has been a process of altering my perceptions and creating a constructive dialogue-space between myself and members of the transsexual community. I will never be able to fully understand this very complex issue; however, I fully acknowledge my position and responsibilities to the communities I represent in my work.

It is a difficult challenge for an audience to view personal work and to allow room for a number of voices to be heard without feeling threatened or guilty for historic and systemic sexual discrimination or racism. A friend recently said to me, "seeing *The Displaced View* becomes like taking cod-liver oil, it's preventive medicine." I would not like to think of my films as Buckley's cough syrup—it tastes like shit but it's good for you.

I want my work to cause my audiences to challenge their ideas and their perceptions. I want my work to create a dialogue, to expose complexities and contradictions. I want my audience to ask questions.

Polite silence is a Canadian disease.

3

WOMEN IN THE SHADOWS
Reclaiming a Métis Heritage

Christine Welsh

W HEN I was invited to speak at the "Feminisms in the Cinema" conference at York University in November 1990, I very regretfully declined as I
was in the final throes of completing the script for my documentary film
Women in the Shadows, and I felt unable to step back from that process
and to speak about it with any kind of clarity or objectivity. Happily, that
is no longer the case. What follows is the story of the film—and of how I
came to make it—as well as my thoughts about the role such films are
playing in giving voice to the rich and multifaceted experience of aboriginal women in Canada.

Women in the Shadows is a very personal film. It tells the story of my
search for my Native identity and my ongoing struggle to reclaim my past
and my heritage—an odyssey into the past and a process of discovery in
which the making of the film ultimately played an integral part. It reaches
back across time to examine the lives of my own foremothers, Native
women who were remarkably representative of the time and place and society in which they lived and whose lives illustrate the sometimes painful
choices that confronted Native women throughout the turbulent history
of the Métis in western Canada. The film records my struggle to understand the choices my grandmothers made—to recognize that, for many
Native people, denial of their Native heritage and assimilation to the
"white ideal" was largely a matter of survival—and to accept them for
who and what they were: Native women who struggled to make a better
life for themselves and their children and whose strength, courage, and
resilience were fundamental to the evolution of a people and a nation.

Women in the Shadows is my/their story. As a film it is but an extension
of an enduring oral story-telling tradition that is both ancient and contemporary and which, in its totality, encompasses the entire story of a people,
both past and present. It is not a story which presumes to speak for all

Native women, for we come from many nations and we have many different stories, many different voices. I can tell only my own story, in my own voice. Leslie Marmon Silko, the Laguna poet and storyteller, puts it this way:

> As with any generation
> the oral tradition depends upon each person
> listening and remembering a portion
> and it is together—
> all of us remembering what we have heard together—
> that creates the whole story
> the long story of the people.
> I remember only a small part.
> But this is what I remember. (7)

From the air, the Qu'Appelle Valley of southern Saskatchewan is an aberration—a great green gash that slices crookedly across a precise geometric patchwork of yellow wheat fields and brown summer fallow. The muddy stream that snakes across its flat bottom widens here and there to form broad, shallow lakes, creating an oasis of cool greenery in an otherwise arid and treeless plain. Before the coming of the Europeans, the valley provided a welcome haven for the Plains Indians and the wildlife upon which they depended, and at the height of the fur trade in the old Northwest it formed an important link in the system of waterways and cart trails that began at the forks of the Red and Assiniboine Rivers and ran west and north to Fort Edmonton and south to the Cypress Hills and Montana. And it was here, in the late 1860s, that Métis buffalo hunters from Red River, in pursuit of the great herds that were being pushed farther and farther west, established temporary winter camps that would eventually become the permanent settlement of Lebret.[1]

My great-grandparents were among the first Métis families to set up camp down on the flats beside Mission Lake where the village of Lebret now stands. As long as the buffalo were plentiful they continued to live from the hunt, wintering in the Cypress Hills and returning to Lebret each summer to sell their buffalo robes, meat, and pemmican at the Hudson's Bay Company post at Fort Qu'Appelle. With the disappearance of the buffalo they no longer wintered out on the plains, choosing to remain at Lebret and earn their living by trading, freighting, farming, and ranching. They are buried there beside the lake among their kinfolk, and the names on the headstones in that little cemetery—Blondeau, Delorme, Desjarlais, Ouellette, Pelletier, Welsh, and many more—bear silent witness to the diaspora of the Red River Métis.

Of course the word *Métis* meant nothing to me when, as a child, I accompanied my parents and grandparents and brother and sisters on our annual midsummer pilgrimage to Lebret. We all piled into my father's car and made the trip out to the valley in a state of high spirits that was nonetheless leavened with a note of solemn observance. The saskatoons would be ripe, and there would be plenty of berries to pick in the deep gullies of the valley—not to mention the milkshakes to be had at the Valley Café in Fort Qu'Appelle before we started back to the city. But first there would be the obligatory climb to the little white chapel that perched high above Lebret—a hot, dusty trek up a narrow trail cut straight into the side of the hill and marked at intervals by towering white crosses signifying the Stations of the Cross that could be seen for miles up and down the valley. The chapel was invariably locked in a futile attempt to discourage vandals, so after catching our breath we would make our descent, sliding and scrambling, grabbing tufts of sagebrush to break our fall. After that there would be a visit to the big stone church down on the flats beside the lake and then a tour of the adjacent graveyard during which my grandmother would pray for all our relatives, both living and dead. I still remember the taste of the berries and the milkshakes, and the smell of dust, sagebrush, and incense. And I still remember those headstones with all the strange-sounding names. "French," my grandmother said. "French." That was all.

I don't know when I first realized that among those ghostly relatives there was Indian blood. It was something that just seemed to seep into my consciousness through my pores. I remember my bewilderment when the other children in my predominantly white, middle-class school began to call me "nichi" on the playground. I had never heard the word before and was blissfully ignorant of its meaning, but it wasn't long before I understood that to them it meant "dirty Indian." Snippets of family mythology reinforced my growing sense that this was something to be ashamed of— especially the story of how my other, Eastern European grandmother had not wanted my mother to marry my father because he was part-Indian. By the time I was in high school I had invented an exotic ethnicity to explain my black hair and brown skin and I successfully masqueraded French or even Hawaiian, depending on who asked. But I lived in mortal terror that the truth would get out because, no matter how hard I tried to hide it, my native background seemed to be written all over me.

The 1960s gave rise to a new pride in Native identity among Native people across Canada, and even though I had no contact with other Native people I was swept up by the spirit of the times and began to feel that it was no longer necessary to try to hide who I was. But who was I? By the time I reached university in the early 1970s, denial of my Native ancestry had given way to a burning need to know. My curiosity was fueled by the discovery of a much-worn volume entitled *The Last Buffalo Hunter*, a biography of my great-grandfather, Norbert Welsh, which had been written in the 1930s and rescued by my mother from a secondhand bookshop. I reveled in the references to Norbert's Indian mother and his part-Indian wife, but they were shadowy figures—half-formed, incomplete—who seemed to inhabit only the margins of Norbert's story. And even though I was clearly interested in tearing away the shroud of mystery that seemed to surround them, my attempts were largely futile. Whenever I tried to raise the subject, strenuous attempts were made, especially by my grandmother, to diminish and deny any connection we might have to Native people. She actively discouraged my burgeoning interest in and involvement with "things Indian": "we" were very different from "them," she implied, and such associations would only bring me grief.

In spite of my grandmother's dire predictions, I spent much of the next fifteen years traveling to Indian communities across Canada and making documentary films on issues of concern to Native people. The work was enormously satisfying and rewarding, but my personal goal—to find out who I was and where I belonged—remained elusive. I soon realized that, while I might have Indian blood in my veins, I had no natural claim to understanding or participating in Indian culture: my family's rejection and denial of its Native heritage and my own "white," middle-class upbringing had seen to that. I was naive enough to think that I could bridge the gulf by sustained effort and sheer force of will, but no matter how hard I tried to fit into Indian society I always had the sense that here, too, I was an outsider—this time because I was "too white." I learned the hard way that one who swims between cultures can get stranded from either shore: I found myself adrift in a treacherous current of confusion, self-loathing, and despair, and I began to wonder if perhaps my grandmother had been right after all.

I saw very little of my grandmother during those years. I was living in Toronto, she was in Regina, and our contact consisted of occasional letters and brief visits once or twice a year. But the passage of time and my own lonely struggle to try to understand and come to terms with my Native heritage gradually led me to see her in a whole new light. Whereas in my youth I had felt nothing but contempt for the values that had led her to deny her Native heritage, I now began to feel a genuine bond of compassion and respect for this formidable old woman who seemed to visibly shrink and grow more fragile with each passing season. I was acutely aware that, just as we were getting to know each other, we would soon be separated for good. She was my only living connection with the past, my only hope of finding out who I really was, so even though she was still reluctant to talk about the past I kept on asking my questions. While she continued to steadfastly maintain the distinctions between our family and other Native people, she must have had some sense of how important this was for me because she began to try to give me some answers. And so began a series of long afternoons, often separated by intervals of several months, during which she told me about her parents and grandparents, about growing up in Lebret and being sent to school at the convent in St. Charles, about raising her family during the Great Depression and sending two of her sons to fight in World War II, never to see them return. We spent hours poring over old family photographs, putting names and faces to those ghostly ancestors who had haunted my childhood. And then, quite suddenly, she died.

I was uncomfortably pregnant with my first child and was unable to undertake the journey from Toronto to Regina for my grandmother's funeral, but I was there in spirit as she made the trip out to the valley for the last time and was laid to rest in the little cemetery on the flats down by the lake. She never saw my son, Daniel; he was born a few months after she died. Somehow those two events marked a turning point for me. I was determined that my child was not going to grow up as I had, cut off from his past. But how could I give him a sense of who he was and where he came from if I didn't know myself? And with my grandmother gone, how would I ever find out? The only thing she left me was a child's sampler, mounted in a faded gilt frame, that had been embroidered by my great-grandmother and that bore her name: Maggie Hogue. It seemed like such an insignificant thing at the time, but in fact my grandmother had bequeathed to me the very thing she had been unable to give me while she was alive—the key to unlocking the mystery of my past.

I put my great-grandmother's sampler up on the wall in my kitchen, but with the demands of being a new mother I scarcely gave it a moment's thought during the months that followed. I had returned to university and was pursuing my deepening interest in Native history by studying the recent work that had been done on the role of Native women in the North American fur trade. For almost 200 years, beginning with the founding of the Hudson's Bay Company in 1670, the fur trade dominated the history of what is now western Canada. From it there emerged a unique society which drew upon both Indian and European customs and technology. Though it has been traditionally regarded as an exclusively male pursuit, I learned that women—Native women—in fact played an essential economic, social, and political role in the fur trade. Initially, very few white women were permitted to brave the perils of the "Indian country," so most fur traders took Indian (and later mixed-blood) women as "country wives." These "marriages à la façon du pays" were socially sanctioned unions, even though they were not formalized according to the laws of church or state. But with the establishment of the first settlements in the early 1800s white women began to go west, and it soon became fashionable for the traders to legally marry white women and to try to sever their ties with their Native country wives.

In the forefront of this trend was Sir George Simpson, governor of Rupert's Land[2] and, by all accounts, the most important personage in the Canadian fur trade, who had taken as his country wife a mixed-blood woman named Margaret Taylor. Though she bore him two sons, Margaret Taylor was abandoned by Simpson when he married his English cousin, a move which signaled the widespread rejection of Native women as marriage partners by "men of station" in fur-trade society and reflected the increasing racial and social prejudice against Native women throughout pre-Confederation Canada. Clearly, Margaret Taylor's story epitomized a crucial chapter in the history of Native women in Canada, but I was equally intrigued by its epilogue—her hastily arranged marriage to a French Canadian voyageur whose name was startlingly familiar: Amable Hogue.

On the basis of my great-grandmother's faded sampler and a rather incidental footnote in a history book, I began a search that eventually verified my connection to my great-great-great-grandmother, Margaret Taylor—a search which culminated in the making of Women in the Shadows. For me, finding Margaret was the beginning of a journey of self-discovery—of unraveling the thick web of denial, shame, bitterness, and silence that had obscured my past and picking up the fragile threads that extended back across time, connecting me to the grandmothers I had never known and to a larger collective experience that is uniquely and undeniably Métis.

My search for my Native grandmothers was hampered both by the inadequacies of traditional historical sources with respect to women and by the code of silence that existed in my own family with respect to our Native heritage. But, after venturing down a couple of blind alleys, I finally called my great-aunt Jeanne, who is my grandmother's youngest sister and the only surviving female relative on that side of my family. When I was growing up, Aunt Jeanne hovered on the edge of the family and her infrequent visits were characterized by an atmosphere of tension that you could cut with a knife. When I called Aunt Jeanne I hadn't seen or spoken to her in more than twenty years, yet she was surprised and touched that I remembered her and seemed eager to help me in any way she could. Aunt Jeanne knew about Margaret Taylor, and knew that she had some connection to Governor Simpson, but said that this had never been discussed because, in the words of Jeanne's mother, it had brought shame on the family. Nevertheless, Aunt Jeanne was able to tell me the names of Margaret Taylor's daughters and grandaughters, and in the act of naming them I finally had the sense of reaching back and grasping hands with all my grandmothers and great-grandmothers—right back to Margaret Taylor.

Like most Native women of her time, Margaret Taylor left no diaries, no letters, no wills—no written record that might have helped me reconstruct her life as *she* perceived it. Her voice is not heard in the historical record, and so I was forced to rely on the logs, journals, letters, and account books that form the written history of the fur trade for the few maddening snippets of factual information to be found about her life. For it was the men of the fur trade—our European forefathers—who wrote the story of the historic encounter between Indian and European on this continent. And because they wrote it, the history that has been passed down to their descendants—the history that has been taught to generations of half-breed children, including me—is their story, from their point of view. In the absence of any other version of the story, we have identified with them—with their struggle, their courage, their triumph. But what about our Indian foremothers? What about their struggle and their courage? The fur traders wrote almost nothing about the Indian women who shared their lives. And thus the voices of our grandmothers remain silent, leaving us to wonder about the story *they* would have told if they had been able to write it down.

The existing records show that my great-great-great-grandmother, Margaret Taylor, was born on Hudson's Bay in 1805. Her mother was an Indian woman who was known only as Jane. Jane is almost nameless, certainly faceless, but I can make some reasonably well-informed assumptions about what her life might have been like. She was probably one of the Homeguard Cree—the "Great House people" who, by the late 1700s, had forged close ties with the traders who lived in the isolated trading posts on the shores of Hudson's Bay. In exchange for the European goods that had revolutionized their lives—guns, knives, axes, kettles, cloth, beads, and brandy—the Cree traded their furs and supplied the posts with country provisions to help the traders survive the long, cold winter months.

It was incomprehensible to these people that the fur traders had brought no women with them, for women were the strength and backbone of aboriginal society—those with the power to give life and the wisdom to sustain it. In offering their women as wives for the newcomers, the Cree were making a remarkable gesture of friendship and goodwill, one that drew the white men into the heart of aboriginal society in a way that nothing else could and established bonds of kinship, understanding, and trust that formed the very foundation of the fur trade. For it was the women who taught their new husbands the skills needed to survive in the wilderness, and it was their comfort and companionship that made life bearable for the fur traders in this strange new land. As guides, teachers, helpmates, and wives they occupied an important and privileged position as "women in between" two worlds, and it was they who bridged the gulf between the old ways and the new.[3]

Margaret Taylor's mother, Jane, was one of these women. I do not know when or where she was born, but I do know that sometime in the late 1790s she became the "country wife" of one George Taylor, the Hudson's Bay Company's sloopmaster at York Factory on Hudson's Bay. But what did she feel, my Indian grandmother, at the prospect of marrying a white man? Was it enthusiasm, indifference, dread? I'll never know for sure. All I know is that their union produced at least eight children, including Margaret, and that when George Taylor retired from service with the Hudson's Bay Company in 1815 he returned to England, leaving Jane and their children behind.[4]

It seems that Jane remained at York Factory, at least for a time, for the post journal indicates that she continued to receive provisions during the following winter—some damaged salt pork, a little flour, a few biscuits. But after that, nothing—no record of where she went or how she managed. Most likely she returned to live with her own people, taking her daughters with her. There they would have learned to live according to her ways—to know the animals and birds, and to recognize the voices of their ancestors. Yet they carried within them the spirit of two peoples: they remembered other voices, other ways, and they must have known that they were different. Not Cree like their mother, though they spoke her language; not English like their father, though they bore his name; but something else, something unique—a new people.

It must have been Jane who taught her children to make the best of who and what they were—to take from two cultures the things they would need to make their way in a world that was shifting and changing before their very eyes. No longer could her daughters rely on those skills that had made her so indispensable to her husband—those things that had been passed from mother to daughter among her people for as long as anyone could remember. The fur traders no longer needed Indian wives to help them survive in the wilderness: they now looked with pleasure on the light-skinned, mixed-blood daughters of their own kind for the womanly qualities they sought in a wife. With no father to look to their future and pave the way for a suitable marriage, it must have been Jane who painstakingly groomed her daughters to survive in the only way that seemed possible—by becoming all that the traders most desired, shining examples of European ideals of beauty, modesty, and virtue. And in time her diligence paid off, for it was *her* daughter who eventually caught the eye of the governor himself, George Simpson.

Margaret Taylor was just twenty-one years old when she became the "country wife" of the governor of Rupert's Land. Her brother Thomas was George Simpson's personal servant, and it was probably through him that Margaret first came to the governor's attention. Though George Simpson was notorious for indulging in short-lived liaisons with young Native women, his relationship with Margaret Taylor appeared to be different. He relied on her companionship to an unusual degree, insisting that she accompany him on his historic cross-continental canoe journey from Hudson's Bay to the Pacific in 1828. Not only did Simpson recognize and assume responsibility for their two sons, but he also provided financial support for Margaret's mother and referred to Thomas Taylor as his brother-in-law, thus giving Margaret and the rest of fur-trade society every reason to believe that their relationship constituted a legitimate "country marriage" (H.B.C.A. fo. 10, 346). Nevertheless, while on furlough in England in 1830—and with Margaret and their two sons anxiously awaiting his return at Fort Alexander at the mouth of the Winnipeg River—Simpson married his English cousin, Frances Simpson.

It is not hard to imagine Margaret's shock when she learned that the governor was returning with a new wife. No doubt she and her children were kept well out of sight when Simpson and his new bride stopped at Fort Alexander during their triumphant journey west from Montreal to Red River. Once the Simpsons were installed at Red River the governor lost no time in arranging for Margaret's "disposal," and a few months later she was married to Amable Hogue, an event which drew this comment from one contemporary observer: "The Governor's little tit Bit Peggy Taylor is also Married to Amable Hog what a down fall is here . . . from a Governess to Sow."[5]

Amable Hogue, who had been among Simpson's elite crew of voyageurs, was hired as a stonemason on the construction of Simpson's new headquarters at Lower Fort Garry. From her vantage point in the Métis laborers' camp just outside the walls, Margaret would have been able to watch the governor and his bride take up residence in their magnificent new home. For his service, the Hudson's Bay Company gave Hogue a riverfront lot on the Assiniboine River just west of its juncture with the Red—a piece of prime real estate that now lies in the heart of downtown Winnipeg. And it was there that Margaret Taylor spent the rest of her life, raising her family, working beside her husband on their riverfront farm, and joining with her neighbors in the buffalo hunts that were the lifeblood of Red River Métis.

My great-great-great-grandmother's life spanned the rise and fall of the Métis nation. By the time she died in December 1885—just a few weeks after the hanging of Louis Riel—the world that she and other Métis women had known had changed irrevocably. Rupert's Land had become part of the emerging Canadian nation, and immigrants from eastern Canada and Europe were pouring into the old Northwest to lay claim to homesteads on land that had been the home of Indian and Métis people for generations. The buffalo were gone, the fur trade was no more, the Indians were confined to reserves, and the Métis had lost their land and their way of life. The Métis resistance that had begun at Red River in 1870 and that ended at Batoche in 1885 resulted in the final dispossession and marginalization of the Métis people. In the dark years that followed, very few Métis people spoke about being Métis and there was widespread denial of Métis identity among the generations of Métis who survived that troubled time and who grew up in its aftermath.

It is impossible to know when the process of denial and assimilation began in my own family, but I feel in my heart that it goes right back to what happened to Margaret Taylor. Here, I believe, are the roots of our denial—denial of that fact of blood that was the cause of so much pain and suffering and uncertainty about the future. Is it such a surprise that, many years later, Margaret's own son would choose to describe his mother as "a sturdy Scotswoman" rather than the half-breed that she really was?[6] Perhaps Margaret herself perpetrated this myth, if not for her sons' sake then certainly for her daughters', to try to spare them a fate similar to her own and that of her mother. I'll never know. But I do know that the denial of our Native heritage, which has been passed on from generation to generation of my family, is explicable in light of those events that took place so long ago, and I am finally able to see it not as a betrayal but as the survival mechanism that it most certainly was. For we *did* survive—even though, for a time, we were cut off from our past and our people—and we did so largely because of the resourcefulness, adaptability, and courage of my grandmothers.

Unlike Alex Haley, whose search for "roots" was prompted by obscure snatches of stories passed from generation to generation of his family and pumped into him like plasma from the time he could remember, my search for my Native grandmothers was prompted by silence—the silence that is the legacy of assimilation. When I began, I assumed that no such fragments, no messages from the past, had survived in my family. Yet in my Aunt Jeanne I found incontrovertible evidence that this was not the case. For Aunt Jeanne, the answer to the question "Do you remember?" was like coming up from very deep water, giving voice to things which had not been forgotten but which had been deliberately submerged in a process of alienation from her Native heritage and assimilation into the dominant society which had become more firmly entrenched with each new generation. Yet for me, for Aunt Jeanne, and for all the other Native women who participated in the making of *Women in the Shadows*, the act of remembering—of reclaiming that which had been lost to us—was a process of affirmation: affirmation of the importance of Native women's experience; affirmation of the strength, courage, and resilience of our grandmothers; affirmation of our ability to speak both our past and our present, and to make our voices heard.

Thus, in the end, *Women in the Shadows* is about one Native woman's reconciliation with her past, her people, and herself. It is both a coming-to-terms with loss—the price that has been paid for assimilation by countless numbers of indigenous people in Canada and indeed throughout the world—and a celebration of survival. Yet, as Métis poet and historian Emma LaRocque pointed out during the making of the film, our survival carries with it certain responsibilities:

> You and I are survivors. We're here because the generations that came before us survived, and maybe generations a hundred years from now will be there because we survived. We have to go on, and part of going on is that we are creating and re-creating and freshly creating. That's our role right now. But unlike Margaret and your grandmothers and my grandmothers, the challenge for us today is to survive—to be who we are—without paying the price of hating ourselves and rejecting a part of ourselves. That's the big issue—not just that we survive, but that we survive well and healthily without having to abandon anything that is of us.

Contemporary aboriginal women are responding to that challenge. Our stories, poems, songs, and films have a recurring theme—that of survival, continuance. It is a theme born of what Emma describes as "a haunting and hounding sense of loss" that is unique to a people dispossessed and that compels us to keep saying over and over again: "I remember" (LaRocque, xxviii). For our words and music and images are testaments to the remarkable fact that *we are still here*—that we have survived near-annihilation, and that we continue to resist—and though they necessarily give voice to our pain, they also express our vision for the future, and in so doing they become tools for healing, for empowerment, and for change.

As we continue to raise our voices—to write, to sing, to teach, to make films—we do so with the certainty that we are speaking not only for ourselves but for those who came before us whom history has made mute. We have a responsibility to our children and our people to ensure that the voices of our grandmothers are no longer silent. And so the voices of my grandmothers are alive today, for they speak through me.

Notes

1. Métis: In Canada, the name given to the mixed-blood population that resulted from the intermingling and intermarriage between Indians and Europeans that followed the European invasion and colonization of the Americas. Written with a small "m," métis is a racial term for anyone of mixed Indian and European ancestry. Written with a capital "M," Métis is a sociocultural or political term for those originally of mixed ancestry who evolved into a distinct indigenous people during a certain historical period in western Canada. This latter group includes the Métis to whom this paper refers—the descendants of Hudson's Bay Company men and the predominantly Cree women with whom they founded families in the decades following the coming of the HBC traders to Hudson's Bay in the 1670s.

2. Rupert's Land: The vast drainage basin of Hudson's Bay given by royal charter to the Hudson's Bay Company in 1670.

3. For a thorough discussion of the role of Native women in the Canadian fur trade, see Sylvia Van Kirk, "Many Tender Ties": Women in Fur-Trade Society, 1670–1870 (Winnipeg: Watson and Dwyer Publishing Ltd., 1980).

4. For information on the family of George Taylor, see Hudson's Bay Company Archives (H.B.C.A.) biographical file on George Taylor; also H.B.C.A. D4/113, fo. 146-d.

5. This is what W. Sinclair says to E. Ermatinger, August 15, 1831; quoted in John S. Galbraith, The Little Emperor: Governor Simpson of the Hudson's Bay Company (Toronto: Macmillan of Canada, 1976), p. 109.

6. Article in the Winnipeg Free Press, January 11, 1919: "Mr. and Mrs. Joseph Hogue, Both Born in Manitoba, Wedded 60 Years Ago Today."

Works Cited

Galbraith, John S. The Little Emperor: Governor Simpson of the Hudson's Bay Company. Toronto: MacMillan of Canada, 1976.

H.B.C.A. B239/C/2; B239/C/1.

LaRocque, Emma. "Here Are Our Voices—Who Will Hear?" in Joanne Perreault and Sylvia Vance, eds., *Writing the Circle: Native Women of Western Canada*. Edmonton: NeWest Publishers Ltd., 1990.

Marmon Silko, Leslie. *Storyteller*. New York: Seaver Books, 1981.

4

"WHO IS SPEAKING?"

Of Nation, Community, and First-Person Interviews

Trinh T. Minh-ha

Interview conducted by Isaac Julien and Laura Mulvey after the screening of *Surname Viet Given Name Nam* at the London Film Festival, November 1989.

Isaac Julien: *Apart from the title being a pun, a play on, or a parody of naming a country, a nation, there seemed to be a play with documentary form in the first instance—interviewees talking as first subjects—and then this deconstruction in the middle where we saw it break down, that it was really a constructed interview, rather than something that was first person, subjective. Then the third part was really a catharsis, subjective, a number of different voices coming together, a whole break down, and I just wanted you to elaborate on the kind of form, because it is different from* Naked Spaces—Living Is Round, *and harks a little more to* Reassemblage, *in terms of questioning documentary form, and deconstructing a number of devices.*

Trinh: You are the first viewer to talk about the naming of the country—or the attempt to name a country—and to relate that to a questioning of the first-person interview in the film. It's a most perceptive reading; one that is pivotal, but that I have not yet had the opportunity to discuss, because it has not come up in the audiences' questions so far. The film, structured by multiple strategies of cultural identification, is very much about how, even and especially for insiders, the naming of their own culture (the national narrative) remains plurally unstable. Viet Nam cannot be homogenized nor subsumed into an all-embracing identity. Not only the explicit enumeration of all the names of the nation in the last third of the film recalls the different moments in its history, but the title itself, *Surname Viet Given Name Nam*, invite explanations and interpretations that differ according to gender, political affinity, and subject positioning.

This title, taken from a gendered context of recent socialist tradition in Viet Nam, suggests both a personalization of the country and a differential construction of the culture from within. It can also be read in the film's framing, as a feminist necessity to rethink the questions of community, nation, and identity, and to challenge nationalist assumptions of cultural mastery. On the one hand, *Viet* is the name of origin of the land and the ancestors of the Vietnamese people whom it is said migrated from meridional China, while *Nam* designates their further southern relocation in relation to China—whose historical domination of Viet Nam continues bitterly to mark popular memory. On the other hand, Viet Nam as a name stands for the nation's (feminine-masculine, north-south) totality: to the question "Are you married yet?" of a man who makes advances to her, an unwedded woman would *properly* imply that she is at the same time engaged and not engaged by answering, "Yes, his surname is Viet and his given name is Nam." It requires wit to reply that one is married to the state; but such wittiness speaks volumes for what it both is supposed and not supposed to say on the question of gender and nationalism. And the risk incurred in this form of feminine-nationalist in/directness is, for me, the same risk taken in the simultaneous filmic construction and deconstruction of the first-person interview in documentary practice.

In the making of this film, the politics of the interview emerges fraught with uneasy questions. As you point out very clearly, the first part of the film deals with interviews that set out to be first-person witnesses to women's condition, but then, as they unfold, not only is it more apparent that their materialization borders the dialogue and the monologue, but it also fundamentally raises the question "who is speaking?" Although the interviewee does address an ambiguous "you" (a "you" that is directed not only at the original interviewer and the filmmaker but also at the English-speaking viewer, including here the Vietnamese viewer in exile), what is offered to the viewer in this part are long socio-autobiographical criticisms whose unconventional length and use of spoken language allow each woman her own space. It is, for example, at the difficult pace of her English utterances that the story of her life is unrolled, and the film structured. Lighting, setting, framing, camera movement, shot duration, and the use of visualized words are other strategies indicative of the carefully constructed nature of the interviews. The attentive viewer is bound at one point or another to puzzle over the voice of the film. I wanted to keep the reenactment ambiguous enough in the first part so as to solicit the viewer's sense of discovery, which may grow with means other than plot, story, or message—means unique to cinema as a medium.

The interviews are made to look gradually less and less "natural" as the film advances. Only halfway through it does the staged quality of the visualized speech become more manifest: when a woman is seen pacing back and forth while she delivers her thoughts; when another woman is also seen speaking with her back to the camera in a denuded setting; or when the reflexive voice-over is heard with the synchronous voice, thinking aloud the politics of interviews. Thus, interviews which occupy a dominant role in documentary practices—in terms of authenticating information; validating the voices recruited for the sake of the argument the film advances (claiming however to "give voice" to the people); and legitimizing an exclusionary system of representation based on the dominant ideology of presence and authenticity—are actually sophisticated devices of fiction.

The play on the fictions of documentary is differently layered throughout the film. This is conveyed to the viewer, among others, by the diverse cinematic means mentioned earlier, which became all the more perceptible in what you could call the third part of the film: when the active-reductive, more documentary-like editing and cinematography of the "unstaged" life activities and snatches of conversation sorely stand out in relation to those of the "staged" material offered in the first part; hence this statement by a voice-over: "By choosing the most direct and spontaneous form of voicing and documenting, I find myself closer to fiction." It is certainly nothing new to say that every documentary practice fundamentally involves elements of fiction, just as every good fiction film has a profound documentary quality to it.

IJ: *I know in my practice, and in Laura's practice as well, in using documentary there's always this tension if one wants to comment on the way documentary films are constructed, but then the way your subject is positioned within that text is a problem. Then there is the extra, what I would call the burden of representation—making films about subjects that have not been given voice—that you face in relationship to trying to give that subject in some way its own voice without it being the "authentic" voice. In your film I felt these tensions. I avoided it because I didn't interview anybody, really. That was my way of dealing with it, but I know that to a certain extent that didn't work as well. I thought that your attempt was a brave one.*

T: This raises another issue that came up, on a more simple level, when I approached the women for this film. In the casting process, it was important for me to hear about their own life stories before I decided on the voices that they would be incorporating. Within the range of their personal experiences, which were sometimes worse than those they were reenacting, they could drift in and out of their roles without too much pain. But in selecting them for who they are rather than simply for who they can play, I was not so much looking for authenticity as I was interested in seeing how they would draw the line between the differing fictions of living and acting. What the film tries to set into relief is precisely the fact that whether they act or whether they are telling us about their own stories, speech is always "staged" (or "tactical," as a statement in the film says).

Direct speech does not transcend representation. To a certain extent, interviewees choose how they want to be represented in what they say as well as in the way they speak, dress, and perform their daily activities. To push the limits of self-representation a bit further, the second and, even more so, the third parts of the film are organized around "documented" scenes that materialize the choices the women made when, as a structural device, I asked each of them how they would like to see themselves represented, after having been put through the ordeal of incorporating other women's pain, anger, and sadness. My own role thus shifted from that of a director in the first half to that of a coordinator in the last half. Hence you move here to what you called earlier a "catharsis"—or what I myself would see as the height of "documentary" fiction: the place where the diverse fictions of representation and self-representation come together. The result in this last half is a fabric of "excess"—of scenes that were sometimes fantasized and could be judged at first sight as being gratuitously unrelated: for example, a woman is merely cooking or quietly drinking tea; another is jogging solitarily in a park; yet another is sitting next to a fish pond; and a fourth one is performing her Tai Ch'i or doing a public presentation on the Vietnamese dress. These are things that, in a way, embarrass me (laughter)—at least initially, but afterward I understood, because they are so much a part of myself as well. They embarrass me because I have problems with forms of presentation that tend to commodity ethnicity. This was for me the case with the live exemplification of Vietnamese women's historical and customary attires (the *ao dai* in its evolution). But seen in the context of this film, where women's bodies and the way they are clad constitute one of the critical threads woven through the entire texture of the work, it really adds a dimension to the critique and does not come out as just a commodification of ethnicity.

IJ: *No. . . . In the beginning, where this question comes up about pleasure, where for me the beginning is very sensuous, there are the colors, the way this works to create a mood for it, I think, is important.*

T: Yes. Commonly enough, I had to learn to give up much in this film and to burn all the intentions during the making process. In the reenacted interviews, we (the art director and I) were partly going after the feminist "natural look"; thus, the women involved are clad in very simple clothing, which is what they would wear in socialist Viet Nam. But in the "real-life" shooting situations where they had a choice, they would all prefer to wear makeup and to dress up with showy colors. For the viewer, especially the Western viewer, this has been misleading in terms of class, because of the habit of attributing fancy garments to the bourgeoisie and practical, if not drab clothes to the working class. Not only such a habit is itself class-defined, hence indicative of the viewer's middle-classness; but it is also oblivious of circumstances and contexts. So while I was still trying to be "truthful" and to hang on to some vestiges of documentary practice in my choices as director, the women were, in fact, opening it up by insisting on what, in certain cases, is an imaginative flight from their working-class daily realities. As I state elsewhere, the legacy of dressing down in public occasions (here, on film) belongs in all probability to middle-class women who wish to ally with the cause of the working class.

IJ: *That's very interesting, because for me that's about desire, and wanting to fictionalize yourself in a particular way, because to a certain extent they realize they want to present themselves in a way that may be different from the way they may be every day. Because its a special experience. Andy Warhol spoke about this, "fifteen minutes of fame...."Those things are unavoidable really once you start interviewing people not familiar with different technologies.*

Laura Mulvey: *I've got a few general questions, then some specific things. The first thing is a way in which the film could be read, and judging from what I've heard you say in discussion afterward—I'm not sure if this is the way in which you intend it to be read, and that is that there is a before-and-after structure in the film. Actually, not a before and after, more a kind of here-and-there structure: the experiences women are undergoing in Viet Nam, seen or understood through a comparison with women in the U.S. Is that a false reading?*
T: I was not so much comparing—

LM: *Would you say a kind of juxtaposition?*
T: Yes, a juxtaposition, but with no linear intent in mind, so that's why

I prefer it when you said here and there, rather than before and after, because there is no before and after.

LM: *Yes, exactly. Because that's your point—a very beautiful point about people thinking that there's a moment when things start, but in fact they're just a continuum.* I think you had the sound of a train on the soundtrack . . . the sense of something running along on it's own momentum, outside the way people may read history. I wanted to ask you about the politics of that separation—juxtaposition—between the U.S. and Viet Nam, especially as you were talking about the commodification of the traditional culture in the U.S., but then at the same time the picture of Viet Nam is very much one of oppression—the state of women in Viet Nam is one of oppression. So in some ways it's a rather bleak picture, of sexual oppression on one side and the commodification of sexuality on the other side.*

T: Actually, I would also see sexual oppression happening in the context of the United States. It's not only the commodification of ethnicity, but also the perpetration (with refinement) of many of the oppressive concepts in traditional Vietnamese culture. Despite its specific focus, this film is not in fact only about Viet Nam and the Vietnamese diaspora. Certainly, some elements in the film are more accessible to those who are familiar with the culture; nonetheless, many viewers, especially yesterday after the screening, have come to me individually and said that they didn't feel the film was just about Vietnamese women, but also about themselves and about the condition of the women they know. These viewers, mostly women of color from diverse nations, but also white American women, recognized the experiences of the women featured as their own. This is more important to me. When I put forth the fact that the question of women is still very much at issue in socialist Viet Nam, I do not see it as a problem of socialist Viet Nam alone, but as one that cuts across the borderlines of nations and cultures. It is with this in mind that I have selected the strategies and information advanced in the film.

The same problem exists in other socialist countries of the Third World and in any libertarian movement. This is nothing new because feminists of color have repeatedly been very vocal in pointing out how, within revolutionary movements, sexism remains a problem. One cannot simply

---

* Laura is referring here to a statement in the film, which says: "There is always a tendency to identify historical breaks and to say 'this begins there,' 'this ends here,' while the scene keeps on recurring, as changeable as change itself." (T. M-h.)

equate Left with feminist, just as the question of gender cannot be collapsed with the question of race; the differentiation of these issues has been very alive in feminist debates. The fact that one is a socialist does not mean that one is freed from patriarchal values; although, of course, there can be at an institutional level more caution and more of an effort to ameliorate the condition of women. This is not denied in the film; nonetheless that effort in Viet Nam has been reduced, for example, to texts that are written by men to be read by women in women's unions. With all these speeches on equality, what is more blatant is the fact that no women are in the political bureau. That socialist Viet Nam is still caught in the patriarchal system is nothing particular to Viet Nam. The criticism of the film is therefore not directed toward socialist Viet Nam per se; it is directed toward the condition of women—whether in socialist or capitalist context, whether back home in the nation-space or over here in the community-space. In forgetting this, I feel that the tendency is always to *obscure* the question of gender by reverting it to a question of communism versus capitalism and salvaging it in a binary system of thinking.

LM: *What I thought was very interesting was the way that the question of women came out as taking a different form in each country—the way in which I thought it was important to show the Miss Viet Nam pageant, in the U.S., so you could see the Vietnamese community and traditions becoming Americanized, as well as becoming kitsch. There was one monologue I felt was perhaps the most moving and the most difficult to interpret in the context of the overall subject of the film. That was the one with the women doctor—very beautifully filmed. The one who talks about the problems at the hospital after the liberation, the disorganization of the hospital, the husband's arrest. I found it difficult to interpret because you bring on another soundtrack, during the interview, which is about the condition of being a wife in Vietnamese culture, and I became confused at that point, the text became too textured.*

T: I use that strategy more than once in the film, albeit differently each time. Aesthetically speaking, there is a moment within that passage which doesn't work for me either. That's when we hear, over the interviewee's voice, a poem read rather than sung; it's mainly a problem of distribution of dynamics that could be solved in mixing the sound. Since the aesthetic always acts on the politics, such a minor problem does influence the reception of the text. This being said, I'm glad you bring up this point, because one of the issues the film also addresses is that of translation. I am not really talking about the various meanings that one comes up with in translating, but of translation as a theoretical problem—the production of meaning, of identity, culture, and politics. The point you make reminds me of the time when I came to Paris for the International Women's Film Festival in Creteil. The translator for the festival ran up to me, and was at the same time excited, worried, and upset. She told me that it was a most challenging task to translate my film, because in many instances there are simultaneously two texts, and which one to choose! She was all worked up by that, so I said, well, you couldn't do otherwise but make a choice, and in making the choice she was very aware that translation not only determined the way the viewer would read the film; it could also not strive for mere likeness to the original without betraying the latter. Although the situation is slightly different, this is partly what I wanted to achieve myself: to problematize both the role of translation in film and the role of film as translation.

To come back to the point you made about being confused, because the two texts come at the same time—

LM: *It isn't just that they come at the same time, they seem to be also to some extent in contradiction with each other. She is talking in a sense not about her oppression as a woman, but the oppression of the southerners by the new administrative cadres.*

T: Oh yes, I see. That's a very nice reading; it also tells me that I have never seen the two as contradictory, only as supplementary. On the one hand she talks about the country, on the other she exposes the pathos of the family; and actually what appears as a representative case of a woman's and her family's distress also reads as the condition of woman in relation to the husband and the family. She was, in other words, suffering from a double cause. Although her story evolved around the deterioration of the hospital and the lack of competence of the new regime's staff, her real suffering began when her husband was taken away to a camp of reeducation. It was then that her entire perception of the working environment changed; so did her relationship with the hospital and her attitude toward her job and her children. The discovery of fear and the lonely endurance of humiliation on her side did not help the family. Finally, as she told us, she quit her job and got out of that situation, simply because she decided she had nothing to lose, except some ration tickets. So I thought the two oppressions fed on one another.

LM: *I see. I think I understand more now. So what she was exemplifying was the extent to which a Vietnamese woman who is middle class and a doctor internalizes her position of wife, and identifies with her very special position of wife.*

T: Yes. But you see, the difficulty in that case was, I was not simply criticizing. Because I think it would be very abusive in such a case to be merely critical. The challenge was to present the plight critically without condemning. For someone who is in that kind of situation, it seems important to be caring at the same time as one is critical. That's something I find most difficult in working on this film. The same applies for many of the scenes of the Vietnamese community in the U.S., of which the Miss Viet Nam pageant event that you mentioned is an example. How can a critique also be a compliment without being any less of a critique?

LM: *That's what I think was a bit confusing for the viewer, because I think one felt that the emotion that this woman suffered when she lost her husband is not something that one would criticize anyone for feeling. So to what extent you were associating it with an aspect of the position of wife as subordinate to the husband, which seemed to come in on the soundtrack at a certain point, did you think so?*

T: No, even the proverb that is sung on the soundtrack at that point simply evokes the loyalty and the sadness of the hard-working wife, who has to nourish her children while her husband is away. So once more it's not something that simply says she has submitted to her condition, but rather speaks of two sadnesses: one sadness that is proverbial and one that is historical, and the two go together. That's why even the word "criticize" here is not quite adequate, as you point out, because at the same time as one cannot condemn one can still show to what extent we—women of Viet Nam and elsewhere—are internalizing the four virtues, which are introduced and directly commented upon only later in the film, in the context of Vietnamese women in the U.S. The traditional four virtues prescribe how to behave to one's husband and by extension to the society. She must know how to manage the household skillfully; maintain a compliant appearance; speak properly and softly; and be faithful and respectful—all this to save the husband's face. In other words, a woman's identity is entirely defined by her demeanor toward her husband and/or, to recall the title of the film, by her adeptness at saving the nation's face.

Understanding this, how is one to look at this woman doctor? Her story is deeply moving; so are some of the proverbs and songs that tell us poignantly about the fate of women. But the doctor carries the four virtues in her very resistance and suffering. And, to a certain extent, we all do. I cannot help but notice how these oppressive criteria remain imprinted in my everyday behavior. Many of us, Vietnamese women living in the U.S. and in Europe, who have access to work and individual "liberty," may laugh when we hear of the three submissions and the four virtues, but that's only because the higher we climb, the more multiply sophisticated the forms of oppression prove to be. So in looking at this doctor, or at any other women in the film, I also see myself; one cannot criticize here without getting caught in the criticism itself. This also applies to the viewers in the audience.

IJ: . . . *the way it brings us to the inside-out-outside-in dichotomy that you speak a lot about in your work. You speak about it in relation to nations—in every First World there's a Third World, and vice versa. And then this is brought up again in the nexus of the problematic where you're talking about subjectivities and the way in which patriarchy has destroyed that. But I wonder if you could maybe speak a little about the way—I mean, I was very sympathetic to the film, because it's the whole thing about having ruled subjects and then the whole thing around the responsibility of the filmmaker, kind of boring questions in a sense, but they are questions that are important. This is not really different from my first question that I asked, but, I mean, how does one resolve that? This may be asking for closure on this king of discourse, because maybe it not being resolved is a good thing, but it's like the relationship in this country to documentary practice, where the burden of representation, if you're a black filmmaker or a woman filmmaker, is very great still, and the grip of realism hasn't quite loosened from people's visions of seeing themselves, and I wondered what they thought when they actually saw it, because that's in the film as well.*

T: You mean the response of the women acting in the film? They did watch themselves acting on video during the rehearsal of the reenacted parts. Although one can certainly say that video doesn't quite have the same impact as that of film. They were aware of their acting, and, actually, they were the ones to criticize themselves most harshly. But with regard to how they come out in the entirety of the film, none of us—including myself—really know. I started out with that limited body of interviews carried out in Viet Nam by Mai Thu Van, but the way the film developed and got "scripted" came with the making of it, and I really didn't *know* it beforehand. So when the film was shown and the women saw themselves on the large screen, I guess it was a great surprise for them. On the one hand, it has always been an odd experience to look at oneself and one's self-consciousness as spectator; they had no flattering words for themselves and

tended to laugh at what they perceived as their own awkwardnesses in acting. On the other, they didn't anticipate how complex all the issues were
in relation to their own role, and how powerful film could be as a medium.
They were somewhat intimidated by the packed audience at the premiere
of the film, and one of them told me: "we just realize now with fright that
thousands of people will be seeing this film."

Of course, there are some parts that also worried them, and it has to do
with the way they wanted to be represented—which brings us back to your
question. I love the way you keep on asking and saying at the same time
that the questions (of responsibility and of non/representation) raised cannot simply be resolved. Precisely because the challenge is renewed every
time one makes a film. The part the women seemed to prefer were the
places where they chose how they wanted to present themselves. There is
always a problem in relation to the part that they didn't choose; it was no
fun to play the "ordinary" or to take on the role of a sixty-year-old woman.
Some of them were even worried, as I said earlier, because if to the outsider
these reenacted interviews can be highly critical of the government in Viet
Nam, to the Vietnamese viewers they are very nuanced. What is also apparent in these interviews is the fact that the women are not just aspiring
for capitalism in criticizing socialism—there was none of that in their re-
ponses. On the contrary, they were saying very clearly that between two
exploitations of man by man they don't know where to stand. Again, this
is nothing unique to their situation in Viet Nam, especially when one
takes into consideration what is happening right now in Central and Eastern Europe, where the changes the peoples are fighting for have nothing to
do with any simple transfer to the ideology of the "free West." With this
nuance being very much present in the interviews, as well as the questioning of the feminine lady-maid-monkey condition, the women were quite
concerned about how the community would judge them. These are examples of the kind of preoccupations they had at the first viewing, but with
more viewings they apparently felt proud of the work they contributed and
they wanted the film to circulate in the community like the commercial
videos. . . . Two of the husbands said they were very moved by the film.

LM: *How did you choose the texts that you used at the beginning? What
criteria did you use?*
T: As one of the voice-overs in the film states, some of the criteria are:
the age, the work or the profession, the economic situation, the cultural
region where the interviewee grew up, her critical ability, and, sometimes,
the question of personal affinity. When I first started out I was a little more

"politically correct," in the sense that I was looking for a diversity of views and trying to include a wider range of professions, such as having a musician and a fish breeder, in addition to the employee in the restaurant service for foreign embassies, the two doctors, and the health technical cadre whom you heard in the film. I chose the last three right from the start because of the scope that their stories and analyses covered. I think the fact that these women are helping other women—devoting their skill to relieving not only the physical but also the psychological pains of other women—makes them stand out as those whose interactions with women's bodies and mental health allow them to evaluate women's condition with both depth and scope.

Whether I agreed with their viewpoints or not, their stories struck me as being informed, rich, and penetrating—at once social and utterly personal. This, despite their critical denial of any intimate knowledge of their patients. Whereas some of the other interviews such as that with the fish breeder would come out in the context of the film as being merely personal, hence reductive. Since the film was quite long, I had to cut down on the choices. The fact that the fish breeder's account was too personal could not do justice to what she was trying to say, and it could be easily misread as some simplistic form of anticommunism. She was criticizing the system, but according to food metaphors, such as comparing the change of staple foods, from rice and fish sauce to bland potatoes, to the imposed consumption of the foreign doctrines of Marx and Lenin.

I would rather not have a representative of the manual-labor class here, and maintain the integrity of the work by pursuing the links generated within the body of the diverse materials included. For example, the film also deals with the multiple appropriation and expropriation of women's bodies and, by extension, of Viet Nam as a nation—her being possessed and dispossessed at different historical moments by different outside forces. In addition to the many stories of the beloved historical heroines of Viet Nam, one epic poem occupies a pivotal role in the film: it is the popularized story of Kieu, a woman who sacrifices herself for her father and becomes a prostitute, selling her body to save his honor. All these elements tightly interact with the choice of the doctors—one from the north, one from the south, and the third being the northern health technical cadre whose ideological control over the doctors is strongly evoked in the latter's analyses.

Finally, such a choice takes into consideration regional differences to which the Vietnamese remain extremely sensitive: culturally and politically speaking, the voices of the film must represent the three regions of Viet Nam—north, south, and center. This determines not only the choices of the texts as related to the interviewee's cultural background but also the selection of the actors, whose accents differ markedly, especially when they speak Vietnamese, and, last but not least, the singing of the folk poetry.

LM: *So for example the woman that comes from the center spoke English with a voice that was accented differently from the others. . . . I missed that.*

T: It's normal. This is one aspect of language that remains inveterate and irreducibly idiomatic; I can't bring it out to the English-speaking viewer, and that's a limit of translation. For the Vietnamese, it is very evident since, by the feedback that I have had, I understand their attention is largely focused on this. As I just mentioned, such regionalist determination is also heard in the folk poetry, which was sung by one person, but in three accents, according to the context. However, if the demand for regionalism often springs from a hierarchically divisive attitude among certain members of the Vietnamese community, it can also be politicized and applied as a critical strategy. I found it very useful, for example, in trying to avoid reducing the Viet Nam reality to a binary opposition between communism and capitalism, to bring in the cultural role of the center precisely in order to decentralize the north-south duality.

Nowadays, the center part of Viet Nam does not, as in the Western sense of the term, represent power and stability. On the contrary, physically speaking, it no longer constitutes the location where the seat of the government is situated; and politically as well as culturally speaking, it stands as the unstable ground between First-World and Second-World regulations. The central region has always been the one that remains closest to traditional culture, while the southern region adopted the modernization program of the West, and the northern region, under the influence of Russia and China, works at eliminating traditional practices considered to be "feudal and backward." So what's happening to this "tradition"—which people from all three regions keep on claiming in defining the Vietnamese identity? It is here that one realizes the potential of the center as site of resistance—not in reinstating the authority of a national patrimony, or of an essentialist identity (a mere recovery of the authentic past is in any case an "inauthentic" and unrealistic goal), but in offering an "empty," nonaligned, always-and-not-yet-occupied space where the tension between past and present is politicized, hence neither negative nor simply positive.

LM: *I've got a couple more things on the content, then we can talk about the form, because the form is so stunning. I had a problem as well with having set up the interviews—the monologues—at the beginning to show their fictionality, which I thought of not so much as a fiction but as a showing that the testimony that was being given was not coming from the people that were speaking. It was to make a separation between the actresses and the words, to show that it was not authentic subjectivity that was speaking. As a critique I felt that that became rather difficult at the end when the actresses spoke as themselves. It somehow came back to an idea of an authentic subjectivity, so that a relation appeared between the actress and the part which kind of brought back the question of authentic speech.*

T: That goes quite against what I said earlier in relation to Isaac's questions about the structural positions of the film. Of course, your reading can be just as valid, but I hope that there are enough cues in the film to engender another reading as well. I think speech is tactical, and with the unveiling not only of the fictionality of the reenacted interviews but also the fictionality of the general nature of interviews in documentary practice the subsequent words of the women in the "real interviews" cannot no longer be considered as being simply "truthful." Unmediated access to authentic reality via the interview has been questioned, so that the viewer's critical ability is solicited before the "real interviews" are introduced. These interviews in which a camera and a microphone are set up to catch the "spontaneous words" of a woman while she is having lunch, for example, are no less staged than the reenacted ones; but now the "staging" may be taken more for granted by the viewer, it's more hidden, concealed, because it is no longer perceptible via the mise-en-scène or the language, but more via the situating, framing, editing, and contextualizing. Furthermore, when the women spoke, they mostly "chose" how to be heard, and perhaps—

LM: *Can you give us an example?*
T: The last interviews in Vietnamese with the two women who worked, one in a hydroelectric power company and the other in a hi-tech electronics company. When they were asked the question why they accepted to be on film, one replied that she had consulted her husband who encouraged her to contribute to "our native country"; and this was how she overcame her shyness to appear on film. She went on relating also how a friend of her husband teased her, saying: "Who knows, maybe you'll act so well that the Americans will notice you and you'll be a Hollywood star in the future." The other woman interviewed also considered her contribution not to be "an individual matter but one that concerns a whole community." She

went on relating, similarly, her friends' reactions and how they "were taken aback when they heard I was acting the role of a sixty-year-old woman."

What stands out for me in these answers is the fact that the women were extremely aware of both the role they played earlier in the film and the role they were assuming as they spoke "for themselves." They were clearly addressing, not the individual filmmaker, but the community and its authority. And, in a way, they were also voicing their desire as actors to a cinema public. There was no such thing as catching "life on the run," or capturing the words of "truth." Clearly, one truth that did not seem to come through their "real" lines was, for example, the tremendous difficulty one of the two women had to overcome when the time came for her to answer "on her own" and to speak as first subject. She was absolutely stuck in front of the camera and couldn't utter a single word in response to the questions. In between long uncomfortable stretches of silence she said, "What should I say?" "How should I answer? . . . I can't talk." And, typically enough, I said, just answer it the way you usually talk to me; say anything that comes through your mind. But it took her a long long time finally to come out with speech. There is no question, really, of soliciting and reproducing the "ordinary" (or the authentic) in an "unordinary" (or inauthentic) situation. So whether it was by choice or by lack of choice (it was both), this "truth" didn't come out in the delivery; what materialized was not just "anything" that crossed the women's mind but what they wanted the viewers to hear. It is in this sense that I find it difficult to see the last part of the film as a return to the voice of authenticity.

IJ: *It is a whole process really, I mean, your art must enter into that process with you in this kind of journey. . . . I know these questions are unresolved for myself. My practice is—since everything is fictional—to escape in fiction. And enter the realm of fantasy, then, within those spaces, to try to talk about politics or representation. At the same time I'm drawn to documentary film as well because I'm interested in that kind of tension. They all have their different laws—*
T: —and different sets of problems.
LM: *Can't escape. No way out.*
IJ: *I wondered if you could talk about the use of text and image in juxtapostion, where you have the subject speaking, when in some cases they were using English, in the same way that my mother and father use English—it's half their own language and half English, so there's this kind of hybrid taking place, and then you use text as well when they talk, and*

when you think it might be difficult to decipher and disseminate what's being said, so I wondered if you could talk about the use of text and image in your film.

T: Sure. Since the film tackles the problems of interviews and of translation, it cannot avoid dealing with language and with the relationship between languages. Beside deliberately using English for the interviews carried out in Viet Nam, and Vietnamese for those conducted in the United States; and beside juxtaposing different instances of English as used by Vietnamese Americans, I have also worked on the relationship between what is read, what is heard, and what is seen on screen. The duration of the subtitles, for example, is very ideological. I think that if, in most translated films, the subtitles usually stay on as long as they technically can—often much longer than the time needed even for a slow reader—it's because translation is conceived here as part of the operation of suture that defines the classical cinematic apparatus and the technological effort it deploys to naturalize a dominant, hierarchically unified worldview.

The success of the mainstream film relies precisely on how well it can hide (its articulated artifices) in what it wishes to show. Therefore, the attempt is always to protect the unity of the subject; here to collapse, in subtitling, the activities of reading, hearing, and seeing into one single activity, as if they were all the same. What you read is what you hear, and what you hear is more often than not what you see. My desire, on the contrary, was to "unsew" them and to present them as three distinct activities endowed with a certain degree of autonomy. Since the task of translation is more than to impart information, the viewer is made aware, in this film for example, of the gap between what is said or sung and what is read, through the minimal appearance of the burnt-in subtitles.

The necessity to free these activities from the "stickiness" of sameness can also be found in the relation between the verbal and the visual, and between writing and speech. Although differently materialized in each case, the word-image relationship in my films has always been one that refuses the use of the voice as being homogeneous to the image, and vice versa. In such a relationship, the role of an element is never simply to *serve* another—that is, to explain, to illustrate, or to objectify. For example, voice-overs need not be "fastened" to the visuals in an all-knowing mode; and the predicament of interviews lies here in their difficulty to solve the problem of talking heads, or to undo the fixity of synchronous sound and image—hence the name of "flat cinema" given to the talking film, and the need of a filmmaker like Marguerite Duras to break away from the habit of "screwing" (as she puts it) the voices to the mouths in realist cinema practices.

This discussion on the nonsubmissive relation between word and image leads us to the use of the text over the image in *Surname Viet*. The slight difference between the activities of reading and listening and its resulting tension is here created by the visibility of the small discrepancies between the text and the women's speeches (which are actually oral modifications of the text by the women themselves). The difference is also perceived in the fact that not only does the text not always enter at the same time as the speech, but its shorter duration on the screen also makes it quasi-impossible for the viewer to hear and read at the same time without missing parts of both. The tension that the viewer experiences in trying to synchronize the two activities is, at another level, also the tension that the women experienced in reenacting a speech that has been transcribed and translated. The effort required from them is both that of transferring a written text into a spoken one and that of delivering in a language that they have not mastered.

English as spoken by diasporic and Third World peoples has been widely treated by the media merely as a foreign language whose subtitling is a commonplace. I can't perpetrate such a hegemonic attitude, but I also can't ignore the amount of effort I require of English-speaking audiences. So as you rightly point out, I did use the text to help the viewer at moments when the women's foreign accents and articulations may start to make it difficult to follow the interview. But the texts are not presented as mere subtitles; they have a function of their own as discussed, and, aesthetically speaking, they are treated as a visual superimposed on another visual. Framed and composed over and in relation to the image of the woman speaking, they often invade it in its entirety.

LM: *About the rephotography, which you've used before. . . .*
T: No, I haven't used it in any other film.

LM: *So it's the first time you've used rephotography; what does it mean to you in this context? Why did you use it, and what were it's resonances?*
T: There are a number of meanings possible. First, the question of time. Working in the realm of stories and popular memories, I was not interested in a linear construction of time, and I was not attempting to reconstruct any specific period of Viet Nam history. Like the reenacted interviews, the archival images are indicative of the times, the places, and the contexts to

which they owe their existence. (One of the functions of the visual quotes preceding the interviews is also to date the women's accounts.) But the relations they generate among themselves as well as with the verbal texts of the film continually displace the notion of fixed time and place. Hence, the challenge is to use the very specificities of the black-and-white news footage and photographs to reach out both to a plural past and to an unspecified present and future.

An example: the 1950s footage of the north-south movement of the refugees is juxtaposed with a young woman's letter to her sister, reminiscing the time mother and daughters spent in Guam (in 1975) while waiting to be admitted into the states. Here the focus is neither on the plight of the refugees in the fifties nor on that in the seventies; rather, what seems more important to me is the specific nature of the problems women of many times and many places have to undergo—as women. This is brought out in the remembered story, through the mother's anguish and terror of rape in experiencing *again* "fleeing war on foot." So while the viewers follow images of refugees in the fifties with women clad quite unanimously in peasant attire and dark pants, they also hear about the mother's conviction in wearing dark clothes and persuading her daughters to do the same in the 1975 exodus "so as not to draw any attention to ourselves as women."

Another prominent example is the ending sequence of step-printed images of a group of refugees in the 1950s floating amid the sea on a raft, seen with comments on the contemporary condition of the "boat people" and, more recently yet, of the "beach people." The rephotography here stretches both the historical and the filmic time. It materializes the fragility of life, as it sets into relief the desperate and helpless character of such an escape. The insignificance of the tiny human forms on the drifting raft is seen against of the vastness of the sea. But the fact that such a scene was recorded also reminds the viewer of the presence of a seer: the refugees had been spotted in the distance by a camera (and reproduced by another camera). Thus, hope is alive as long as there is a witness—or, to evoke a statement in the film, as long as the witnesses themselves do not die without witnesses. In selecting the archival materials, recontextualizing and rephotographing them while acknowledging their transformations, I was, in other words, more interested in reflecting on the plight of women, of refugee and of exile through images, than in rehashing the mediated horrors of the war and the turmoil of the subsequent fall of Saigon—which accounted for the contemporary disquieting expansion of the Vietnamese diaspora.

To come back to a word you have astutely used, rephotography displaces, and displacement causes resonance. It is extremely difficult, on a certain level, to rationalize such "resonance" without arresting it. As Pushkin would say, "poetry has to be a little stupid." But if I am to further the discussion on another level without denying such a limit, I would add that the use of news footage and photography has its own problems in film practices—especially in documentary practices. The images have both a truth- and an error-value. In other words, they are above all media memories. This is where the desire to create a different look and reading becomes a necessity. In the film, the older news photography is not only selectively reproduced, it is also deliberately reframed, de- and recomposed, rhythmized, and repeated with differences. Needless to say, media images of Viet Nam are not only ideologically loaded; they are also gender clichés. So the point is not simply to lift these news images out of their contexts so as to make them serve a new context—a feminist reading against the grain, for example—but also to make them *speak anew.*

Perhaps an example here is the very grainy black-and-white images of three women moving in slow, truncated motion, right at the beginning of the film. They appear three times throughout the film, each time slightly different in their rhythms, framing, and visual legibility. The third time the viewers see them again, they are presented as they were originally shot, and with the original soundtrack, in which a male journalistic voice informs us that they were captured prisoners, whose bodies were "traditionally used by the enemy as ammunition bearers, village infiltrators, and informers. . . . " A multiple approach to the same image is at times useful to cause resonance in the very modification of the material. Just as the story of Kieu has been, throughout centuries, appropriated according to the ideological need of each government, the media images of women during the war have been shot for causes in which women hardly come out as subjects—never fully witnessing, only glorified as heroines or victimized as bystanders of, spectators to, and exiles in their own history.

II.

THE ROLE OF FANTASY
IN LESBIAN REPRESENTATION
AND SPECTATORSHIP

5

ON THE SUBJECT OF FANTASY

Teresa de Lauretis

O‍N THE subject of fantasy in the cinema, and in feminist work in cinema, much has been said but more remains to be said. My title puns on two meanings of the word *subject*, both of which are current and recurrent in discourses on cinema. The topic, or theme, of fantasy is of course a common one in reference to certain films, certain film genres or styles of film-making, certain traditions within the history of cinema (such as the one traced back to Méliès and opposed to the equally old tradition of realism); and then the idea of fantasy as illusion (and in contrast to "reality") has often served to characterize the phenomenon of cinema in its entirety— whether seen as a production of ideology or as entertainment, commodity, popular culture, or art. When cinema is equated with fantasy, cinema as the dream machine, fantasy may mean utopian promise or artificial escape—more often both at once, and both in contradistinction to "real life," the real of socioeconomic relations and political struggle, the daily business of living, and so forth.

But the meaning of "subject" in my title is more specific: it refers to the notion of subject in contemporary critical discourses ranging from psycho-analysis, film, and feminist theory to others that may be loosely gathered under the heading of cultural theory. When fantasy is predicated of this subject, it usually means a private, subjective, conscious or unconscious, process and a socially inconsequential event (something that takes place behind closed doors, inside one's head, in the dark of the movie theater, between consenting adults, etc.); but occasionally it also means a collective event, public, spectacular, and of enormous social consequence, as when an entire nation or social group is said to be the subject of a fantasy of domination, a fantasy of imperialistic, racial, religious, or sexual mastery (e.g., *Birth of a Nation*, *Triumph of the Will*, *Apocalypse Now*).

In my title, the subject of fantasy is a double trope, a phrase by which I mean to turn the first meaning of fantasy (fantasy as a topic or theme, and as opposed to "reality") into the second (fantasy as a psychic process, a staging of desire, and thus directly involved in the constitution of a subject's identity). But the trope also wants to perform a further semiotic turn from the psychoanalytic notion of subject, with her or his individual psyche, unique personal history, and subjectivity (as the subject of a psychoanalysis is supposed to be), to the notion of social subject: one whose subjectivity and psychic configuration are effectively shaped, formed and re-formed—but also disrupted or even shattered—by social technologies, practices, and representations, inside and outside the cinema, which overdetermine that unique and singular personal history. I place my subject of fantasy precisely in this turn, this slide of meaning between the subjective and the social.

By way of illustration, let me recall Liliana Cavani's film *Il portiere di notte* (*The Night Porter*) (1974): on the one hand, the subjective desire, the very personal passion, of Lucia and Max is inscribed and played out in a fantasy scenario of sadomasochism which is socially instituted and brutally imposed on them by one of the most spectacularized fantasies of racist and sexist domination in recent history; but on the other hand, their perverse desire and sexual passion—perverse by the standards of the whitewashed morality of those aspiring to social normalcy—*subvert* those aspirations and give the lie to the very notion of normalcy, and in particular to a normalcy of desire.

The film's careful construction of the fantasy scenario that is the setting of their desire at once replays and deconstructs for the spectator the terms of that fantasy—provided that she, the spectator, can be engaged by it. For, as the reception of *The Night Porter* showed, when it was first released in the U.S. in 1974, many spectators refused or were unable to be engaged: the fantasy was too threatening, too close to home, or too distanced perhaps. This is an important point, to which I will come back, because it suggests that, first, a particular fantasy scenario, regardless of its artistic, formal, or aesthetic excellence as filmic representation, is not automatically accessible to every spectator; a film may work as fantasy for some spectators, but not for others. Second, and conversely, the spectator's own sociopolitical location and psycho-sexual configuration have much to do with whether or not the film can work for her as a scenario of desire, and as what Freud would call a "visualization" of the subject herself as subject of the fantasy: that is to say, whether the film can engage her spectatorial desire or, literally, whether she can see herself in it.

But I am running ahead of my argument. Let me backtrack and provide some bibliographical notations on the subject of fantasy, which has been the focus of much recent film-theoretical work. For example, *Fantasy in the Cinema* is the title of a 1989 collection of essays edited by James Donald, who with Victor Burgin and Cora Kaplan had co-edited the influential *Formations of Fantasy* in 1986. The importance of this latter collection rests on its reprinting, together with contemporary essays influenced by them, two much earlier texts, Laplanche and Pontalis's "Fantasy and the Origins of Sexuality" (1964) and Joan Riviere's "Womanliness as a Masquerade" (1929). Both of these notions—femininity as masquerade and fantasy as constitutive of sexuality as such—have become central to current work in film, performance, and visual theory (and have directly influenced several of the essays collected in *Fantasy in the Cinema*). Indeed, the essay by Laplanche and Pontalis, which was originally published in *Les Temps modernes* with the title "Fantasme originaire, fantasmes des origines, origine du fantasme" and translated into English in the *International Journal of Psycho-Analysis* in 1968, is singly responsible for the second meaning of "the subject of fantasy" in my title, and therefore for the first turn of my trope. For the second turn, I am indebted to an important essay by Elizabeth Cowie published in 1984 and entitled "Fantasia," which was the first to pursue systematically, in relation to cinema, the implications of Laplanche and Pontalis's notion of fantasy as narrative scenario, mise-en-scène, and structuring scene of desire.

Take One

Rereading Freud's early writings up to and including his famous analysis of the beating fantasy, "A Child Is Being Beaten," in the context of the then burgeoning structuralist thought (of which Lacan was the main representative in psychoanalytic discourse),[1] Laplanche and Pontalis point out the continuous if ambivalent presence of the notion of fantasy in Freud, noting as well its ambiguous status in psychoanalytic theory in general; an ambiguity due to the fact that the term *fantasy* was semantically inscribed in a cultural opposition between illusion and reality which antedated psychoanalysis by centuries but which, like the opposition between mind and body, the psychoanalytic project was, in fact, engaged in undermining.[2] By following up the development of Freud's thought through his various (re)formulations of concepts such as psychic reality, the seduction theory, and the primal scenes (*Urszenen*), Laplanche and Pontalis make a convincing case for the metapsychological status of fantasy and its structural, constitutive role in subject processes.

Rejecting the formal separation between conscious and unconscious fantasies (between, for instance, daydreams and memory traces or fantasies recovered in analysis), Laplanche and Pontalis see a "profound continuity between the various fantasy scenarios—the stage-setting of desire" in the history of the subject. They mention three primal fantasies—the primal scene, seduction, and castration—and call them original fantasies or fantasies of origins (*fantasmes originaires, fantasmes des origines*) because, "[l]ike myths, they claim to provide a representation of, and a solution to, the major enigmas which confront the child": the primal scene (*Urszene*), which "pictures the origin of the individual" in the child's imaging of parental coitus; seduction, "the origin and upsurge of sexuality"; and "castration, the origin of the difference between the sexes" (19). But they also add—and this is an important emphasis against the structuralist postulate of universal structures—that, if the primal or original fantasies can be understood as a structure in the subject's prehistory, what Freud called phylogenesis, it is in the sense of a "prestructure which is actualized and transmitted by the parental fantasies" (27). Thus the original fantasies lie "beyond the history of the subject but nevertheless in history—a kind of language and a symbolic sequence, but loaded with elements of imagination; a structure, but activated by contingent elements" (18). The fantasies of origin, in other words, are historically structured as well as structuring of the subject's history; that is to say, the constitutive role of fantasy in subjectivity is both structural and historically motivated, historically specific.

With a brilliant conceptual turn, Laplanche and Pontalis link the fantasies of origin to the origin of fantasy (*origine du fantasme*) which, they argue, cannot be isolated from the origin of the drive itself, which in turn has its origin in autoeroticism; they maintain that autoeroticism is not "a stage of libidinal development" but rather

> a mythical moment of disjunction between the pacification of need (*Befriedigung*) and the fulfilment of desire (*Wünscherfüllung*), between the two stages represented by real experience and its hallucinatory revival, between the object that satisfies [the real object, the milk] and the sign which describes both the object and its absence [the lost object, the breast]: a mythical moment in which hunger and sexuality meet in a common origin. (24–25)

But this "mythical moment," they insist, stressing "its permanence and presence in all adult sexual behavior," is not to be understood in the object-directed sense, as "a first stage, enclosed within itself, from which the subject has to rejoin the world of objects." On the contrary, they argue on the side of Freud, "the drive *becomes* auto-erotic, only after the loss of the object." So that, "if it can be said of auto-erotism that it is objectless, it is in no sense because it may appear before any object relationship," but rather because its origin is in that moment, "more abstract than definable in time, since it is always renewed," when sexuality, "disengaged from any natural object, moves into the field of fantasy *and by that very fact becomes sexuality*" (25; emphasis added).

In other words, it is through their representations in fantasy that the drives become properly sexual, in the psychoanalytic sense, and hence it is only through fantasy that desire is sustained. Thus, while any part, organ, activity, or function of the body can acquire erogenous value, "[i]n every case the function serves only as support, the taking of food serving, for instance, as a model for fantasies of incorporation. Though modelled on the function, sexuality lies in its difference from the function" (26); not in the sucking of milk or in the function of feeding, but in the pleasure of sucking as such. And hence, they suggest, the ideal image of autoeroticism is "lips that kiss themselves" (26). And they conclude:

> By locating the origin of fantasy in the auto-erotism, we have shown the connection between fantasy and desire. *Fantasy, however, is not the object of desire, but its setting. In fantasy the subject does not pursue the object or its sign: she appears caught up herself in the sequence of images.* She forms no representation of the desired object, but is herself represented as participating in the scene although, in the earliest forms of fantasy, she cannot be assigned any fixed place in it (hence the danger, in treatment, of interpretations which claim to do so). As a result, the subject, although always present in the fantasy, may be so in a desubjectivized form, that is to say, *in the very syntax of the sequence* in question. (26; emphasis added, pronominal gender altered)

This is the passage that has seemed so strikingly pertinent to theorists of spectatorship, myself included, and indeed it is, for its figuration of the subject "caught up" in the sequence of images—a sequence, moreover, articulated (as) in a syntax—not only is an eminently cinematic figure in itself, but actually reads as a quasi-paraphrase of the theoretical accounts of the relations of spectatorship in narrative cinema. Compare, for instance, Stephen Heath's brilliant formulation:

> What moves in film, finally, is the spectator, immobile in front of the screen. Film is the regulation of that movement, the individual as subject held in a shifting and placing of desire, energy, contradiction, in a perpetual retotalization of the imaginary (the set scene of image and subject). This is the investment of film in narrativization; and crucially for a coherent space, the unity of place for vision. (53)

This congruence between the psychoanalytic subject of fantasy and the film spectator is hardly surprising in view of the profound, foundational influence of neo-Freudian metapsychology on the elaboration of the theory of spectatorship.[3]

Reading Laplanche and Pontalis from the vantage point of that film-theoretical elaboration, Cowie's "Fantasia" speculates on the parallelism between the forms and processes of private fantasy that they articulate in relation to the psychoanalytic subject and the *"public* forms of fantasy" that are made available by a dominant apparatus of representation such as Hollywood cinema; and, I would also add, by other cultural and subcultural representational practices—not only avant-garde and independent cinema, theater, performance, and visual art but also less formal or formalized representational practices such as clothing or hair styles, gay and lesbian subcultural practices, and so on. Cowie proposes (and I agree wholeheartedly with her here) that the cinema, with its highly developed generic and formal conventions—visual, narrative, acoustic, thematic, etc.—is a major apparatus for the production of popular scenarios or public forms of fantasy, and thus the structuring of spectatorial desire through representation. She then proceeds to analyze two Hollywood films of the forties, *Now, Voyager* and *The Reckless Moment*, arguing that in both cases the subject of the film's fantasy, of the film as fantasy, is not only the main character(s) but the spectator as well. Of *Now, Voyager* (1942), for example, Cowie writes:

> The scenario, the *mise-en-scène* of desire thus emerges for us not just in the story, but rather in its narrating. . . . The pleasure then not in *what* wishes Charlotte obtains but *how*. . . . [As the film's ending shows,] Dr. Jacquith and Jerry are both substitutes for the phallic mother, and they are finally unnecessary once the conditions are set for Charlotte herself to be the phallic mother. . . . [Thus, while] Charlotte is both mother and daughter, Mrs. Vale and Tina, this is not Charlotte's fantasy, but the "film's" fantasy. It is an effect of its narration (of its *énonciation*). If we identify simply with Charlotte's desires, that series of social and erotic successes, then the final object, the child Tina, will be unsatisfactory. But *if our identification is with the playing out of a desiring, in relation to the opposition (phallic) mother and child,* the ending is very much more satisfying. (90–91; last emphasis added)

Let me emphasize that *if*, which is just the question I raised earlier about *The Night Porter*: Does this fantasy work for me, spectator? Cowie acknowledges this question:

Such a reading [she adds] implies a homosexual desire played across the film, and if this is the case (and [if] my reading is not too far-fetched), it is also a way of understanding the pleasure for the *masculine* spectator, since the film figures the eviction of the father and the re-instatement of the now "good" phallic mother. By suggesting this I am assuming that the place of the spectator is not one of simple identification with Charlotte Vale. (90–91)

But the question lingers: can a *masculine* spectator (by which I assume that Cowie means a *male* spectator, otherwise her argument would not make sense)—can a male spectator, then, identify anywhere in the film, in the specified positions of mother, daughter, and phallic mother, or in their so-called homosexual relations, which retroactively become "pre-Oedipal" after the "eviction" of the father? Can he (that male spectator), or I, or you, identify "with the playing out of [that particular] desiring"? Obviously, these are empirically unanswerable questions, but they are theoretically necessary nonetheless.

For me, moreover, yet another question comes up, naggingly: What does Cowie mean by "homosexual desire" when she is speaking of a daughter's pre-Oedipal relation to the mother? Isn't the term "homosexual" vastly ambiguous in this context? And just as ambiguous—and strangely so, for a writer as lucid and precise as Cowie—is the designation *masculine* for a spectator who, in the logic of the argument, we must take to be a man, but whose desire, supported by the film's scenario of paternal eviction and fetishistic-maternal desire, perhaps unwittingly suggests a "masculine woman": a spectator who feels addressed by, *and is responsive to*, the particular desiring that Cowie reads from her own location as spectator of the film and subject of its fantasy. In other words, I am suggesting that her reading of *Now, Voyager's* fantasy, theoretically sophisticated as it is, may also be quite subjective, even personal; and that, therefore, such a reading may be possible from her particular spectatorial position but not from others, a position some spectators may fit in or identify with, as Cowie does, but nonetheless not a subject-position open to occupancy by all and sundry.

In this regard, it may not be coincidental that her analysis of *Now, Voyager* ends with a reference to masquerade: if Charlotte's transformation into a beautiful and desirable woman seems to recuperate her for masculine desire, Cowie argues, nevertheless the narrative works to represent (her) "femininity as the masquerade." Now, you will perhaps remember that Riviere's notion of femininity as masquerade was developed in her analysis of a heterosexual woman with a strong and anxiety-producing "masculinity complex," as Freud(ians) called it. Could this be, I wonder, the "*masculine* spectator" (the "masculine woman" spectator) whose pleasure is produced by the masquerade of *Now, Voyager*? Undoubtedly, my own reading (or projection) of a fantasy scenario into Cowie's text may also be rather farfetched, but the point I want to make is that her viewing Charlotte's femininity as masquerade, while convergent with a narcissistic fantasy of phallic motherhood, casts a further burden of doubt and ambiguity on the alleged "homosexual desire" that Cowie sees played out across the film. What *homosexuality* can be fantasized, I ask, in the masquerade of femininity, which is by definition addressed to men, or in a surrogate motherhood that reconstructs for the subject the pre-Oedipal phallic mother?

As if in answer to these questions, by one of those coincidences not infrequent in academic life, a conversation with Stanley Cavell alerted me to his recent essay on *Now, Voyager* which, although apparently unaware of Cowie's "Fantasia," could well be read as its companion piece. Cavell's "Ugly Duckling, Funny Butterfly" is both a testimonial to the pleasure *Now, Voyager* may afford a "masculine spectator" and the confirmation that a sophisticated, finely nuanced, and quite compelling response to the film can come only from a particular spectatorial position, one sustained by a very personal set of identifications and a subjective engagement in the film's fantasy scenario. Moreover, while it supports Cowie's assumption "that the place of the spectator is not one of simple identification with Charlotte Vale" (90), in that the male critic's identification with Charlotte Vale is not at all simple, as I shall suggest, his reading at the same time refutes that assumption, in that its spectatorial identification is most emphatically *with* Charlotte Vale and/as Bette Davis. As Cavell puts it, "I find that to say how I take the films I must from time to time speak for their central women. I feel that I am amplifying their voices, listening to them, becoming them" (232). The essay bears witness to a male spectator's passionate identification with "Bette Davis and her memorable ways of walking and looking and of delivering lines" (218)—Bette Davis and/as Charlotte Vale, the actress and her character, the woman and her powers:

> a certain hysteria, or hysterical energy, about her character on film. It taps a genius for that expressiveness in which Freud and Breuer, in their *Studies on Hysteria*, first encountered the reality of the unconscious, the reality of the human mind as what is unconscious to itself, and encountered first in the suffering of women. It is Bette Davis's command and deploy-

ment of this capacity for somatic compliance, for the theatricalization of desire and of its refiguration or retracking that, so it seems to me, made her one of the most impersonated of Hollywood stars. (227)

As for Charlotte Vale, to Cavell she is a figure of transcendence, of meta-morphosis and ironic transfiguration, rather than of sacrifice, reaching a "level of spiritual existence" so beyond the "second-rate sadness" of Jerry's world that by the end of the film he "no longer knows where to find her" (230), and "his last protestation of passion for her has become quite beside the point, no longer welcome" (232). With the famous closing line, "Oh, Jerry, don't let's ask for the moon. We have the stars," spoken from her place of attained transcendence of his conventional world, she is tactfully and "gallantly providing the man, quite outclassed, outlived, with a fiction that they together are sacrificing themselves to stern and clear moral dic-tates." But for herself, she is not giving up something that she no longer wants, and perhaps never did want. "In her metamorphosis she is and is not what she is; in his incapacity for change, for motion, he is not what he is not. . . . So one may take the subject of the genre of the unknown woman as the irony of human identity as such" (234). It is this subject, the fantasy of this subject with its ironic, unfixed, mobile identity, that appears to draw the critic's spectatorial identification (Cavell cites Whitman's lines from which the film's title is taken and his metaphor of the open road for the overcoming of fixity and conventionality); it is the "feminine voice that the male philosopher is refusing to let out" and to acknowledge in himself (283) that Bette Davis/Charlotte Vale re-presents for Cavell through the film's narrative and her woman's body.

But what of the phallic mother and "homosexual desire"? Here, Cavell's reading is amazingly consonant with Cowie's, not only in locating Camille/Charlotte's defiant strength in "her identification with her mother's power" (21) but in further suggesting that her appropriation of Tina, Jerry's child, for her own is sustained by the Oedipal fantasy of receiving a child from the (phallic) mother: "If Charlotte undergoes a fantasm[at]ic 'deliv-ery' then she can have produced a deferred understanding of her fatness as (fantasied) pregnancy. Since . . . her fatness is her mother's doing ('My mother doesn't approve of dieting') then something her mother had put into her has now come out of her" (243). And of Charlotte's identification with Tina as her own younger self, Cavell writes, "I assume that both men and women are capable of tracking desire in a fantasy of parthenogenesis" (244). Which spells out, in more clearly gendered terms, Cowie's "if our identification is with the playing out of a desiring, in relation to the opposition (phallic) mother and child, the ending is very much more satisfying" (92).

How gender does make a difference in spectatorial identification and desire becomes apparent when Cavell is led to speculate further on what he calls "Charlotte's homosexual possibility" (282), which he infers from several clues in the film (e.g., "Bette Davis's invitation to camp," Charlotte's self-avowed "idiosyncrasy" and her refusal to marry Livingston, the slip of paper with Whitman's title "The Untold Want" that Dr. Jaquith hands Charlotte at the termination of her treatment with the words "If old Walt didn't have you in mind when he wrote this, he had hundreds of others like you" [282]); but he infers it, as well, from his own spectatorial intuition that Charlotte "has transcended this man's [Jerry's] realm" and "is contemplating, perhaps refusing, a homosexual possibility, hence perhaps for that reason all future erotic possibility" (279).

Now, it would be difficult to remind Dr. Jaquith that "old Walt" did not have anyone *like* Charlotte in mind as he was almost certainly thinking of male-desiring men when he wrote the poem. But I will suggest to Cavell that Bette Davis's invitation to camp and to impersonation may clue the spectator to a *male* rather than a *female* homosexual possibility; and that male homosexuality does not usually require the sacrifice of one's erotic possibilities as the price for ironic transcendence, a price that Charlotte has to pay, contrary to Cavell's thesis and yet by his own reading. For if it is the case that Charlotte no longer wants "a man of my own, a house of my own, a child of my own" (279), and thus is not making the banal sacrifice—the renunciation—that is commonly attributed to her, nevertheless, the refusal of "all future erotic possibility" that Cavell sees in her "homosexual possibility" would be an even greater sacrifice, and one whose effects of transcendence would liken it to the sacrifice—the execution—of a Joan of Arc.

Again, the intimation of a female sexuality that entails a denial of all present and future erotic possibilities (at present with men, in the diegetic context of the film, and in the future perhaps also with women, in the spectator's fantasy scenario) appears to be predicated on a sexually inactive or even (oxymoronically) nonsexual female homosexuality bound to the pre-Oedipal relation to the (phallic) mother, in Cowie's terms, or, in Cavell's, to the specific feature of melodrama that is "the woman's search for the mother" (279). However, as I will try to show, these seemingly parallel readings ultimately subtend different, gender-related fantasies, although the parallelism between the terms *homosexual desire* in Cowie's essay and *homosexual possibility* in Cavell's appears to be sustained by their common reference to masquerade.

Expanding the contours of "homosexual possibility" and its effects on the relationship between Charlotte and Jerry by a detour through the crossdressing personae of Marlene Dietrich and Greta Garbo, Cavell writes: "Their male dress would accordingly declare that they have, among others, the same tastes in bodies that the male they will choose has, and they wish his gratification as well as, so to speak, their own, as if their own bodies are an instance of what they desire" (281). This can be taken as a perceptive rendering of the effects of feminine narcissism and of the masquerade of woman-as-phallus on the men to whom it is addressed; but its not-so-hidden implication is that if Garbo and Dietrich in drag appear to desire women's bodies (their own and other women's), the men they attract must be men who really want men but will make do with women provided that they at least look like men.[4]

Indeed, when he subsequently recasts the *Now, Voyager* scenario with Jerry as "a feminine object" for Charlotte (the film itself does feminize him, he insists), Cavell wonders whether their relation would be constituted as homosexual or heterosexual. His answer is all the more remarkable for being virtually the only instance in the essay where Cavell assumes the point of view of Jerry, whom he otherwise treats rather unsympathetically: "It *needn't be* that she is . . . a masculine object for him. Here, rather, her morbidity must come into question, that is . . . he takes her as homosexual" (282; emphasis added). This at first surprising reading (they can't get it on, so someone must be homosexual; but if someone has to be homosexual, it cannot be he, so it must be she) finds its logic, I suggest, in the idea that Charlotte's "wish for a passionate existence" gives her "a male direction" or valence; in other words, makes her a masculine woman (and thus a safe anchoring point for male spectatorial identification). This idea will then justify the appropriation of her feminine voice and hysterical expressiveness, together with that masculine "compulsion to desire," for the ironic identity of the philosopher—not the masculine philosopher who refuses his "woman's voice," but rather the skeptical, Nietzschean philosopher who, like the Spencer Tracy character in *Adam's Rib* (the example is Cavell's), can shed real tears, just like a woman, and hence partake of that double, mobile, ironic subjectivity that marks "human identity as such" in the persona of Charlotte Vale.

I might put it this way: the "homosexual" possibility in Charlotte literalizes Dante's figure of the "screen woman," "*la donna dello schermo*." It is the possibility for a male spectator to identify with a desiring figure that combines the distinctive features of both genders, but that identification is the projection onto Charlotte of a male and not a female homosexual "possibility," akin to the "masculinization" Mulvey attributes to the female spectator in relation to the image of woman on the screen.[5] Like her "compulsion to desire," then, Charlotte's transcendence of the conventional man's world is, paradoxically, a male achievement. For Cowie, on the other hand, "Charlotte is 'phallic' for the narrative in being bound to pre-Oedipal relations, rather than because of any male, 'phallic' imaging of her" (93), and the spectator's desire is positioned in the "oscillation between mother and child." Which seems to outline a fantasy of woman's desire as a desire to be the virgin mother. In both readings, then, Charlotte's identification with the phallic mother results in her desexualization—her refusal of "all future erotic possibility" (Cavell) and her regression to a pre-Oedipal fantasmatic (Cowie).[6]

Returning to my earlier question—*What homosexuality* can be fantasized in Charlotte's transcendence (Cavell) or in her phallic motherhood (Cowie)?—the answer I have found in these two texts is either a fantasy of male homosexuality (rejected in actuality but achieved fantasmatically through identification or impersonation) or a fantasy of phallic femininity whose sexual threat to both men and women must be neutered by desexualization (pre-Oedipal motherhood) or make-believe (the masquerade). In neither case, it seems to me, is there any "possibility" of actual homosexual desire or of *female* homosexuality as such.

The implications of the two essays for the theory of spectatorship, however, differ. Cavell's reading of *Now, Voyager* and the spectatorial subject position that subtends it are marked as a singular, I would even say personal, response to a film most critics have interpreted otherwise. One may or may not share it, depending on one's own subject position, but one has a clear sense of the subject position from which this reading, this spectator's desiring, proceeds. On the other hand, after the brief parenthesis in which her personal location as spectator and desiring subject is acknowledged ("if . . . my reading is not too far-fetched"), Cowie's essay goes on as if her particular desiring were fully generalizable, universally available. And the theoretical ambiguity of her conclusion takes back the advantage gained by complicating the notion of identification and no longer assuming that the spectator simply identifies with the protagonist.

"In each film," Cowie concludes, "the subject-positions shift across the boundary of sexual difference but do so always in terms of sexual difference. Thus while subject-positions are variable the terms of sexual difference are fixed." Or, put another way, "while the terms of sexual difference are fixed, the places of characters and spectators in relation to those terms are not" (102). This, to my mind, is a very ambiguous conclusion. In the first draft I actually wrote "ambiguous to hysteria," and I still think that, like the notion of oscillation proposed elsewhere by Parveen Adams in relation to Dora's hysterical identification but then directly applied to female subjectivity period, the conceptual ambiguity of "Fantasia" invites reduction and has in fact already spawned reductive textual applications.[7] This seriously undercuts, in my opinion, the theoretical step forward that can be made in the feminist theory of spectatorship by rearticulating (not simply transposing or applying) the psychoanalytic concept of fantasy to the processes of spectatorial desire and identification, processes which are formed, but also shattered, disrupted, or reshaped, by the discourses, practices, and representations that surround and traverse each spectator as the subject of a social, racial, and cultural, as well as personal, history.

Let me say explicitly what concerns me here. This essay is usually cited to promote the view, now popular among some feminist critics, that every spectator can identify with any character or with his or her relational position in a film's narrative. Cowie's carefully argued theoretical proposal is invoked by others to buttress the optimistically silly notion of an unbounded mobility of identities for the spectator-subject; that is to say, the film's spectator would be able to assume and shift between an undefined "multiplicity" of identificatory positions, would be able to pick and choose any or all of the subject-positions inscribed in the film regardless of gender or sexual difference, to say nothing of other kinds of difference. Moreover, the spectator is collapsed into the psychoanalytic subject of fantasy, and spectatorial identification is equated with unconscious identification. One critic, for example, states:

> An important emphasis has been placed [by recent film theory] on the subject's ability to assume, successively, all the available positions in the fantasmatic scenario. Extending this idea to film has shown that spectatorial identification is more complex than has hitherto been understood because it shifts constantly in the course of the film's narrative, while crossing the lines of biological sex; in other words, unconscious identification with the characters or the scenario is not necessarily dependent upon gender. (Penley, 73)[8]

The patent oversimplification in the first two sentences, compounded by the misleading implication of the third, that spectatorial identification is only unconscious, is based on the equation of spectator and the psychoanalytic subject who, according to Laplanche and Pontalis, "is [her]self represented as participating in the scene although, in the earliest forms of fantasy, [s]he cannot be assigned any fixed place in it [and] although always present in the fantasy, may be so in a desubjectivized form" (26). What is lost in the equation, however, in the direct transposition of the psychoanalytic subject of fantasy to the film spectator (as subject of the film's fantasy), and in the reduction of fantasy to original (unconscious) fantasy, is the difference between those two subjects and their differential location in the analytic situation and in the movie theater, respectively; that is to say, their differential location in the relations of production of fantasy. In this manner, the question of who produces the fantasy, of whose fantasy the film represents, is preempted or mystified, leaving the theory of spectatorship with a re-found universal subject unmarked by gender, class, racial, sexual, or other differences, and free to move in and out of subject-positions at its leisure.

It is one thing to say that I am the subject always present in my own fantasies, which sustain my desire; but it is quite another thing to say that a film, any film, addresses or constructs me as the subject of its fantasy, whatever *it* may be. This is not to invoke some notion of intentionality on the part of the film(maker), or to deny that heterogeneous effects may be produced in spectatorship by the multiple agencies involved in the making of the film (e.g., the particular contributions of actors, director, screenwriter, editor, sound editor, camera, etc.). But it is to reaffirm the historical situatedness of the spectator in the movie theater, as well as Cowie's emphasis on the specific narrative and enunciative strategies employed in any given film, its manipulation of the cinematic codes, and its particular form of address.

For example, working with the psychoanalytic concepts of fantasy and masquerade in my reading of Sheila McLaughlin's film *She Must Be Seeing Things* (1987), I have suggested that McLaughlin uses the film-within-the-film device precisely to recast the primal fantasy in relation to lesbian subjectivity and spectatorship: by rearticulating fantasy, masquerade, and voyeurism in lesbian terms, the film constructs a lesbian subject as the subject of its fantasy, and thus addresses the spectator in a lesbian subject-position. The film, I argue, does not simply provide the fantasy but, by its particular manipulation of cinematic codes (the film within the film, for instance), it provides a particular means of spectatorial access to it; thus it effectively inscribes a lesbian subject-position in its very mode of address, not merely diegetically, in the story or in its images and sounds (see de Lauretis, "Film and the Visible"). This is not to say, however, that such a position is necessarily accessible to all viewers, or even to all lesbian-identified viewers, because the film's fantasy may very well *not* be their own.

The lack of attention this film has received in heterosexual feminist circles and its divided and controversial reception among lesbians certainly suggest that the latter is the case.

Finally, then, my quarrel with Cowie is that, while she cannot be held responsible for the banalization of her argument by other critics, nonetheless the structured ambiguity of her essay does leave ample room for such an effect; and her equivocation of fixed and variable terms (*sexual difference* and *subject-positions*, respectively) can rightly be held accountable for the eventual eviction of sexual differences, and in particular of lesbian-homosexual difference, not from the film (*Now, Voyager* or any other film) but from the spectator herself. If the pre-feminist discourse on film ignored the cinematic production of spectatorial positions in sexual difference (to say nothing of racial and other social differences), this application of the subject of fantasy to film theory would render sexual difference, and in particular lesbian difference, altogether irrelevant. Begun as a critique of Laura Mulvey's alleged eviction of the female spectator from the movie theater, this recent (I would say, post-feminist) theory of sexual indifference reverses the direction of feminist film criticism and attempts to get rid of both gender and sexual difference, again, not only from the cinema but from the spectator as well.

Take Two

A more attentive reading of "The Origin of Fantasy" shows how the figure of the subject of fantasy is more complex both in psychoanalytic terms and with regard to mass-produced or public forms of fantasy. Even as they insist on the homology between different levels of fantasy, from daydreams and reveries to the delusional fears of paranoiacs and the unconscious fantasies of hysterics, Laplanche and Pontalis distinguish between the unconscious fantasy, distorted and yet revealed under the dream-facade, and the form it takes as the secondary elaboration reworks it into a fantasy more acceptable to consciousness. In the daydream—or what they call Freud's "model fantasy," the reverie, "that form of novelette, both stereotyped and infinitely variable, which the subject composes and relates to [her]self in a waking state"—"the scenario is basically in the first person, and the subject's place clear and invariable" (22). On the other hand, the original fantasy "is characterized by the absence of subjectivization, and the subject is present in the scene: the child, for intance, is one character amongst many in the fantasy 'a child is beaten'. Freud insisted on this visualization of the subject on the same level as the other protagonists" (22).

Now, spectatorship does not consist of purely unconscious processes, and, while film almost certainly engages the spectator in its fantasy, the processes of secondarization and conscious or preconscious identification can hardly be discounted. If it is rare to see a film that fits our own individual reverie so closely as to mark our spectatorial subject place clearly and utterly compellingly, surely it must be equally rare for a spectator, going to the movies on a Saturday night, to respond to the images on the screen with nothing but the raw materials of her or his primary processes. (Were that the case, the entertainment industry could hardly prosper as it does, or else the psychoanalytic/therapeutic profession would not.) Hence Freud's insistence on the visualization of the subject in clinical practice acquires relevance for the practice of film viewing, as well as the theory: How do I look at the film? How do I appear in its fantasy? Am I looking on? Can I be seen? Do I see myself in it? Is this my fantasy? (I discuss this at greater length in "Film and the Visible.")

Another instance of controversial representation that bears a close relation to fantasy is pornography. In order to articulate further the distinction between the psychoanalytic subject and the social subject, between subjectivity and subjecthood, between fantasy and representation, and between private and public forms of fantasy, I will refer to another essay that draws on Laplanche and Pontalis's work to argue in behalf of pornography as fantasy. Judith Butler's "The Force of Fantasy" is a critique of the "discursive alliance" of antipornography feminists with the New Right in their respective efforts, the former to secure legal measures against the pornography industry, and the latter to push through the passage by the United States Congress of a bill prohibiting federal funding of artwork deemed "indecent" or "obscene." Both groups, Butler maintains, share a common theory of fantasy, or rather, a "set of untheorized presumptions" about fantasy; they rely "upon a representational realism that conflates the signified of fantasy with its (impossible) referent and construes 'depiction' as an injurious act" (105–106), and thus see fantasy (pornography) as "the causal link between representation and action" (112). Arguing, on her part, for pornography as fantasy, but with another understanding of fantasy and its effects, Butler also quotes the famous passage in Laplanche and Pontalis:

Fantasy is not the object of desire, but its setting. In fantasy the subject does not pursue the object or its sign; one appears oneself caught up in the sequence of images. One forms no representation of the desired object, but is oneself represented as participating in the scene although, in the earliest forms of fantasy, one cannot be assigned any fixed place in it (hence the danger, in treatment [and in politics] of interpretations which claim to do so). As a result, the subject, although always present in the fantasy, may be so in a desubjectivized form, that is to say, in the very syntax of the sequence in question. (Butler, 109–10)[9]

Butler remarks:

> There is, then, strictly speaking, no subject who has a fantasy, but only fantasy as the scene of the subject's fragmentation and dissimulation; fantasy enacts a splitting or fragmentation or, perhaps better put, a multiplication or proliferation of identifications that puts the very locatability of identity into question. In other words, although we might wish to think, even fantasize, that there is an "I" who has or cultivates its fantasy with some measure of mastery and possession, that "I" is always undone by precisely that which it claims to master. (110)

The reading would be quite plausible if Laplanche and Pontalis had written only the passage Butler quotes. However, distinguishing this (unconscious) form of fantasy from the conscious reverie or daydream, they also wrote that in the latter forms of fantasy "the scenario is basically in the first person, and the subject's place clear and invariable. The organization is stabilized by the secondary process, weighed by the ego: the subject, it is said, lives out his reverie" (22). Laplanche further writes:

> [A]fter all, "life has to be lived" and a human being can supplement a love of life that is occasionally deficient only by a love of the ego or of the ideal agencies which are, in turn, derived from it, but also—if the essence of the ego function is indeed *binding*, before being adaptation—because a minimum of intervention by that function is indispensable for even an unconscious fantasy to *take form*. (*Life and Death in Psychoanalysis* 125–26)

On the strength of this theory of fantasy, therefore, there is *also* a subject who fantasizes herself in the scene and whose *fantasy* (precisely) is one of mastery; even as that fantasy may be in contradiction with her own unconscious fantasy. And indeed what else if not such contradiction would bring about the splitting of the subject or the undoing of the ego's self-possession? In Freud's analysis of "A Child Is Being Beaten," the unconscious ("transitional") form of the fantasy ("I am being beaten by my father") is an interpretation or a reconstruction in analysis, and is never remembered by the subject; whereas the two remembered forms—the "objective" and the "voyeuristic" forms, as Freud calls them—would correspond respectively to the pornographic text and the pornographic text viewed by the subject. The point is that "the subject" is *both* conscious and unconscious. In fact, Butler's own argument suggests as much.

"Fantasy is the very scene which *suspends* action and which, in its suspension, provides for a critical investigation of what it is that constitutes action" (113), she states, adding that, insofar as it opens up "interpretive possibilities" (113), she sees "the pornographic text as a site of multiple significations" (114). But surely the subject of such critical investigation is much closer to the conscious end of the fantasy spectrum than to the unconscious one. The *interpretation* of a text's or a scene's multiple significations is the work of analysis, of secondarization, whose subjective purpose *is* mastery and self-possession. And these, I suggest, acquire all the more weight in the interpreter's confrontation with a "pornographic" text (the representation of a sexual scene) which by its very content (the sexual scenario) is likely to engage directly the subject's unconscious (repressed) fantasy and thus present the threat of fragmentation and undoing of the interpreter's ego. In other words, Butler's is not a silly notion of the nature of fantasy, but it is still an optimistic or, rather, a voluntaristic one. For, in asserting that fantasy suspends action by fostering at the same time a disruption of identity and a critical distance in the viewer of pornography, Butler would have her cake and eat it too: fantasy (pornography) can do no harm. In part, this may derive from her taking the other side in the "political" opposition against the antipornography feminists represented in her text by "Dworkin" (I put this name between quotation marks to indicate that I am not referring to the person or the author Andrea Dworkin but to the character in Butler's fictional dialogue, the antagonist in her argument):

> Indeed, if pornography is to be understood as fantasy, as anti-pornography activists almost invariably insist, then the effect of pornography is not to force women to identify with a subordinate or debased position, but to provide the opportunity to identify with the entire scene of debasement, agents and recipients alike. . . . The pornographic fantasy does not restrict identification to any one position, and [Andrea] Dworkin, in her elaborate textual exegesis, paradoxically shows us how her form of interpretive mastery can be derived from a viewing which, in her own view, is supposed to restrict her to a position of mute and passive injury. (114)

Butler's polemic against "Dworkin" misses its target by ignoring the obvious, if contradictory, fact that feminist analysis and politics have always proceeded concurrently with—indeed have been prompted by—the social injury suffered by women, but the strength of feminism, or what social power it may have, does not disprove that injury. When Butler suggests that the argumentative power or "interpretive mastery" of a feminist critique of pornography can derive only from an identification with the pornographic fantasy and its representation of aggression, I want to think it is because she, too, simply transposes the theory of the psychoanalytic subject of fantasy to the viewer of a public, industrially produced representation. In equating the pornographic text with the pornographic fantasy, or pornography with fantasy, she conflates fantasy with representation and disregards the different relations of production of fantasy that obtain for the subject in a private or analytic situation, on the one hand, and for the subject in a public context of representation, on the other. In the end, Butler's equation of (pornographic) representation with (unconscious) fantasy is the obverse of the move to equate pornographic representation with action. One side ignores the possibly heterogeneous effects of fantasy within the subject vis-à-vis representation; the other side disregards the contradictions within the subject and denies the effects of fantasy with regard to action, which (after all) is an important dimension of the political. While both pornographic representation and action do have an intimate relation to fantasy, and to each other, in the realm of the senses and in that of the law, in sexual practices as well as in the juridical-legislative realm, nevertheless, it seems to me, retaining the distinction among the three terms—representation, action, and fantasy—is important, not only theoretically but also politically.

Quite correctly, in my opinion, Butler reads "Dworkin's" interpretive mastery as a form of feminist sociopolitical subjecthood; but she does not acknowledge that subjecthood—conscious, affirmative, even willful, and based on a political and collective identity—is not the same as subjectivity, which is permeated by repression, resistance, ambivalence, and contradiction. Obviously, subjectivity and subjecthood are never dissociated in the subject, just as the psychoanalytic subject is always a social subject, but the two terms stand to each other in a conceptual relationship analogous to that of private representation (fantasy) to public representation. By not distinguishing between fantasy and representation, or between the psychoanalytic subject of (unconscious) fantasy and the social or the political subject, what Butler loses sight of, ironically, is precisely the imaginary (unconscious?) force of fantasy in "Dworkin's" subjectivity. For it is the hold of a socially constructed and subjective internalized identification with the victim's or "feminine" position that, I would speculate, prevents "Dworkin" from fantasizing herself in the other place and taking up the aggressor's or "masculine" position which Butler projects onto her. It is that imaginary identification with the victim's position that both limits the interpretive possibilities for "Dworkin" as viewer of the pornographic text and makes her feel constricted in a fantasy scenario that her subject-hood will not accept as hers. In other words, it is not, as Butler suggests, that "Dworkin's reading draws its strength and mastery" from "an identification and redeployment of the very representation of aggression [the "masculine" position] that she abhors" (115); but rather that "Dworkin" resists seeing herself in the mass-produced pornographic fantasy, in which yet she does see herself. In short, what Butler sees as masculine aggression, to another may look more like feminist resistance.

If, therefore, "Dworkin" does not lend support to the theory that "fantasy does not restrict identification to any one position," this may be so because she is neither the subject nor the producer of the fantasy in question; in short because the pornographic text is not her fantasy but a fantasy produced by others and which, as she sees it, seeks to interpellate her with a certain identification, to assign to her a place that she will not or cannot occupy. Much in the same way as "Dora" resisted Freud's interpretation of her Oedipal wish. And much in the same way, again, many spectators of Cavani's *Night Porter* so strongly refused to enter Lucia's sadomasochistic fantasy that they actually misread the film and, despite the explicitly stated reason for her internment in the concentration camp as a political prisoner (a socialist), they left the theater believing that she was a Jew (see de Lauretis, "Cavani's *Night Porter*"). Their identification in the film's fantasy was apparently restricted by other representations and constructions of identity, both subjective and social, conscious and unconscious, which they brought to their viewing of the film; and these overdetermined those spectators' reception of the film and their particular path through its multiple significations.

Ideology is a quaint word now, in disuse, but its effects are still at work in the spectator-subject of public fantasy, as is secondarization in the psychoanalytic subject. The work of unconscious fantasy, important as it is for our understanding of psychic contradiction and divisions in the social subject, cannot simply replace the complex intersections of conscious and unconscious processes in the subject of fantasy. Nor can a theory of film spectatorship, a theory of representation, collapse the social into the subjective by equating representation with fantasy. Finally, the theory of fantasy I have been discussing should not serve to legislate spectatorial identification and desire. Its value resides, I have tried to argue, in the possibility it offers for a more nuanced understanding of the heterogeneous and often contradictory effects of representation in the subject. This in turn reaffirms the historical, particular situatedness of the spectator in a given configuration of the social field, and makes spectatorship an important site of articulation of individual subjectivity with social subjecthood and of fantasy with representation.

Notes

1. Nineteen sixty-four was the year of Lacan's seminar on *The Four Fundamental Concepts of Psycho-Analysis*, originally published only in 1973. On fantasy, Lacan also writes: "The phantasy is the support of desire; it is not the object that is the support of desire. The subject sustains himself as desiring in relation to an ever more complex signifying ensemble. This is apparent enough in the form of the scenario it assumes, in which the subject, more or less recognizable, is somewhere, split, divided, generally double, in his relation to the object, which usually does not show its true face either" (185).

2. We need only think of Freud's redefinition of the instinct or drive (*Trieb*) in the "Three Essays on the Theory of Sexuality" (1905): "By an 'instinct' is provisionally to be understood the psychical representative of an endosomatic, continuously flowing source of stimulation, as contrasted with a 'stimulus', which is set up by *single* excitations coming from *without*. The concept of instinct is thus one of those lying on the frontier between the mental and the physical" (168); and then again, in "Instincts and Their Vicissitudes" (1915): "an 'instinct' appears to us as a borderline concept between the mental and the physical, being both the mental representative of the stimuli emanating from within the organism and penetrating to the mind, and at the same time a measure of the demand made upon the energy of the latter in consequence of its connection with the body" (121–22). On Freud's radical reconceptualization of the sexual drive, see Davidson.

3. On the relation of montage to what may be called the syntax of film language (the "*grande syntagmatique*" of narrative cinema), see Metz, *Language and Cinema*; and on the relations of film and spectatorship theory to psychoanalysis, see Metz, *The Imaginary Signifier*, in particular part III, "The Fiction Film and Its Spectator: A Metapsychological Study," as well as Heath, Mulvey, de Lauretis, Cowie, Doane, Mayne, and others.

4. In its classic definitions, Riviere's and Lacan's, the masquerade of femininity is addressed to men. Here is Lacan's: "Paradoxical as this formulation might seem, I would say that it is in order to be the phallus, that is to say, the signifier of the desire of the Other, that the woman will reject an essential part of her femininity, notably all its attributes through masquerade. It is for what she is not that she expects to be desired as well as loved" ("The Meaning of the Phallus" 84). Of instances of masquerade addressed to women, such as the butch and the femme performances in a lesbian subcultural context, which obviously have quite different valences, see my "Film and the Visible." In the two instances here in question—the feminine masquerade of Bette Davis in *Now, Voyager* (Cowie) and the crossdress masquerades of Dietrich and Garbo (Cavell)—the arguments of the two critics assume, respectively, a male address and a male point of view.

5. Another male spectator has suggested that possible reasons for male homosexual identification with the Davis persona and with Charlotte Vale in particular include "the

ability to be expressive during the repressive 1940s and 1950s, sense of style, sexual self-assuredness, and (somewhat tragically or ironically) the fact that women like Charlotte don't get the man *either*" (Earl Jackson, Jr., in a personal communication). I am indebted to Jackson for his acute comments on an earlier version of this paper.

6. Cf. Freud's view that "the transformation of object-libido into narcissistic libido" through parental identification (that is, a former object-cathexis that has been given up and introjected to become an identification) "implies an abandonment of sexual aims, a desexualization—a kind of sublimation, therefore" (*SE* 19: 30).

7. I use the term here in the sense of word-processing format, as my Macintosh manual puts it: "an application is a software program that helps you perform your work": like Microsoft Word, for instance, or WordPerfect. When the application is punched in, we have something like this: "The desire represented in the time travel story, of both witnessing one's own conception and being one's own mother and father, is similar to the primal scene fantasy, in which one can be both observer or one of the participants. (The possibility of getting pregnant and giving birth to oneself is echoed in *Back to the Future*'s TV ad: 'The first kid to get into trouble before he was ever born.')" (Penley, 72). Not coincidentally, what is alluded to here is a *male* subject's fantasy.

8. Various other criticisms of this position are articulated by Copjec (241), Mellencamp ("Responses," 235), and Doane ("Responses," 145).

9. The somewhat different wording of the passage would suggest that the translation has been altered by Butler, although the reference given is "*Formations [of Fantasy]* 26–27" (incorrectly, as it is only 26) without further comment.

Works Cited

Adams, Parveen. "Per Os(cillation)." *Camera Obscura* 17 (1988): 7–29.

Burgin, Victor, James Donald, and Cora Kaplan, eds. *Formations of Fantasy*, London: Methuen, 1986.

Butler, Judith. "The Force of Fantasy: Feminism, Mapplethorpe, and Discursive Excess." *differences: A Journal of Feminist Cultural Studies* 2.2 (1990): 105–25.

Cavell, Stanley. "Ugly Duckling, Funny Butterfly: Bette Davis and *Now Voyager* Followed by Postscript (1989): To Whom It May Concern." *Critical Inquiry* 16 (1990): 213–89.

Copjec, Joan. "Cutting Up." *Between Feminism and Psychoanalysis*. Ed. Teresa Brennan. London: Routledge, 1989. 227–46.

Cowie, Elizabeth. "Fantasia." *m/f* 9 (1984): 70–105.

Davidson, Arnold. "How to Do the History of Psychoanalysis: A Reading of Freud's *Three Essays on the Theory of Sexuality*." *The Trial(s) of Psychoanalysis*. Ed. Françoise Meltzer. Chicago: University of Chicago Press, 1987–88. 39–64.

de Lauretis, Teresa. *Alice Doesn't: Feminism, Semiotics, Cinema*. Bloomington: Indiana University Press, 1984.

———. "Cavani's *Night Porter*: A Woman's Film?" *Film Quarterly* 30.2 (1976–77): 35–38.

———. "Film and the Visible." *How Do I Look? Queer Film and Video*. Ed. Bad Object-Choices. Seattle: Bay, 1991. 223–76.

Doane, Mary Ann. *The Desire to Desire: The Woman's Film of the 1940s*. Bloomington: Indiana University Press, 1987.

———. "Responses." *Camera Obscura* 20-21 (1989): 142-47.

Donald, James, ed. *Fantasy and the Cinema*. London: British Film Institute, 1989.

Freud, Sigmund. " 'A Child Is Being Beaten': A Contribution to the Study of the Origin of Sexual Perversions." 1919. *The Standard Edition of the Complete Psychological Works of Sigmnd Freud*. Trans. and ed. James Strachey. Vol. 17. London: Hogarth Press, 1955, pp. 175-204. 24 vols. 1953-74.

———. "Instincts and Their Vicissitudes." 1915. *The Standard Edition*. Vol. 14. 109-40.

———. "Three Essays on the Theory of Sexuality." 1905. *The Standard Edition*. Vol. 7. 123-245.

Heath, Stephen. *Questions of Cinema*. Bloomington: Indiana University Press, 1981.

Lacan, Jacques. *The Four Fundamental Concepts of Psycho-Analysis*. Trans. Alan Sheridan. New York: W. W. Norton, 1978.

———. "The Meaning of the Phallus." *Feminine Sexuality*. Ed. Juliet Mitchell and Jacqueline Rose. Trans. Jacqueline Rose. New York: W. W. Norton, 1982. 74-85.

Laplanche, Jean. *Life and Death in Psychoanalysis*. Trans. Jeffrey Mehlman. Baltimore: Johns Hopkins University Press, 1976.

Laplanche, J., and J.-B. Pontalis. "Fantasy and the Origins of Sexuality." Burgin 5-34.

Mayne, Judith. *The Woman at the Keyhole: Feminism and Women's Cinema*. Bloomington: Indiana University Press, 1990.

Mellencamp, Patricia. "Responses." *Camera Obscura* 20-21 (1989): 235-41.

Metz, Christian. *The Imaginary Signifier: Psychoanalysis and Cinema*. Trans. Celia Britton et al. Bloomington: Indiana University Press, 1975-82.

———. *Language and Cinema*. Trans. Donna Jean Umiker-Sebeok. The Hague: Mouton, 1974.

Mulvey, Laura. *Visual and Other Pleasures*. Bloomington: Indiana University Press, 1989.

Penley, Constance. "Time Travel, Primal Scene, and the Critical Dystopia." *Camera Obscura* 15 (1986): 66-85. Also in Donald 196-212.

Riviere, Joan. "Womanliness as a Masquerade." Burgin 35-44.

6

GOVERNING LESBIAN DESIRE
Nocturne's Oedipal Fantasy

Patricia White

WHEN IN *Alice Doesn't* Teresa de Lauretis wrote that "the most exciting work in cinema and in feminism today . . . is narrative and Oedipal with a vengeance," she was rejecting any easy equivalence between experimental film practices and new forms of female subjectivity or relations of looking. She was also concluding a compelling analysis of "desire in narrative": how stories inscribe the male hero's Oedipal desire into their very structure and allocate woman to a position of obstacle or goal in his journey. De Lauretis was "not advocating the replacement or the appropriation of . . . Oedipus" but "an interruption of the triple track by which narrative, meaning, and pleasure are constructed from his point of view." This feminist work, she argued, "seeks to stress the duplicity of that scenario and the specific contradiction of the female subject in it" (157).

It is perhaps unnecessary to rehearse that the female Oedipus complex is "by nature" duplicitous. Unlike the little boy, who must simply displace his love for the mother to other women and thereby consolidate his identification with the father and all that he represents, the little girl is asked to change her object from mother to father, her disposition from active to passive, and her sexual zone from clitoris to vagina, in order to become woman, post-Oedipal, and heterosexual. Since this transition is so difficult her desire remains double, even "bisexual."

But although de Lauretis gives examples of "remakes and rereadings" of "his story," her claim remains a riddle. She was referring in part to feminist critical work in film—Oedipus, a tragic male hero, has lent his name to the domestic, familial, and "feminine" thematics of the film melodrama, a genre that has been the object of much of this work. De Lauretis's phrase might recall in particular the title of Tania Modleski's book, *Loving with a Vengeance*, which, although characterizing the presumably heterosexual women readers of popular romance novels, would also be a good title for a book on lesbian culture.

Oedipal inquiry has proceeded with a vengeance among feminist film critics since the publication of *Alice Doesn't*. Laura Mulvey, in a recent essay on the actual Oedipus myth, elegantly describes the project of her *Riddles of the Sphinx* (a film de Lauretis had singled out), made with Peter Wollen in 1977:

> The film used the sphinx as an emblem through which to hang a question mark over the Oedipus complex, to investigate the extent to which it represents a riddle for women committed to Freudian theory but still determined to think about psychoanalysis radically, or, with poetic license. (177)

Riddles of the Sphinx also figures as a central text in Kaja Silverman's argument for the importance to feminism and to feminist theory of the negative Oedipus complex, defined as the subject's desire for the same-sex parent and rivalry with the opposite-sex parent, which, together with the more familiar, "positive" complex, comprises the complete version (120; see Freud, *The Ego and the Id* 23). No longer simply a triangle, the Oedipus complex is a complex edifice, sheltering deviant desires and cross-gender identifications under the familial roof. The notion of a negative Oedipus complex might be appealing to feminists, lesbians, and gay men reluctant to acknowledge that they have one at all.

For *lesbian* work in cinema and feminism today to be "narrative and Oedipal with a vengeance" is to open a new set of contradictions. On one hand is the understandable suspicion gay people have toward psychoanalysis—as great as the well-documented resistance of feminists. On the other is the keen interest—shared by popular culture, science, *and* lesbians and gay men—in uncovering the origins of homosexuality, and the not infrequent "discovery" of those origins in the family. (The popular imagination seems less compelled to explain the origins of heterosexual object choice and identity.) Clearly homosexual subjects are governed by the psychic processes that affect "everyone else"—there can be no argument but that homosexuality is indeed within psychoanalysis, each having contributed to the other's very invention. At the same time psychoanalysis is a representational system that produces homosexuality as its outside (it is not the only discourse to have done so); thus it can never simply be improved upon to include us. Lesbianism can not be fully "explained" within its terms.

In the spirit of this contradiction, this essay aims to hang both question and quotation marks over the Oedipus complex.[1]

It is of course within narrative that Oedipal models of lesbianism are most prevalent—and most compelling. Freud himself gives us Dora as a classic heroine. For examples of self-representations of the Oedipal lesbian we can cite characters like Stephen Gordon in *The Well of Loneliness*, who take up and pervert the *male* trajectory. The woman's picture, not least its maternal variant, is arguably the classical cinematic genre in which the repressed discourse of lesbian desire can most easily be discerned. Three seminal lesbian films, *The Children's Hour*, *The Killing of Sister George*, and *The Bitter Tears of Petra von Kant*, could themselves be argued to be latter-day women's pictures in which the familial mise-en-scène of desire is revamped.

One might argue that the mother/daughter bond exploited in many of these films is derived more precisely from the pre-Oedipal relation so popular in contemporary feminist thinking (see, for example, Williams). As lesbian critics have begun to argue, however, this scenario might itself be duplicitous for lesbians, not just because the pre-Oedipal is posited only vis-à-vis the Oedipal (and thus within the family and sexual difference), nor simply due to its fundamentally dyadic nature (see Mayne 153–54; de Lauretis, "Film and the Visible" 1991). For in stressing the mother/daughter connection as the foundation of relationships between women, lesbian specificity, the dynamic of desire between women, is subsumed into identification.

It is in part as a response to the romanticization of the pre-Oedipal realm in feminist psychoanalytic writing that Silverman has returned to and rigorously developed the notion of the negative Oedipus complex—not so much to revive the gay Oedipus, but, perhaps even more ambitiously, to locate therein the "libidinal basis of feminism" (102). In Silverman's account, the female subject sustains both an identification with and a desire for an Oedipal mother, a mother possessed of language, desire, and symbolic agency. This relation of desire is *negative* not only because of the lack and loss—what Silverman understands as symbolic castration—that constitute the mother as object of desire, but because of the acute cultural devaluation of the feminine position and of homosexuality (120–24).

However, the considerable interest Silverman's thesis might generate for those attempting an analysis of the psychic contours of lesbian desire is not entirely sustained by her argument. While lesbians and other feminists might be pleased by her description of a female position of speech, as well as a relation with the mother crisscrossed by the law of desire rather than relegated to an unrepresentable symbiosis, they might find her reliance on Julia Kristeva troubling. For Silverman's forceful account of the psychic role of the female negative Oedipus is based not upon the description of such a relation but upon a reading of the Kristevan *chora*—that is, not upon the daughter's relation to an Oedipal mother but upon the narcissistic mother's relation to a male child. (Although the films Silverman analyzes include a female child or child surrogate, the maternal fantasy they invoke originates in the "half-light of the imaginary" [Mulvey 15] rather than within the vigorously symbolic field of Silverman's own intervention.) In what she acknowledges as a "highly unorthodox reading," Silverman interprets the "desire that fuels" Kristeva's "choric fantasy" rather than the letter or spirit of the Kristevan text. Her argument is an ingeniously *negative* one, staked around the lack in Kristeva's thought of any position of female discursive agency or symbolic autonomy besides Kristeva's own.

De Lauretis sees the reliance on maternal identification in Silverman's film analyses as ultimately bespeaking "the heterosexual nature of this feminist fantasy." She notes: "I would insist that failing to distinguish object-choice, of whatever type, from narcissistic-maternal identification can only lead to . . . a vision of female-bonding, homosocial collectivity under the sign of 'a primary and passionate desire for the mother' [Silverman 139]. This is all well and good as a feminist utopia, but what about lesbians?" ("Film and the Visible," 262n35). A virtual obsession with the mother in a great deal of feminist writing, particularly on the pre-Oedipal, has led not only to the dangers pointed out by Silverman—a privileging of a position with no purchase on the symbolic—but to a writing out of lesbianism. An identification with the mother is also a desire for the paternal phallus, and the valorization of motherhood participates in the heterosexual reproduction of the universe. At the same time, celebrating the "passion" for the mother is a way of encompassing within feminism a female "desire" that is homosexual (that is, same sex), while warding off its sexual nature, its otherness. This chapter is motivated by two related questions: first, how does female homosexuality function within feminist psychoanalytic theory? and, second, how is the Oedipal fantasy inscribed in lesbian representation and even in lesbian identity?

For definitions of lesbian desire bound up with the mother, long nurtured by psychoanalysis and by feminism, are not easy to dismiss out of hand. A passage from Helene Deutsch's essay on female homosexuality, written in 1932, illustrates both the perverse appeal of the mother/daughter paradigm and the prickly business of separating out identification from object-choice, sexual desire and fulfillment from infantile sexual disposition. Deutsch describes the analysand (who was referred to her after a suicide attempt) as a "blond and feminine" married woman with children who, though long aware of her homosexuality, never acted on her desire: "She was kind and gentle and showed unmistakable obsessional neurotic traits, such as exaggerated decorum and propriety" (209–10). Deutsch referred her for the finishing touches (i.e., renunciation of her homosexual object-choice) to a male analyst "of the fatherly type," with whom the woman's transference was unsatisfactory. "About a year later I met the patient and saw that she had become a vivid, radiant person." Deutsch continues:

> She told me that her depressions had entirely disappeared. . . . At last she had found happiness in a particularly congenial and uninhibited sexual relationship with a woman. The patient, who was intelligent and conversant with analysis, informed me that their homosexual relationship was quite consciously acted out as if it were a mother-child situation, in which sometimes one, sometimes the other played the mother—a play with a double cast so to speak. . . . No "male-female" contrast appeared in this relationship; the essential contrast was that of activity and passivity. The impression gained was that the feeling of happiness lay in the possibility of being able to play *both* roles. (214)

That the informant was conversant with analysis explains how she might "quite consciously" assert that her sex life confirmed the analyst's conjectures about lesbianism. The relationship plays with a double cast in many senses: there are two actors for each role; there are two settings, the sexual and the familial; two scripts, the one reversing the action of the other. Most interesting, the passage highlights—"so to speak"—the double cast of, the play of meanings within, the described scenario. On one hand there is an emphasis on sexual pleasure, "happiness," rooted itself in doubleness—two women, playing both roles. On the other is an undoubtedly problematic reinforcement of psychoanalytic presumptions about female homosexuality: the naming of sexual roles as mother/child, the classic active/passive distinction—though here explicitly extricated from the male/female binarism.

Finally, there is a second arena, outside the lesbian relationship, in which the play is staged. In the psychoanalytic session, the understudy for the lover is the analyst:

> Everything that had come to the surface so clearly in the analytic transference was now detached from the person of the analyst and transferred to other women. . . . It was evident that the overcoming of her hostility to-

wards the analyst had brought with it the overcoming of her anxiety and, consequently, a positive libidinal relationship to women could appear in place of the anxiety and hostility which had caused the neurotic symptoms—only, of course, after the mother-substitute object had paid off the infantile grievances by granting her sexual satisfaction. (214)

Contrary to this passage, the originary anxiety and hostility toward the mother had *not* been played out in the analysis—if this earlier statement is to be trusted: "Her transference to me was very pronounced and was characteristic of that type whose actions as well as conscious response over a long period of time reveal nothing except tenderness, respect and a feeling of safety. The patient was very happy and felt as if she had at last found a kind, understanding mother" (210). Could it be the analyst's own anxiety we read here? Does she fear the counter-transference, the inscription of desire in her own role? The feeling of happiness in the possibility of being able to play both parts?

To anchor these speculations on the relevance of Oedipal inquiry for lesbians, I would like to turn to a discussion of the 1989 film *Nocturne*, directed by Joy Chamberlain and written by playwright Tash Fairbanks for Britain's Channel 4. As we will see, it is most literally a film with a double cast. Like the classic woman's picture, *Nocturne*—made-for-TV and narrative with a vengeance—exhibits a strange fascination with the vicissitudes of intrafamilial female desire. My analysis will put aside the question of what kind of Oedipal fantasy the film invokes—whether positive or negative, pre- or post-, revisionist or reactionary—and argue that *as* a fantasy, and as an instance of lesbian self-representation, it may effectively and affectively engage the lesbian spectator.

At the opening of the one-hour chamber drama, Marguerite (Lisa Eichhorn), a straight-laced, forty-five-year-old woman, returns to her childhood home after her mother's funeral. The orderly, proper house has been cared for for many years by Mrs. Ruddick (Helena McCarthy), an efficient, though meddlesome, housekeeper. Marguerite sits at the piano and begins to play a Chopin nocturne. Here and throughout the film, flashbacks reveal scenes from her childhood centering around the arrival and ultimate dismissal of Miss Carpenter (Jackie Ekers), a kindly governess from the north of England. (The flashbacks are shot in an eerie bluish light and generally offered as the reverse field of Marguerite's angle of vision, lending them a visual and spatial sur-reality.) As Marguerite discusses arrangements with Mrs. Ruddick, it becomes apparent that she is attempting to free herself of the influence of her repressed and repressive mother (Maureen O'Brien).

She is ultimately able to do so, fully to remember her childhood and to reveal the nature of her mother's secret (a secret she hadn't realized she shared), through the intervention of two lesbian runaways with a penchant for role-playing (Caroline Paterson and Karen Jones). Uninvited guests in her (mother's) house, Sal and Ria educate her—about her own desire—in a way neither her mother nor the adored Miss Carpenter was able to do.

Nocturne can be read as a classic case history—the key to the repressed character of the adult single woman is found by revisiting scenes of childhood trauma. Marguerite's reminiscences and revelations come about not in analysis but in a different sort of transferential situation. The film's plot is Oedipal in that it enacts the daughter's assumption of the mother's place in fantasy, through the interplay of desire, prohibition, and transgression.

Marguerite's case, however, is not a prototypical one. The father is *in*conspicuously absent from the film. He does not figure in the flashbacks and is indeed only mentioned as the owner of the wine in the cellar: bottles the mother is said "never—ever" to have touched. A framed family photograph that figures prominently in the drama depicts mother and daughter only. The paternal absence can perhaps be referred to the presumed historical period of the flashbacks—postwar Britain. Indeed, the flashbacks evoke the women-on-the-homefront cycle of the woman's picture, which enacts the eviction of the father from the mother/daughter dyad—thus the film inscribes a fantasy of a time when the father's absence did not need to be accounted for. The citation of the woman's picture is also notable in that, as Mary Ann Doane and others have documented, the genre was preoccupied with psychoanalysis.

The Oedipal triangle to which Marguerite's adult memories obsessively return unfolds among mother, daughter, and governess. In fact, the nurturing maternal position is occupied by the governess, and the paternal, prohibitive function is filled by the mother. It should be stated at the outset that the film does stage extra-familial signs of difference, particularly class, and less systematically race, as components of its erotic fantasy.

Nocturne has a curious feeling of timelessness. The ambiguous period of Marguerite's prim clothing—indeed, she shares the "exaggerated decorum and propriety" of Deutsch's patient—makes the lipstick-lesbian look of the visitors seem almost futuristic (Kennedy 62). The isolated setting, the arrival of the guests as if by fate, the disciplinary scenarios and social class inversion that ensue, render the setting a quasi-pornographic one.

Elizabeth Cowie, in her important essay "Fantasia," relates the psychoanalytic notion of fantasy to several levels of film spectatorship. "Firstly, fantasy scenarios involve original wishes which are universal. Secondly they are contingent, so that just as we draw on events of the day to produce our own, so we can adopt and adapt the ready-made scenarios of fiction" (85). Thus the strong appeal of the cinema lies in its staging of primal fantasies in a multitude of narrative and visual forms that enlist the identification and desire of particular spectators in particular ways. Cowie's analysis of *Now, Voyager*, discussed by de Lauretis in this volume, suggests that the heterosexual romance plot itself is on the order of a secondary revision of an originary homosexual maternal fantasy.

In *The Language of Psychoanalysis*, Jean LaPlanche and J.-B. Pontalis usefully define the term *fantasy*:

> a. . . . [P]hantasies are scripts (*scenarios*) or organized scenes which are capable of dramatization—usually in a visual form.
> b. The subject is invariably present in these scenes; even in the case of the "primal scene". . . .
> c. It is not an *object* that the subject imagines and aims at, so to speak, but rather a *sequence* in which the subject has his [/her] own part to play and in which permutations of roles and attributions are possible. . . .
> d. In so far as desire is articulated in this way through phantasy, phantasy is also the locus of defensive operations: it facilitates the most primitive of defence processes, such as turning round upon the subject's own self, reversal into the opposite, negation and projection.
> e. Such defences are themselves inseparably bound up with the primary function of phantasy, namely the *mise-en-scène* of desire—a *mise-en-scène* in which what is prohibited (*l'interdit*) is always present in the actual formation of the wish. (318)

Particularly apt for the study of film, LaPlanche and Pontalis's conceptualization has been most interestingly developed by de Lauretis in a reading of *She Must Be Seeing Things* (Sheila McLaughlin, 1987) that discusses the deployment of primary fantasies in a notably contingent way. According to de Lauretis, the film produces and solicits the *lesbian* subject of fantasy though the narrativization of a primal fantasy framed and rendered meaningful by the film's representation of desire between two women (de Lauretis, "Film and the Visible," 236–37).

Nocturne's very action is the dramatization in visual form of an "original wish" through a "ready-made scenario" for Marguerite and, at one remove, for the spectator. For Marguerite plays out the Oedipal relationship to her mother and governess, from the multiple and shifting place of her desire and its prohibition, by reenacting organized scenes from her childhood (presented as flashbacks, these scenes are themselves fantasies) in a new form—the negotiation of a *ménage à trois* with her houseguests. Having proclaimed triumphantly to Mrs. Ruddick "I am not my mother," Mar-

guerite puts herself precisely in the place of her mother, who is both literally dead and fantasmatically killed off.

Nocturne's "fantasy as mise-en-scène of desire" is also a fantasy of
mise-en-scène as desire. Erotically invested objects and sounds from Marguerite's past, privileged parts of the house—the nursery, the drawing
room—elicit Marguerite's fantasy and function within it. And cinematic
codes such as point-of-view structures, the flashback narration, and the
use of music are deployed in the construction and evocation of the fantasy.
Just as Mrs. Ruddick follows Marguerite around the drawing room in the
opening scene, putting knickknacks back in their proper place, Marguerite
assigns herself and her guests to their proper places, admonishes Ria to
behave "properly." Mrs. Ruddick remarks "we've got a lot of sorting out to
do in here. . . . " It is not coincidental that Marguerite's psychical "sorting
out," her assumption of a proprietary relation to the house and to her own
desires, entails the physical upheaval of the house and the crossing of all
bounds of propriety by the end of the film.

The structural similarities between present and past, and the place of
lesbian desire within each plot, are established with the arrival of the two
guests. Marguerite insists that the French doors in the drawing room remain open in spite of the threat of a gathering storm and the housekeeper's
reminder: "Your mother kept it locked shut, winter and summer!" When
rain comes in through the window, Mrs. Ruddick exclaims hyperbolically,
"It's too late, it's come in already! . . . Once in, you can never get rid of it,
it rots the fabric, it destroys it!"

The incident provokes Marguerite's memory of Miss Carpenter and herself as a child, drenched from a sudden downpour during their afternoon
walk, bursting in on her mother through the window. (Curiously, this
flashback is not the first in the film which, although initiated by a traditional subjective shot of Marguerite, inscribes the mother's point of view
within the flashback. This scene opens and closes on the mother alone, a
privileged subjective moment impossible as Marguerite's literal memory
[Dorenkamp 104].) The mother's arousal at the sight of Miss Carpenter in
her wet, clinging dress is made patently clear. Mrs. Tyler masters her desire (for the moment), but transfers her sexual excitement to her daughter,
giving her permission to ride her rocking horse for ten minutes after tea.
(Marguerite's favorite game, she has confided to Miss Carpenter and, reluctantly, to her mother, is riding her horse "to the moon." Her mother
cautions her not to break it.) The cinematic stereotype of the cold, repressive mother is given a completely new significance as locus of lesbian lust.
The flashback reveals that she didn't always "keep [the door] locked," and

we assume she began to do so only after she recognized what it was she wanted to shut out.

In the present, what gets in through the open window causes not only water damage but structural damage—it rots the very fabric of the family. Ria and Sal, soaking wet from the storm, burst into the drawing room, inevitably "dripping on [Marguerite's] nice carpet." The shot of their entrance is canted; the framing device registers the affirmative answer to Sal's sly question: "Are we disturbing you?"

The crooked framing reappears subsequently in the film on shots of Sal and Ria, signifying the jarring introduction of their wild world into Marguerite's ordered one. This strangeness is echoed on the soundtrack, as the bird and animal noises associated with the lovers from their introduction in an outdoor setting become audible in the domestic scenes. In contrast to Marguerite's primness, the lesbians are uninhibited, very physical with each other, given to carnivalesque laughter that Ria's very name recalls.

Nevertheless, there is a psychical "fit" between the earlier triangle and the contemporary trio. To replace the girls' wet clothes, Marguerite digs up the summer dresses she and Miss Carpenter had worn the day they got wet. (They've been saved in a hatbox all these years, through a tacit collusion of mother and daughter's desire.) "These are the only clothes in the house," Marguerite states, " . . . that will fit." Sal's northern accent suits her for the role of the governess, and it is Ria, significantly portrayed by a black actress, who is reluctantly cast as the young Marguerite and asked to wear the little girl's dress.

In the role of the daughter, ostensibly the privileged point in an Oedipal reconstruction, Ria must take on the very position of powerlessness that led Marguerite to fantasize herself in the place of the mother. (As a mark of the lack of connection between mother and daughter, the film contains no two-shots of them together—save the framed snapshot.) Ria has the power only to refuse or to misbehave, which is circumscribed within her role as child. Within the clichéd fantasy of seduction by a member of the uninhibited white lower class are inscribed stereotypes of the eroticized and of the infantilized black woman. At best, the casting of Ria/Karen Jones as child doubly dramatizes exclusion and implies the inadequacy of the familial drama as account of the subject in ideology. By using the black woman's body as a marker of the limits of its own fantasy, the film raises questions—what if she were the subject of this tale? how do its power dynamics, the relations of repression, punishment, illicit desire, servitude, unravel for her?—that cannot be resolved within its terms.

When Ria performs for Sal (and Marguerite as bystander), she displays a

sexuality and assertiveness that Marguerite is denied, over which the latter's recently assumed powers of prohibition are insufficient. Sal and Ria
direct their sexual desire primarily toward each other and authorize, ultimately author, the fantasy. And Ria's resistance is registered in her gaze,
which encompasses defiance, pity, humor, and her judgment of Marguerite. Though the story of Marguerite's repression seems something of a
joke and a shame to Sal and especially to Ria (a less sentimental spectator
might also find it so), they cannot help but recognize its script.

Marguerite's "part" is divided into two roles, but the adult Marguerite
takes her place as the mother only through putting herself in the place of
the child, in order to identify Sal with Miss Carpenter. Several low-angle
point-of-view shots reveal this process. In one instance Marguerite is helping Sal to put on the dress—playing governess, in fact. Although the positions in the reenactment are set from the beginning—and immediately
understood by Sal ("She's a little girl, and I look after her, isn't that
right?")—the control of the fantasy shifts among the players—from Marguerite, to Sal, and to Ria, who has veto power over her lover's actions. The
lesbian spectator might identify with each of the positions or with the un-
folding of the fantasy itself—what will happen next?—with her own position, one of "looking on," the "de-subjectivized" subject position discussed by Freud in "A Child Is Being Beaten" (see de Lauretis, "Film and
the Visible," 135–37). The following exchange inscribes the spectator's
complicity within the film:

> Sal: "Do you want to watch?"
> Marguerite: "Watch what?"
> Sal: "A lesson, of course. I presumed you'd want to watch."
> Marguerite: "I presumed you'd let me."

Spectatorial identification is solicited by the fact that the originary
Oedipal seduction fantasy is overlaid and played out through lesbian sexual fantasy. The dialogue is full of double entendres bringing the levels
together. When Ria is playing chopsticks on the piano, Sal tells Marguerite: "She can play the bottom part, or the top part—whichever you like."
We identify with Sal in her function as reader of the fantasy, and our reluc-
tance to participate is centered around the figure of Ria.

The repeated play of two-shots and shots of single characters—child and
governess are paired against the mother, Marguerite and Sal against Ria,
Sal and Ria excluding Marguerite—underlines again that the Oedipal
structure—the working of desire itself—is triangular. When Mrs. Tyler
joins Marguerite and her governess for tea in the nursery, Miss Carpenter

explains: "When it's just the two of us we don't stand on ceremony." Psychoanalysis tells us it is never just the two of us. Indeed, even in this scene Marguerite's doll Camilla has a place setting at the tea table; her mother displaces the doll, eats the piece of cake set aside for her, and stirs her tea with a doll-size spoon. In the *mise-en-abîme* fantasy structure, the players play house.

As the evening's ceremony progresses, Marguerite, Sal, and Ria—the play's other cast—share a meal highly charged with sexual and other tensions. When Marguerite finally blurts "I want to join in," Ria concedes: "You can play—the piano, while I dance." As Marguerite plays, a different, nonsubjectively marked order of enunciation of the relationship between past and present takes over. We see quick flashes of an earlier scene at the piano, for the first time binding the affect of the present relationship to the childhood scene *for* the spectator. The lesbian couple kisses passionately at the culmination of Ria's dance.

Mrs. Ruddick intrudes at this moment, and, under the mocking gaze of the embracing couple, runs finally from the house. The eviction of Mrs. Ruddick obviously symbolizes that of the mother, whose interests she represents. And as a servant, she had on some level replaced Miss Carpenter in the household. The scene reinstates the other servant.

"We're going upstairs; you can come if you like . . . and say good night," Sal suggests to Marguerite coyly. Marguerite mounts the staircase just as her mother had in an earlier shot. A flashback intervenes at this moment— the moment of the fade, the ellipsis, which marks what really happens that night among the three women. The film fills this lack for the spectator with a primal scene, dramatized around saying goodnight. This final flashback, one assumes, is no longer part of Marguerite's point of view, as she is otherwise occupied.

Mrs. Tyler walks in as the governess is putting Marguerite to bed with kisses and caresses. She refuses her daughter's extended arms, and, as revealed in the mirror across from Marguerite's bed, plants a kiss firmly on Miss Carpenter's lips instead. Mrs. Tyler then fires the governess and shuts Marguerite's door, thus blocking her own image as reflected in the mirror to her daughter, and thus to the camera/spectator occupying the same position. The shot setup indicates that Mrs. Tyler would in turn have been able to see Marguerite's reflection in the mirror, and thus whether her daughter's eyes were open to witness the kiss.

The same setup was used earlier in the film at a crucial moment of the relay of desire between mother and daughter. Marguerite witnessed a telling exchange between the two women in her bedroom mirror. In reply to

Miss Carpenter's suggestion that she might be too hard on her daughter, Mrs. Tyler admonishes: "Remember, you are just a servant in this house." "I will," the governess responds, "if you will." This scene sums up the ambiguities of the governess's position, as she is effectively reprimanded to remember her place in the fantasy: the mother has made her own only too apparent.

The goodnight scene is clearly a kind of primal scene: a fantasy from the point of view of the child, who also betrays her position as eavesdropper. It figures the mother as unwelcome intruder on the relationship between Marguerite and the governess. The drama takes place in the mirror, representing the classic scene of (self-)identification. The mirror shot also signifies the likeness between and reversibility of the positions of mother/ daughter, and constructs two exchangeable points of enunciation of the fantasy. Again, as in the flashbacks, although the content of the film is not sympathetic to the mother's position, on some level the enunciation is. Finally, the fantasmatic nature of the scene is foregrounded: offered in a mirror—itself a figure of unreliability, mediation, "turning round upon the subjects own self"—to a little girl whose eyes may be closed.

In the film's next scene the adult Marguerite really opens her eyes. In bed the morning after, she stretches her naked body and smiles radiantly. She looks just as satisfied when she goes downstairs to find that Sal and Ria have trashed her house and stolen her silver (and probably her car).

Structurally, it seems as if it is the content of the "primal scene" that has been repressed, and its memory that is liberating to Marguerite. The scene is offered to the spectator as a key. But the presumption of lesbianism in the film (the display of sexuality by the houseguests, the codes of the coming-out drama), the disengagement of the flashback from Marguerite's enunciation, as well as the very literalness of the scene, undercut any privileging of its content (i.e., the kiss itself). Affect is concentrated *après coup* on the other kiss, the one between Ria and Sal that is the most "sex" the film ever shows.

If it is Miss Carpenter's knowledge of the mother's desire that the latter ultimately feels compelled to expel from the house, Marguerite can now meet that knowledge with her own, carnal knowledge. Her mother may have "never—ever," but she now has. To which the spectator may add her knowledge—and speculation.

The Oedipal cast of a film like *Nocturne* is self-consciously drawn from similar plots (often clichéd and heavy-handed) in cinematic history. The revelatory flashback is a device inextricably identified with the hermeneutic of psychoanalysis in cinema. Think, for example, of the tour-de-force depiction of childhood trauma in *Marnie*, a film that blames a stereotypi-cally stern, unfeeling mother for the daughter's neuroses, including "fri-gidity." The memory of Miss Carpenter's dismissal coincides with psychic release for Marguerite, as if she is rid of her ghosts and can now displace her desire onto new objects. Rather than adjusting the subject to normalcy (in *Marnie*, abandoning the mother for the rapist husband, albeit in a state of near catatonia), in *Nocturne* the cathartic flashback, together with the transferential and "uninhibited" if not "particularly congenial" erotic en-counter with the lovers, enables Marguerite to embrace a present reality in which the possibility of lesbian desire and identity is the imaginary frame.

In moving from Oedipal triangle to lesbian three-way the film perhaps recalls *The Killing of Sister George* and *The Bitter Tears of Petra von Kant*, also melodramas about role-playing and class conflict among three women. As much as they ostensibly share with the decadent figures of eros in Pa-solini's *Teorema* (in which a guest seduces each member of a bourgeois household) or of evil in Losey's *The Servant*, the runaways in *Nocturne* are primarily signifiers of lesbian liberation. That is, the film's condition of possibility is a feminist fantasy that also grounds and directs the desire and identification of its spectator in a manner distinct from that in which the Aldrich or Fassbinder film might engage even the same spectator.

Ultimately, as a film by, about, and (though not exclusively) for lesbi-ans, *Nocturne* revisits recognizable cinematic paradigms just as it restages universal fantasies—within a different frame of reference, a different order of recognizability. The film suggests that the Oedipal fantasy is not a suf-ficient governess of lesbian desire, which is unruly and manages to exceed the familial boundaries. *Nocturne* offers two alternative fantasies to a strictly Oedipal (ir)resolution. The first shifts focus to the third term of the triangle. The second points to the outcome of refusing to be Oedipal, with a vengeance.

The governess is a point of tension on the Oedipal model, first through her appearance on the scene of psychoanalysis in Freud's case histories and in the bourgeois family upon which his theory was based, and second through her literary and cinematic "pull" toward the representation of dif-ference, class difference, and a-sexual difference, which, if not identifiably lesbian, can at least be identified with by lesbians. I have commented else-where on the film gothic's lesbian-coded governesses and companions (167–69). One might also mention Miss Puddleton (Puddle) in *The Well of Loneliness*, who is always pointing to a secret that Stephen, belonging to the younger generation of inverts, never bothers to ask about.

As Jane Gallop has noted in her "Keys to Dora": "The family never was, in any of Freud's texts, completely closed off from questions of economic class. And the most insistent locus of that intrusion into the family circle . . . is the maid/governess/nurse" (144). In *The Newly Born Woman*, the text by Hélène Cixous and Catherine Clément upon which Gallop draws, she is called "the seductress . . . the hole in the social cell . . . the repressed of the boss's wife" (150). Mary Poovey, in her interesting essay "The Anathematized Race: The Governess and Jane Eyre," looks at popular discourses on the role of the governess in nineteenth-century England and points out that the ideological "problem" of the governess is in part the *question* of class. That is, the governess must be from a "good family," must be similar in breeding and manners to her female employer. Her class position is a result of misfortune, not of origin.

Gallop collapses maid, nurse, and governess, figures who clearly serve very different practical and, one would assume, fantasmatic functions within the household. The difference in class position of Miss Carpenter, and of Sal and Ria, in *Nocturne* is a structural aspect of the fantasy. When Ria dresses up as daughter and Sal as governess, they perform a travesty. And the inscription of racial difference in *Nocturne* overlays the class division. Director Chamberlain, in an interview with Monica Dorenkamp, responded to a question about the casting of a black actress in the film:

> *Chamberlain*: I have a commitment to multiracial casting as much as possible. This one was problematic because the film's very much an allegory for the class system in Britain. . . . Some of the characters needed to be white because it was about the white middle-class, so it was a case of casting one of the two girls as Black. . . . If one of them is a woman of color, then it's more to do with the inter-relationships of the characters. I wanted it to be incidental.
>
> *Dorenkamp*: The problem, of course, is that it never is, . . . especially since this is a film about role-playing—it gets incredibly loaded.
>
> *Chamberlain*: The whole film is loaded. But I thought it'd be worse if I cast her as Sal because then she'd be playing the nanny. (105)

The director suggests that "governess" (or tutor, as Miss Carpenter is called in the film) is also a white position—if the character were black, she would be seen as a nanny, a historical, sociological, and subjective position carrying a different set of connotations and contradictions. One of the ways in which the film remains "loaded" is that Ria's being played by a black actress can do no more than stand in for the possibility of a story that would be about race (would this be a "colonial allegory"?)—or be seen as "incidental."

Poovey emphasizes that it is the resemblance between governess and mistress that is the source of anxiety in the nineteenth century: "If the fallen woman was the middle-class mother's opposite, the middle-class governess was her next of kin, the figure who ought to ensure that a boundary existed between classes of women but who could not, precisely because her sexuality made her resemble the women from whom she ought to differ" (250). This "sexuality" is understood in terms of the domestic ideal—the ideology of the white, middle-class woman's lack of sexual desire and her innate maternal instinct. The governess's "position" is the performance of this ideology for money. According to Poovey, "the governess not only revealed what the mother might otherwise have been; she also actively freed mothers to display desires that were distinctly *not* maternal, thus setting up the unsettling possibility that a mother's 'jealousy' and her energies might find an object other than the one 'nature' had decreed" (249). To suggest that this object might be the governess herself, that the similarity/difference threatened by the governess is lesbianism, is to go beyond the scope of Poovey's analysis.

Gallop writes: "[The servant] is so much a part of the family that the child's fantasies (the unconscious) do not distinguish 'mother or nurse' "; and she concludes that it is in the interest of the family to maintain this identification: "If the nurse is assimilated to the mother . . . then the family cell can close up again." If this does not happen, if the woman's alterity is insisted upon, "it is not enough [for the father] to seduce her. She must be expelled from the family" (145–46). In *Nocturne* the governess is expelled because she crystallizes the mother's difference from herself, her own lesbianism. For Cixous and Clément and Gallop, the point of identification between the women in the household is their oppression by men; the interchangeability of the women as sexual objects in the Dora case is striking. In another case history, that of Deutsch's patient mentioned above, what is emphasized is the relay of *lesbian* desire along the chain of female figures—from daughter to mother to servant to lover (and ultimately to analyst). Deutsch's patient "came into analysis on account of neurotic difficulties. She had suffered for years from depressions and feelings of anxiety with a particular ideational content: she could not find the courage to assume the fitting authoritative attitude towards women in her employ" (209–10). Psychoanalysis is called upon to restore the meaning of this boundary. The patient's anxiety is revealed to be derived from her disposition toward her mother and thus toward her potential sexual partners (by whom she fears she will be psychically subjugated).

Gallop's "Keys to Dora" concludes with a postscript or "supplement" to the main argument, a portion of the text signaled as poetic. "Having reached a definite conclusion, I find more remains to be said. The 'more' revolves around Dora's love for Frau K., around her lesbianism" (148). Although no explicit link is made between the discussion of the governess in the body of the text and the topic of female homoeroticism in the "supplement", the progression of the argument suggests one might be found.[2] Yet Gallop goes on to say less about this "more" than we have been led to expect: what is here introduced as lesbianism is next called feminine homosexuality, then bisexuality, then an "other bisexuality": "neither the fantasmatic resolution of differences in the imaginary, nor the fleshless, joyless assumption of the fact of one's lack of unity in the symbolic, but an other bisexuality, one that pursues, loves, and accepts both the imaginary and the symbolic, both theory and flesh" (150). Gallop speculates, "Perhaps in a theoretical text one can never do more than say 'There is more, there is love and beauty,' which is a necessary affirmative supplement to the murderous negation that theory must be" (148). But since "more" has been identified with lesbianism, are we to understand that it is a rhetorical figure, supplemental to, or murderously negated by, theory?

The alterity of the governess—Gallop recognizes her as a threshold figure (146)—might have motivated a consideration of lesbianism in the "theory" portion of the text. Instead the governess is seen as "a threatening representative of the symbolic, the economic, the extrafamilial" (147), opposed, apparently, to female homoeroticism, "cited as an instance of the imaginary, which is to be taken as a criticism" (148). Although Gallop quickly deconstructs this binary opposition, valorizing elements of the imaginary and the maternal, the female servant is safely ensconced elsewhere, as a signifier of class, albeit within a phallic sexual economy. And, more problematically, lesbianism is actually missing from the "postscript." To whom is bisexuality other? Indeed, the bisexuality to which Gallop's is opposed appears to be one defined by sexuality, and specifically by its homosexual component.

I have discussed Gallop's text as an example of the cachet lesbianism can have in psychoanalytic feminist theory. Pointing a way out of psychoanalytic descriptions of femininity as lacking subjectivity and a proper desire, lesbian difference risks reinscription as not other, indeed, not lesbian. The ambiguous figure of the governess might represent this uneasy relation between lesbian difference and the Oedipal scenario. In *Nocturne* the mother may identify with Miss Carpenter—as a sensual being, or even as the object of her daughter's desire. But, more important, and more obviously, she *desires* her. It is not even necessary that Miss Carpenter be a lesbian (in fact she is something of a cipher); Sal makes manifestly clear the connotations of her position. Marguerite does not confuse mother and governess on a conscious level, although her compulsion to fantasy is the working through of their similarity and difference.

Finally, *Nocturne*'s fantasy activates the *mise-en-scène* of Oedipal desire in the service of the daughter's desire to *have* "something else besides a mother"[3]—the desire, not yet fully realized, for rupture with what de Lauretis names the "Oedipal contract":

> In the term "Oedipal contract" I want to bring together and into view the semiotic homology of several conceptual frameworks: Saussure's notion of language as social contract; Rousseau's "social contract" with its gender distinction; Freud's "Oedipus complex" as the structuring psychic mechanism responsible for the orientation of human desire and the psychosocial construction of gender; the "cinematic contract" that stipulates the conditions of vision by encoding the specific relations of image and sound to meaning and subjectivity for the film's spectator . . . ; and finally, Wittig's "heterosexual contract" as the agreement between modern theoretical systems and epistemologies not to question the *a priori* of gender, and hence to presume the sociosexual opposition of "man" and "woman" as the necessary and founding moment of culture. (1987, 277n1)

The terms of this contract are so closely imbricated that a mere governess cannot stand up to them alone.

Nocturne invokes a second fantasy governing the operation of lesbian desire, one which displaces the familial context, one in which Ria fully—ironically—participates: the fantasy of *running away*. Monique Wittig writes in her essay "On the Social Contract": "I see now that [women] can tear themselves away from the heterosexual order only by running away one by one" (239). Before leaving, Sal and Ria ransack Marguerite's house. They are dressed in their proper clothes, now dry. (We don't know whether they steal the dresses, although Chamberlain recounted that cast and crew members staked claim to these souvenirs!) One of the fetish objects is stolen. Ria picks up the portrait of Marguerite and her mother, wonders if the frame is genuine silver, smashes the glass, tosses the photograph casually aside, and adds the frame to her box of loot. Her definitive, triumphant gesture removes the framing structure, rendering the image of mother and daughter "crooked." She leaves the roles behind her. Wittig writes: "only by running away from their class can women enter the social contract (that is, a new one), even if they have to do it like the fugitive serfs, one by one. We are doing it. Lesbians are runaways. . . . " Sal and Ria, driving a car stolen from a lecherous man, sing, "Keep on running, keep on hiding. . . . " What is prohibited is present in the actual formation of the wish. Their first stop, after all, is the bourgeois home. But they run away *together*.

Nocturne solicits a spectatorial identification with the lesbian as *metteur-en-scène*. Marguerite reinvents and displaces the drama of her own Oedipal constitution, and the viewer is drawn by this ever-resonant fantasy of origins. Yet existing tangentially with it is the fantasy of running away, of breaking the Oedipal contract. The uninvited guests are the perfect figure for lesbian spectatorship. On a narrative level they represent the resolution of psychic conflict through lesbian sex—an ending one might have wished to see in countless conventional women's films. *Nocturne* implies that what is excluded from the family and from classical cinema may already exist as the difference within. We might well wonder what subtle havoc the drama wreaked when invited into the homes of middle-class British audiences on prime-time TV.

Notes

I would like to thank Cynthia Schneider and Teresa de Lauretis for their comments on earlier drafts of this essay. Thanks, too, to Laura Pietropaolo and especially Ada Testaferri for including me in this volume and the conference from which it arose.

1. As de Lauretis puts it: "lesbian sexuality is neither convergent with heterosexual female sexuality . . . nor pre-Oedipal, in the sense of the 'mother-child dyad' dear to much of so-called psychoanalytic feminism, nor finally altogether outside or independent of the Oedipal fantasy structure, as many would prefer to think" ("Film and the Visible," 237).

2. Gallop's postscript self-consciously repeats Freud's gesture of speaking of female homosexuality only in the footnotes to the Dora case. She also notes how Cixous and Clément's comments on female homosexuality are formulated as an afterthought. Again the topic of homosexuality is introduced just after the discussion of the governess: "And to that must be added that in Dora there is a very beautiful homosexuality, a love for woman that is astounding" (Cixous and Clément 154). Interestingly, Cixous refers to the footnote as the "maid's room" of Freud's text (150).

3. This is the title of Linda Williams's essay on the quintessential maternal melodrama, *Stella Dallas* (King Vidor, 1939), and it is derived from an ironic line of dialogue in the film.

Works Cited

Cixous, Hélène, and Catherine Clément. *The Newly Born Woman*. Trans. Betsy Wing. Minneapolis: University of Minnesota Press, 1986.
Cowie, Elizabeth. "Fantasia." *m/f* 9 (1984): 70–105.

de Lauretis, Teresa. *Alice Doesn't: Feminism, Semiotics, Cinema*. Bloomington: Indiana University Press, 1984.

———. "Film and the Visible." *How Do I Look? Queer Film and Video*. Ed. Bad Object Choices. Seattle: Bay, 1991. 223–264.

———. "The Female Body and Heterosexual Presumption." Rev. of *The Female Body in Western Culture*, ed. Susan Suleimen. *Semiotica* 67.3–4 (1987): 259–79.

Deutsch, Helen. "On Female Homosexuality." *The Psychoanalytic Reader*. Ed. Robert Fliess. New York: International Universities, 1973. 208–30.

Doane, Mary Ann. *The Desire to Desire*. Bloomington: Indiana University Press, 1987.

Dorenkamp, Monica. "Joy de Vivre." *OutWeek*. June 17, 1990: 104+.

Freud. "A Child is Being Beaten." *Sexuality and the Psychology of Love*. Ed Philip Rieff. New York: Collier, 1963.

———. *Dora: An Analysis of a Case of Hysteria*. New York: Collier, 1963.

———. *The Ego and the Id*. Ed. James Strachey. New York: Norton, 1960.

Gallop, Jane. "Keys to Dora." *The Daughter's Seduction: Feminism and Psychoanalysis*. Ithaca: Cornell University Press, 1982. 132–50.

Kennedy, Lisa. "Close Your Eyes and Think of England." *Village Voice*. June 5, 1990: 61–62.

LaPlanche, Jean, and J.-B. Pontalis. *The Language of Psycho-Analysis*. Trans. Donald Nicholson-Smith. New York: Norton, 1973.

Mayne, Judith. *The Woman at the Keyhole*. Bloomington: Indiana University Press, 1990.

Mulvey, Laura. *Visual and Other Pleasures*. Bloomington: Indiana University Press, 1989.

Poovey, Mary. "The Anathematized Race: The Governess and *Jane Eyre*." *Feminism and Psychoanalysis*. Ed. Richard Feldstein and Judith Roof. Ithaca: Cornell University Press, 1989. 230–54.

Silverman, Kaja. *The Acoustic Mirror: The Female Voice in Psychoanalysis and Cinema*. Bloomington: Indiana University Press, 1988.

Terry, Jennifer. "Theorizing Deviant Historiography." *Queer Theory*. Ed. Teresa de Lauretis. Special issue of *differences* 3.2 (1991): 55–74.

White, Patricia. "Female Spectator, Lesbian Specter: *The Haunting*." *Inside/Out: Lesbian Theories, Gay Theories*. Ed. Diana Fuss. New York: Routledge, 1991.

Williams, Linda. " 'Something Else Besides a Mother': *Stella Dallas* and the Maternal Melodrama." *Cinema Journal* 24.1 (1984): 2–27.

Wittig, Monique. "On the Social Contract." *Homosexuality, Which Homosexuality?* Dennis Altman et al. London: Gay Men's Press, 1989.

7

FEMALE MISBEHAVIOR

Monika Treut

Whosoever allows himself to be whipped, deserves to be whipped.

—Leopold von Sacher-Masoch, *Venus in Furs*, 1870

If the role of the phantasy is not recognized, masochism is inexplicable. Phantasy is the place of its origin, and in the beginning there is only masochistic phantasy. The meaning of this factor becomes clear insofar as those who possess only a weakly developed phantasy, or no phantasy at all, show no tendency to become sadomasochists.

—Theodor Reik, *Masochism in Modern Man*, 1940

The masochist must believe that he is dreaming, even when he is not dreaming.

—Gilles Deleuze, *Sacher-Masoch and Masochism*, 1967

FROM THE WORK of the sexologists of the nineteenth century, from psychoanalysis, down through the Left and all the way up to its representation in the contemporary popular press, sadomasochistic theater has been understood by enlightened minds to be perverse. It is seen as a deadly serious mise-en-scène, as the manifestation, born of unnatural conditions, of the domination of one human being over another against which it is necessary to struggle.

The language of proper sexuality says: A little dependency and obedience belongs to every erotic relationship, but not too much, please. For too much of that which is good turns bad, and obedience becomes destructive when it is practiced sadomasochistically.

My reflections are directed against such an evaluation, and they attempt to show, paradoxically, that the S/M mise-en-scène is destructive precisely because it undermines that obedience which, through its uncontrolled and unconscious action, is itself destructive.

Ever since the sexual psychologist Krafft-Ebing dismissed masochism as a "psychopathological symptom," the obedience of the masochist, as the writer Leopold von Sacher-Masoch represented it in literature, has been condemned as a destructive abnormality. "By the term masochism, I mean the curious perversion of the psychic *vita sexualis*, which consists in the afflicted individual's being ruled in his sexual feelings and thoughts by the idea of being completely and unconditionally dominated by the will of the person of the other sex, of being treated imperiously, humiliated, and even abused by this person. This idea is erotically accented" (Krafft-Ebing 1907, 99f).

Normal sexual life would thus be destroyed insofar as obedience could enjoy but a modest shadow existence. In no case could it predominate "unconditionally."

Masochistic obedience violates the rules of disciplined sexual behavior. One must be healed and liberated from it.

Such is the common prejudice from the "Psychopathia Sexualis" that accompanies the headway made by the state in asserting the disciplinary power that prescribes norms for bourgeois individuals and for their bodies, telling them what it is that they have to do.

The code of normalization overlooks a constitutive element of the sado-masochistic mise-en-scène: even when S/M practices possess moments of actual violence (the masochist is beaten, he experiences pain and exposes himself to a "cruel" scenario of unconditional obedience), it is in fact fantasy that is its determining factor. Fantasy alone is the birthplace of masochism.

Theodor Reik was the first to protest against the neglect of the role of fantasy as a constitutive element in sadomasochism: "Those who have a weakly developed fantasy, or none at all, show no tendency toward becoming masochists" (Reik 1977: 61f).

This does not preclude the possibility that these same people may in fact be masochists in an uncontrolled and unconscious manner in everyday life. There is good reason to argue that the renunciation of the fantasizing mise-en-scène of masochist obedience brings forth a destructive condition of submission and of blind dependency. Without the imaginative self-scripted mise-en-scène, the subjugated one loses his self-esteem and his pride that, paradoxically, he can preserve and experience self-consciously in the theatrical staging of S/M cruelty.

Wanda, the tyrant of *Verführung: die grausame Frau* (*Seduction: The Cruel Woman*), a film that I made together with Elfi Mikesch (1985), spells out this insight with an ironic grin to the audience at her "Gallery of Obedience":

> The specifically masochistic ambition,
> the pride of the slave . . .
> —yes, you heard right—
> the slave possesses an almost unimaginable pride,
> that compels him
> to demonstrate his submission in its most extreme form.
> How indeed could he better express this desire
> than by seeking intimate contact
> with your excretions?
> He finds new names for them:
> calls them champagne and caviar,
> their stench is for him the most exquisite of perfumes.
> The slave deifies these substances
> that count in our culture as the most disgusting ones imaginable.
> This has to do with the most extreme form of fetishism
> known to us.
> To manage it properly is not easy.
> Neither for the submissive nor for the dominant partner.
> It is a reciprocal process of education.
> Put yourself for once into the mind of the slave:
> his submissive soul clings to you and at the same time to everything
> that surrounds you, even, paradoxically enough, to that
> which you least regard.
> He strives to demean himself.
> Gladly does he fantasize himself in the role of a lowly beast,
> a worm, for example,
> or an inanimate piece of furniture,
> it goes all the way to total invisibility,
> yes, to self-destruction.
> Overcome your loathing and disgust.
> Tell yourself: my excretions are the most normal thing in the world,
> neither especially beautiful nor especially horrible.
> Stand by your shit!
> One last word:
> You cannot offer a crueler punishment and simultaneously a greater joy
> to your slave than your filth.
> Therefore: don't spoil him too much.
> The best thing for both of you is to keep him in a state
> of continual desire. . . .

Wanda's advice provides an account of the structure of masochistic fantasy, replete as it is with theatrical emotions, and which uses, not by chance, theatrical elements for its ritualized mise-en-scène: scripts, stage directions, sets, costumes, fetish objects. . . .

To express it otherwise: the fantasy of masochistic submission draws its effectiveness not from the actual situation of an objectively existing and powerful dependency but rather from playing with the idea of such a dependency. Its structure is more mythic than real. It operates with the historically, literarily, and mythically formed signs of an imaginative energy that those signs use as the primary materials of a script for the production of desire.

To that end, this structure must be subordinated to a temporality whereby change and stasis, tension and release, are brought together in an artistic manner.

"The best thing for both of them is, in fact, to keep him [the masochist] in a state of continual desire."

The S/M mise-en-scène thrives on suspense. Better than any German word, "suspense" indicates the specifically masochistic release of tension. For this has nothing to do with the apparently natural process of a tension that reaches its high point as it is driven by the expectation of a pleasurable release. It is rather an arc of tension that draws its vitality from hesitation, delay, and waiting.

This paradoxical temporal consciousness has as its result that the final pleasurable release is displaced onto an uncertain future, in which the inaugural desire is deferred over an uncertain length of time.

The anxiety of the masochist, his anticipation of pain as the condition of the possibility of desire, repeatedly undergoes the attempt to be extended to the limits of the tolerable, up to the point of an "agony of suspense." In this manner anxiety may be enjoyed and cultivated, which, prior to punishment, exists for the purpose of the orgiastic final release of desire.

The entire work of fantasy consists in the anticipatory imagination of the impending punishments, humiliations, and pains that would arise in the case of the final realization of desire, in order thus to be able to derive pleasure from anxiety itself.

And the mise-en-scène of "perverse" practices serves to give the very anticipation of displeasure a dysphoric countenance, thereby bringing the anxiety toward punishment and humiliation under one's own direction (Treut 1984).

In contrast to sadistic violence, which orients itself toward the goal of the destruction of the victim, masochistic obedience is aimed at the prevention of such destruction.

That specifically masochistic ambition, the pride of the slave, consists in the destruction of such forms of obedience and claims to power as would be uncomprehended and unchecked. Its destructive obedience is the sign of self-conscious fantasy placing into question every form of actual violence and dependency. Thus, the mise-en-scène, the transmutation of values, and the ritualized submissivity. Only in this manner is it possible to control that which in "normal" sexuality most frequently reveals itself simply as unconscious anxiety, without the possibility of really understanding or experiencing it.

The S/M ritual determines first of all the situation in which the partners in this game find themselves. The obedient one knows what he wants from others and what he can expect from them. Paradoxically, it is he himself who lays down the rules of obedience. His submission is therefore not unconditional, but rather is bound to that which he, the slave, demands from his master.

And the master/mistress knows how far he/she may go. Specific rules are followed that are agreed upon.

S/M events are the artful realizations of an "ars erotica" that plays in a sovereign manner with power and powerlessness. It makes the connections between power and desire in a differnent manner than does the "scientia sexualis" that in its turn only submits its subjects to a disciplinary power.

The body, too, is thereby consciously liberated from its normative dependency. It is precisely through the desubjectivization and objectification of the masochistic body, which can be handled "like a piece of meat," that the masochist gains an expanded consciousness of his own body and of its physiological functioning.

This self-control appears to increase proportionally in correspondence to the violence of the "perverse" act. It is a knowledge not to be found in any book or in any sexological explanation, but is rather a knowledge that stems from a nonverbal experience of the body, a semiotics of the body that emerges from the practice of the sadomasochistic mise-en-scène.

And finally, the aggressivity of the one to whom the masochistic slave unconditionally submits will also be held in check. At the same time as the partner's violence and power to inflict punishment is provoked, that very power is brought under control. It would be mistaken to believe that the masochist seeks a real sadist as a love object. What he seeks in the other is the desire for a power that flourishes not in a destructive fashion but rather in the contained manner of the ritual adhered to by both the dominating and the submissive subject.

It is through the obedience of the masochist that the brutality of a possible sadistic aggression is held in check.

This also becomes clear in the verbal utterances of the masochist. For his verbal self-condemnations that he is a piece of shit, garbage and rubbish, a toilet and slimebag, don't express what he is. They are only an appeal to the other to treat him as if this were the case. The masochist doesn't say that he is a toilet, but rather challenges the other to treat him in a certain way. When he repeatedly abuses and devalorizes himself, he attempts to initiate specific actions from his partner.

His language possesses, in other words, not a constative character but rather a performative function aimed toward the initiation of the desired mise-en-scène. This language provokes the aggression of the partner in order to guide that aggression in the desired direction and thus to bring it under control. The verbally expressed wish of the masochist must not be misunderstood as if it were a realistic one. It is functional and meaningful only as a performative act within the sadomasochistic language game. Another scene from the film *Seduction: The Cruel Woman* is apropos here:

Journalist:
A final question, Ms. Wanda,
do you mean that one would be better off living out one's own fantasies?
Or rather just dream about them, to the end of one's life?
Wanda:
I would say that it depends on the fantasy.
Journalist:
My dear Wanda, forgive me,
I have a wish—
since we have now come to the end of our talk . . .
Wanda:
Yes?
Journalist:
. . . in this bathtub, I could . . . dream . . .
Wanda:
Well, go ahead!
Journalist:
I really would like to . . .
Wanda:
Yes?
Journalist:
I would like to be your toilet!
[. . .]
Wanda:

Get to your place!
How many liters can you drink?
He:
As many as you give me, my mistress.
She:
Do you like being a toilet?
Your greatest wish is
to get yourself installed in the women's washroom at the main train
station.
He:
Would you please watch me
when I clean the urinals with my tongue?
She:
Women don't use urinals, you idiot!
He:
Please excuse me,
I really am just a toilet, my mistress.
She:
Don't say **MY** mistress!
I own **YOU**, you thing!
[. . .]

In the discussion about masochistic obedience and the unconditionality of its submissiveness, repeated reference has been made to fascism. The fetishes of the S/M mise-en-scène, black leather, whips, chains, etc., were criticized as fascistoid.

In response to such criticism it must be observed that fascism demonstrated where the *unconscious* entanglement of violence and sexuality, of cruelty and aestheticized power, lead to. Black leather, an allusion to death, is not entirely by chance the favored material for fascistic clothing. It belongs to the essence of fascism that its attire should be aestheticized. Theatricality is the connecting link between fascism and sadomasochism.

Sadomasochistic mise-en-scènes liberate sex from the deep entanglements that have tyrannized it for hundreds of years, and especially in respect to the premises of platonic-christian love. Sadomasochists seize upon this theatrical posture, they take their obsessions to the limit, playing with the cult symbols of S/M, without therefore being fascistic. For its radical blasphemy recognizes but one impulse: the transgression of regulated shame. Nevertheless, there is but one boundary: the respect for the possibilities of those with whom sexual practice takes place. And this deep respect that is sustained by every sadomasochistic mise-en-scène and that makes them possible at all is anything but fascistic.

It ironizes actual human power relationships, insofar as rights of admission are granted only to those sovereign subjects who may, when and if they please, play the role of master/mistress or slave, in order to fulfill their sexual desires. In contrast to actual violence, sadomasochistic violence is anarchic and free, libertarian and unbounded.

In the U.S. I have experienced just what possibilities such violence offers to women. Women in the U.S. have learned how to develop their potential for sovereignty in this shadow game of reality and fantasy.

The search for contemporary libertine women led me to the capital city of the twentieth century, New York. Several weeks of telephone calls, negotiations, and recommendations were necessary in order to be able to attend a meeting of the Secret Society of Cruel Women. In the U.S. there has existed since the beginning of the 1980s a subculture of lesbian sadomasochists. First there was the Samois group in California, later the LSM group (Lesbian Sex Mafia, Lesbian Sadomasochists).

I did a video interview with Carol, a Mafia member, in a bathroom:

> I think women deny that they're sexual. They don't talk about sex, they talk about theory.
> I've been doing S/M for a lot of years, but not calling it S/M, playing dominant and submissive games, dressing up, spanking, bondage . . . I love bondage! When I put someone in bondage, it's sort of an art form for me.
> I identify as a top, but I'm switchable, so that sometimes I'm submissive. When I'm depressed, hurting about something, I have a friend put me into bondage and it makes me feel a lot better, makes me feel very safe. And if I put someone in bondage I take great care for their comfort and their well-being, not only their physical but their emotional well-being. S/M is communication and really getting into people's emotions.

The erotic combination of therapeutic attitudes, the acting out of psychic tensions, together with the mise-en-scène of artistic "shows," is characteristic of the American women. Without grounding or defending themselves in cultural and historical terms, the LSM movement is wagering on an arrangement that appropriates signs playfully, in which something, however unusual it may be, of the self-conscious power of women shows forth. In that Western metropolis, where reality has become hyper-real like nowhere else, they stage their play: controlled, full of fantasy, under their own direction; lesbian, because men, even in the masochistically submissive role, would, nevertheless, still assume the role of the director, and sado/masochistic, because nowhere else as in the fantasies of Sade and Sacher-Masoch does there appear a woman who, in her exaggerated depiction, makes such a straightforward claim to the human right to realize the condition of freedom, in response to its everyday betrayal.

The destructive obedience that has been represented here as "art," as "art form," and as "ars erotica" ironically negates real violence, the actual relationship between domination and oppression. It does not reproduce violence but plays with violence in order to nullify it. Its subversive character consists in this, and not in the destruction of normal sexuality.

Romantic Love: A German Myth?

All cultures recognize the notion of love. One loves one's parents, one's children, God, nature, a woman, a man. Love: this universal phenomenon is as universal as work and language.

People speak, work, and love. But these three anthropological constants are empty if they do not have cultural and historical content. As soon as we attempt to say more than "Yes, of course, love," the differences concerning love, both in itself and as a universal principle, become unavoidable.

Let us remain in Germany for the time being.

No other country has preserved a notion of love so colored by romanticism, a notion that determines, at least in Western cultures, our idea of love. Almost all of the qualities that we ascribe to and hope for from a great love received their characteristic traits during "German romanticism": the wish to merge with the other; the yearning for a redemption that will put an end to hatred and strife; the dream of an ideal life together, in which each desires only the happiness of the other and is ready to sacrifice oneself; the extreme intensification of an emotional stance that defies death and promises to overcome it; the cultivation of a unique passion that in its singularity binds the lovers together. . . .

Germany—it is not only the land of order and cleanliness, of rules and of calculated method. It is also the home of an unfulfillable romantic yearning that brought forth an idealizing language of love, within which feelings might course freely, liberated of all conventional rules and ritualized forms. Romantic love recognizes no rules other than its own. It is a freely circulating system of energy that follows its own impulses and that is prepared to accept only death as a desirable accomplice. Social imperatives lie outside of its ken.

Romantic love is not reality, it is not a socially practiced form of life. It is but the ideal of a dream and of illusionary wishful thinking. This love is not experienced as an idea of pathos, but is simply imagined and felt.

It operates within the unquenchable longing for love, passion, and emotion. It is not by chance that its privileged place is literature. Romantic love was always already romanesque. Its power, sweeping lovers to their deaths, was the power of a literary language that gradually refined itself and that found its full aesthetic form in romantic texts. In reality it can be experienced only as crazy or ludicrous, like a special kind of illness or madness.

Romantic love draws its vitality from the unnegatable separation between real life and verbal hallucination, between real relationships and emotional rapture, between loving couples and writers of romances.

It belongs to its paradoxical structure that it can draw its power only from a discourse of love to which lovers attempt to aspire, without really being able to follow it.

This structure was heralded for the first time in the Minnesongs of the German Middle Ages. It reaches its high point in the lyric poetry and novels of romanticism from around 1800. Today we are experiencing it as a neo-romantic revival, as the attempt of a satiated and bored civilization to secure for itself a final, sentimental thrill.

Inspired by the aristocratic love poetry of the troubadors of Provence and the trouvères of northern France, German Minnepoetry blossomed to its fullest extent between 1180 and 1210 (Friedrich von Hausen, Heinrich von Morungen, Reimar von Hagenau). The times were chaotic and the empire was being broken apart by the rise of territorial principalities. And it was precisely during this period, which also was marked by the murderous campaigns of the Crusades, when the songs of courtly love revealed an inner world cultivated and ennobled by the idea of "Minne-Service," whereby the lover delivers himself unconditionally to his beloved in the unfulfillable hope of a reward that he will never receive.

The lover could come from any and all levels of society. The greatest of kings, such as Henry VI and Friedrich II, found themselves among the ranks of the Minnesingers along with a great many noble and rich burgraves and knights. Yet even poor Minnesingers from the lowest social levels raised their Song of Songs to their beloved one, who in turn withdrew, making a moral elevation possible solely because of this withdrawal.

An antinomic tension that can never be released finds its perfected expression in a poetic form: hope and disappointment, yearning and sorrow, desire and illusion characterize a love that is in fact but an eternal disquietude with neither satisfaction nor fulfillment. Had in fact the idealizing claim ever reached its goal, it would have lost its appeal and its intensity.

Here everything remains bound to a highly stylized system of expression that turns to the beloved "frouwe"[1] as the earthly counterpart to the highest perfection. The pleasure derived from renunciation, elevation through servile abasement: that is the phantasmagoric goal of the Minnesong as it became refined in forms and in tones[2] that are filled with "wan" (illusion).

The love that is thus imagined and stylized is not a sexual desire that strives for fulfillment. It is the codified medium of a yearning imaginative power that is self-reflexive and that consumes itself insofar as its desire cannot be fulfilled. In response to the pressing demands of the lover inherent in the forms of love and service that are characteristic of Minne comes the answer of the beloved mistress: "so that you might be all the more worthy and joyful of mind" (Albrecht von Johannsdorf).[3] Inner elevation and joy of the heart: the intensification of experience is bought at the price of an unbridgeable distance. This distance alone makes possible the unity of reflection and involvement that would be lost through the fulfillment of pleasure. It is only through hope, through yearning, and through that which is unreachably distant that the courtly love of Minne finds its fulfillment.

Everything is wished for and yearned for, painted in glowing colors and displayed in poetic finery. But nothing may be attained. That is the idea of High Minne, the first appearance of that which would find its individualized bourgeois form hundreds of years later in the paradoxes of romantic love, once it had been liberated from moral constraints of courtly culture.

In classical Minnesong it is only the man who speaks. Woman appears solely as the object of an illusion that would lose its attraction if the beloved were verbally to express her feelings.

This does not mean, however, that women in the Middle Ages did not have a language of love. Its proper place, nevertheless, was not that of courtly ceremony. It is instead the ascetic space of the convent where a mystic piety came into being and traversed all the levels, from the simple religious experience up to the transport of ecstasy. It is unmistakable here how language, visual imagery, and, perhaps, the system of virtue of High Minnesong turn into a spiritual form that bursts and transcends the frame of courtly possibility. The antinomic tension of Minne-illusion is taken to its outer limits in that all semantic contradictions between desire and its unfulfillability appear to be resolvable in the perfect amalgamation of a "unio mystica" between the deific beloved and His ecstatic bride.

Shut away from the influence of social life, alone because of an inner necessity, ascetically prepared in expectation of the Deity, there began to burn behind the walls of the convents a mystical energy of receptivity and of love that brought forth the visionary poetic imagery of a union that was completely illusionary.

It is only in the "flowing light of the Deity" (Mechthild von Magdeburg) that women's unfettered liberation of feeling could take place, as it is metaphorically named in the image of the "great river."

In this "great river" the floodgates of worldly inhibitions and denials are opened for the secluded maids of the Lord. It is here that the tension between the ecstatic and the ascetic, between passivity and passion, takes place.

It is the passion of an itinerary that begins with suffering, pain, and "illness"[4] and that by way of many stages finally concludes in the bridal chamber of God. After a wearisome battle against "godless temptations," the yearned-for union with the living God takes place therein. The pure soul experiences itself in a visionary state in a condition of "oneness with God," in the Mysterium of the "unio mystica." Protected from the temptations of the Devil by humility, obedience, chastity, virtue, and love, the exhausted combatants finally receive that reward for which they have yearned.

"Virginity, you stand in the bridal chamber of the King! How sweetly you burn in the embrace of the King, while the sun's rays glitter about you, so that the noble blossom never falls," as it is described by Hildegard von Bingen (d. 1179). And years later, Mechthild von Magdeburg would write:

Lord, for I am a naked soul,
And You, in Yourself, a majestic God.
[. . .]
He gives Himself to her and she to Him.[5]

The history of passionate love, from the beginning of the thirteenth century up to the present time, is the history of a progressive profanization. The cult of the court and the idea of mystical union have made themselves felt ever more strongly in everyday life. This process of transformation is unmistakable: mystical transcendence and High Minne are transmuted into notions of intuitional intensity and subjective passionality. But the verbal figures and the rhetorical patterns of the newly discovered forms of love cannot hide their origins: they are entangled still in the bewildering twilight and the phantom-like promise of happiness found in the medieval discourse of love.

German romanticism in particular played a decisive role in this process. It translated the courtly and mystical language of Minne into its modern form, into the semantics and the rhetoric of love of bourgeois individualism. Romantic love is an imaginary dimension of the poetic power of the imagination. The great lovers are the heroines and the heroes of novels in which the bourgeois readership could find that which was denied to it in everyday life.

More than anyone else, Jean-Jacques Rousseau provided the essential catchwords for romantic love literature. Between 1756 and 1758 he wrote *Julie où la nouvelle Héloise*, a novel of the passions of two lovers who may not love each other. For Julie is already married and bound by "unbreakable chains" to her husband. The only role that remains for the lover is that of the excluded third. But it is precisely this that provokes the enraptured excess, the feeling of a boundless love that can never be fulfilled.

Everything draws its vitality from the unappeasable anticipation of love and from the desire for love. And nothing stipulates this wish more than do the insurmountable difficulties that intervene before the fulfillment of the wish. The beloved must be unattainable in order that the pleasure of loving might be enjoyed up to the deadly end.

Goethe's *Werther* (1744) obeys this same law: his beloved also belongs to another already, in real life (Charlotte Buff, married name Kestner) as in the novel. This situation occasioned the most intense of emotional experiences, as well as a host of ever-renewed complaints and outbursts of self-doubt. Without her nothing has any meaning for him, and his feelings for her consume everything.

Yet he cannot be with her. The happiness for which he yearns is the source of his distress. "I cannot beg: Leave her to me! and yet she often seems to be mine. I cannot beg: Give her to me! for she is another's. I mock myself over and over with my sorrows. Were I to desist, there would be a whole litany of antitheses" (Letter of November 22nd, 1771).[6]

It is Lotte who calls this contradiction by its name. She utters the secret, the riddle of this painful love, the "antithetical humor" which finally destroys Werther. For it is only a self-inflicted death that can lead to the unraveling of that impossibility which heightens the sensation of life to its highest intensity: "Don't you feel that you are deceiving yourself, that you are willingly preparing your own destruction! Why me then, Werther? precisely me, the property of another? precisely that? I fear, I fear that it is simply the impossibility of possessing me that makes this wish so attractive to you."[7]

In no other period of European culture was the ideal of love so codified as it was in Germany toward the end of the eighteenth century. At this time it became the *leitmotif* and the behavioral model of a subjective passion that one had to surrender to, even as an intimate partner was still to be sought for. It often appears as though the lover loved only love itself and not the object toward which love is oriented. As if love moved in a vacuum, as a moral duty, as a poetic idea, or as a religious fantasy. Romantic love came to dominate as a pure code that sucked everything into its verbal maelstrom. Only this can explain how even the smallest of signs, often simply a tiny wink of the eye, could suffice to enflame the most powerful of feelings.

Werther sees Lotte cutting brown bread for her sisters and his "entire soul came to rest on her form, her tone, her behavior, and I had just enough time to recover from my surprise as she walked into the room to get her gloves and her fan."[8]

It comes like a bolt out of the heavenly blue. It is sufficient to perceive the other as in a snapshot, in order immediately to mobilize the desire for love. The adored person is sacrificed to that desire. It is the code of love that conquers here like a mystical power from which there is no turning back.

Both man and woman were subject to this same mechanism. Of course, it was men especially who gave literary and idealizing form to their romantic desire for the affective and the passional. Yet women also surrendered themselves to this model, and often even more intensely than their literary prompters, who sought them as their partners. It is not by chance that women writers occupied the center of the romantic circles: Caroline Schlegel-Schelling, Dorothea Schlegel, Sophie Brentano, Bettina von Brentano-Arnim, Sophie Tieck, Rahel Varnhagen, Karoline von Günderode. And not to be forgotten is Auguste Bußmann, who wanted to live a dauntless life, a life that Clemens Brentano, the man she loved, could only dream and poeticize about. She had to pay for that with her life.

Much has changed since this golden period of German romantic love. Its idealizing pathos was enriched by the reality of sexual needs. The nineteenth century in particular developed further the notion of love as a sublime form of the sexual drive. Love and sex were meant to be brought together in harmonious union in a unique social institution: the love-marriage.

For a long time the choice of a partner was based on the hope of an ideal common life, in which the passion of the lovers would find a safe haven until death parted them.

Both of these ways in which the romantic ideal was meant to be realized have in the meantime revealed themselves to be false paths and to have brought new and unsolved problems into play.

Neither the combination of sexual desire with the phantasmagoria of romantic love nor the long-term transposition of the desire for love into the marriage institution have been successful. They could not, despite all claims to the contrary, offer any protection against the greatest danger to intimate love relationships: insecurity and instability.

Thus did sexuality become ever more forcefully detached from love as it became liberated and desublimated. And love-marriage became increasingly profanized under the reproductive authority of the family, an institution that can only be disturbed by powerful passions.

But these cultural and historical changes have still not been powerful enough to make the romantic ideal of love disappear completely. It has been a hushed and often despairing voice that has expressed the claim that the experience of purely sexual gratification is empty and that marriage is a prison. Today we have to cope with the loss of codified ideals of love. High Minne, mystical union, and romantic dream have disappeared into the reliquaries of cultural history. They have lost their social impetus. Their semantics are antiquated, their rhetoric is worn out. But their impulse is still operative. It continues to function as a critical prod against the unsatisfying offerings of a sex culture that is experienced as loveless, and against an ideology of the family that functionalizes the romantic ideal for its purposes only.

Today romantic love is simply that which is missing still. It has become the supplement of a lack. As such it has found a new medium, beyond the experience of sexuality and of social life forms. If it is "real," then it is so only in the make-believe of the world of the media, in which it is presently experiencing a simulative revival. Advertising, film, and literature are full of neo-romantic offerings in which images of passional love are offered up into the bargain: sentimental love stories and artificial dreams.

These are the modern places in which the old ideal of romantic love lives on so suggestively, laden with a neo-romantic challenge: neither can one live according to it, nor can one free oneself of it.

(Translation by Richard Kidder)

Notes

1. [Trans. note] Middle High German: *vrouwe, vrowe*, lady, mistress, lover, as in "unser vrouwe Maria" (our Lady Mary).

2. [Trans. note] "Tone" corresponds in modern German as well as in English to the Middle High German, *don*, which signifies the whole musical and formal pattern of the poem.

3. "Daz ir deste werder sit und da bi hochgemuot."

4. Middle High German, siechtuom.

5. Herre, nu bin ich ein nakent sele,

Und du in dir selben ein wolgezieret got.
Er gibet sich ir und si git sich ime.

[Trans. note] Book 1, chapter XLIV of *Offenbarungen der Schwester Mechthild von Magdeburg, oder das fliessende Licht der Gottheit.* Herausg. von P. Gall Morel (Regensburg: Manz, 1869).

6. "Ich kann nicht beten: Laß mir sie! und doch kommt sie mir oft als die Meine vor. Ich kann nicht beten: Gib sie mir! denn sie ist eines anderen. Ich witzle mich mit meinen Schmerzen herum; wenn ich mirs nachließe, es gäbe eine ganze Litanei von Antithesen."

7. "Fühlen Sie nicht, daß Sie sich betrügen, sich mit Willen zugrunde richten! Warum denn mich, Werther? just mich, das Eigentum eines andern? just das? Ich fürchte, ich fürchte, es ist nur die Unmöglichkeit, mich zu besitzen, die Ihnen diesen Wunsch so reizend macht."

8. " . . . ganze Seele ruhte auf der Gestalt, dem Tone, dem Betragen, und ich hatte eben Zeit, mich von der Überraschung zu erholen, als sie in die Stube lief, ihre Handschuhe und den Fächer zu holen."

III.

INSCRIBING WOMAN IN
SOCIO-HISTORICAL CONTEXTS

8

NELL SHIPMAN

A Case of Heroic Femininity

Kay Armatage

Historiography

N<small>EW HISTORIOGRAPHICAL</small> approaches are quickly emerging in the current discussions integrating cinema history with film theory. As Tom Gunning writes,

> anyone can see that the apathy toward history evident in film theory in the early and middle seventies has been replaced by a mode of interpenetration. . . . Now . . . film historians have appeared for whom film theory played a vital role and who are as interested in exploring what a fact *is* as in discovering one. Likewise theorists have realized increasingly the importance not only of the historian's facts, but of historical research and speculation in approaching issues of spectatorship, narrative structure, and the role of gender. (1990, 5)

Gunning goes on to say that "It is no accident that much of the exciting new work being done in film history is being done by women. Recognizing their marginalized place in traditional discourses, these scholars have undertaken a rediscovery of women's experience of cinema which has led to a fundamental questioning of the established concerns of history and its dominant methods" (Gunning 1990, 14).

Feminist Historiography

For many years feminist historians in all the arts have questioned dominant historiographical conventions. Within their ranks, a repeated topic of debate has been the efficacy of simply interpellating women historical figures into mainstream history without questioning its historiographical assumptions. Feminist historians have also argued that the conventional emphasis on the role of heroic figures and the master narratives of the past have been significant factors in obscuring the role of women in history. Over a decade ago in *Old Mistresses* (1981), Griselda Pollock discussed the theoretical problems of such simplistic historical interpellation of women artists into fine art history and called for new critical methodologies as well as new historical categories.

In a recent update of this position, Irit Rogoff writes:

> Constructing a speaking position and a narrative voice from which to en-gage with the identity of women culturally constituted on the margins of modernism entails several acute paradigm shifts. Not only do the parame-ters of historical periodicity and historical value need to be shed, but the very interplay of voices and "telling" needs to be reworked. The reconsti-tution of erased voices and their recuperations into existing narratives, structured as "probing models", achieve little more than a similar history gendered female. Perhaps it is not the materials and attempts of their al-ternative marshalling which we need to address but the modes of telling and retelling, the full consciousness that the narrative is endlessly and circularly retold, that the missing voices and erased identities cannot, should not, be robustly reconstituted. (1992, 39–40)

For feminist film scholars there are pressing reasons to make "trouble in the archives" (Pollock 1992, x). Feminist film theory has remained to a large extent situated within the established canon of classic narrative cin-ema. With a few rigorously restricted exceptions such as Sandy Flitter-man-Lewis's *To Desire Differently* (1990) and Giuliana Bruno's *Street-walking on a Ruined Map* (1993), we have not stirred up significant trouble in the archives. In the other humanities disciplines such as litera-ture and art history, feminist scholars began "contest[ing] the canon" (Pol-lock 1992, x) fairly early on, producing a seismic shift in the definition of feminist criticism. As Jane Gallop outlines in *Around 1981* (1992), in lit-erary studies feminist criticism moved in its first half-decade from a con-centration on the examination of representations of women in the canoni-cal (male-produced) literature to the recovery of texts by women writers and a taxonomy of women's literary traditions. By 1981, feminist literary criticism *was* the study of women writers. If such "reconstitution of erased voices and their recuperations into existing narratives" has achieved "lit-tle more than a similar history gendered female," nevertheless we are un-deniably richer for it. By 1993, we not only have a treasure-trove of women writers from the past with which to pleasure ourselves as women readers, but we have produced a more welcoming publishing climate for contem-porary women writers from many geographical and cultural heritages, as well as new theoretical rubrics with which to consider them. When I read Rogoff's disclaimer, "that the missing voices and erased identities cannot, should not, be robustly reconstituted" (1992, 39–40), I am reminded of B. Ruby Rich's ancient complaint about feminist film theory: "How does one formulate an understanding of structure that insists on our absence even in the face of our presence?" (1978, 87). Indeed, we seem to be bent on actively prohibiting our presence in favor of "uncertainty, ambiguity, and disorientation" (Rogoff 1992, 61).

In cinema, a number of factors combine to suggest a historical configuration with rather differently modulated significance for women historical figures and for feminist film historians. The novelty of the medium in its pioneering period, combined with its status as a popular entertainment growing alongside vaudeville and the "legitimate" theater—terrains already occupied by women—resulted in a period marked (albeit briefly) by the presence of women in proportionately greater numbers than in subsequent years until the late 1970s. It would be foolish to argue that cinema was anything like a "free zone" for women, escaping utterly the discrimination against women endemic to the other arts and the culture as a whole. But in its earliest days at least, cinema had not yet begun to effect the deliberate exclusion of women found in the other more established arts such as poetry, music, and painting, in which women were systematically denied access to the educational and professional institutions which shaped the arts. We had to wait about seventy years, until film schools were established all over the world, to feel those effects.

In time, the number of women in cinema would decrease dramatically with the monopoly practices that accompanied the coming of sound, the rise of the large Hollywood studios, and the founding of the immediately powerful technicians' unions which were dominated by organized crime and admitted only men to their membership. All three of these factors came together just at the end of the silent period. For the first thirty years, however, women pioneers in cinema were numerous: Olga Preobrajenskaya, Esther Shub, and Elizaveta Svilova in Russia; Lotte Reineger and Leni Reifenstahl in Germany; Alice Guy Blache, Germaine Dulac, and Marie-Louise Iribe in France; Adrienne Solser in Holland; Lottie Lyell in Australia; Elvira Notari in Italy; and Alla Nazimova, Mabel Normand, Lois Weber, Margery Wilson, Mrs. Wallace Reid, Dorothy Gish, Nell Shipman, and numerous others in the U.S. This period is a site from which we can make "trouble in the archives," as Griselda Pollock writes, by "contest[ing] the canon—the received and authorized version of the stories of modern art and its way of defining the visual image as the expressive site of an authoring self" (1992, x).

Nell Shipman is an exemplary figure, for her story parallels the entry, participation, and finally exclusion from cinema that was experienced by women filmmakers as a group in the first stage of film history.

Biography

Nell Shipman was born Helen Barham in Victoria B.C. in 1892, to a poor family of somewhat genteel British roots. With her mother's permission, Nell left home at thirteen to become a player in a small touring vaudeville company. Eventually instead of bringing money to the family, Nell required help. In a show of support for women's career ambitions at a time when independent single women formed a very new social group, Nell's mother joined her on the road, making her costumes, feeding her, and generally looking after her. By sixteen Nell had played every sort of vaudeville role and circuit. In 1910, at age eighteen, a leading lady, she became Canadian impresario Ernest Shipman's fourth wife and gave birth to a son two years later. She had already written and starred in her first film, *The Ball of Yarn*, which was so bad, she admits, that even Ernie couldn't book it (Shipman 1987, 40). She directed her first film in 1914, "an outdoor yarn" starring a handsome young leading man, Jack Kerrigan, in a buckskin suit (Shipman 1987, 43). She acted in films for Famous-Players-Lasky and Vitagraph, and turned down a seven-year contract that would have made her a star with Goldwyn. Her stated reasons:

> I did not like the way they dressed their contract players. This was in the period of curly blondes with Cupid's-bow mouths; and Wardrobe's main idea was to bind down a bosom with a swatch of shiny material which met yards of floaty gauze at the waistline and looked like a flowery pen-wiper. This long-legged, lanky, outdoors gal, who usually loped across the Silver Screen in fur parkas and mukluks, simply gagged at such costuming. And had the nerve to refuse it. (Shipman 1987, 46)

In 1915 she starred in *God's Country and the Woman*, a James Oliver Curwood–Vitagraph feature that was to become Nell's big break. The film's handsome budget of $90,000 reflects the stature of James Oliver Curwood (1878–1927), a well-known short-story writer specializing in western, wilderness, and animal tales, and Shipman's ascending trajectory as a star. From the moment of her first association with Curwood, Nell was known as "the girl from God's country," driving a team of sled-dogs, snow-shoeing, canoeing, and "undergoing pages of Curwoodian drama" (Shipman 1987, 50). *Baree, Son of Kazan* (1918) was another Curwood feature, followed by *Back to God's Country* (1919). This magnificent adventure set in the Canadian north features Nell as the heroine, saving her invalid husband's life and bringing the villains to justice through her bravery, fortitude, and wilderness acumen, as well as her rapport with animals. Although Shipman did not direct the film, she wrote the screenplay as well as starring as the protagonist of the narrative, and it is evident from historical accounts that she played a central creative role. The film is in every frame a vehicle for Nell Shipman. *Back to God's Country* was an enormous critical and box-office success, reaping profits of 300 percent and cementing Nell's reputation as a star.

During the course of the *Back to God's Country* shoot, Nell began an affair with Bert Van Tuyle, who was working on the film as production manager. When the production was completed, her partnerships with both producer/husband Ernest Shipman and writer James Oliver Curwood ended. Nell was so infatuated with Van Tuyle, a handsome former racing car driver, that she made him co-director of her movies and partner in her company, Nell Shipman Productions, formed in 1921. Between 1922 and 1924, they located in Upper Priest Lake, Idaho, living in a log cabin twenty-one miles from the nearest road and fifty miles from a railway line. To get out in winter, it was dogsled and snowshoe across the frozen lake, a two-day walk in the best of weather and nightmarish in the blizzards. In her autobiography, Shipman describes a heroic real-life adventure, chasing Bert when he left the cabin raving in delirium from frostbite, herself bare-foot for part of the journey because her socks had gotten wet and she knew better than to allow them to freeze on her feet.

Nell and Bert, cast and crew, lived up there in Priest Lake, making movies independently. Shipman was already known for her zoo of wild animals, including the famous Brownie the Bear as well as numerous "untameable" animals such as elks, coyotes, wolves, a cougar, wildcats, skunks, eagles, and owls, and more easily domesticated animals such as raccoons, deer, porcupines, beavers, marmots, muskrats, rabbits, dogs, and cats. A map of Lionhead Lodge, the Shipman establishment at the tip of Priest Lake, indicates the prominence of the ten animal buildings, not counting eight malamute houses and a beaver dam. Nearly all of Shipman's films featured animals in prominent roles, functioning as romantic agent, comic relief, victim, or hero. As I shall argue below, they also figure as central elements in the definition of feminine subjectivity in her narratives.

Shipman wrote, directed, and starred in at least two more feature films, *Something New* (1921) and *The Grub Stake* (1923), using a skeleton crew, doing all her own stunts, wrangling the animals, and supervising the editing. When the films were finished she would trudge across the lake to the nearest town and put on a vaudeville-type show at the local hall to raise money for her train fare to New York, where she would try to sell the films for distribution.

History: Just the Facts

An independent entrepreneurship in cinema was possible at the time. By 1908, 14th Street in New York City was well established as "film exchange row" (Balshofer 1989, 37). By 1912, there were 138 movie theaters in New York City alone (Allen 1983, 170), and the following year saw the formation of many distribution companies with large syndicates. The Protective Amusement Co. offered two features per week to one hundred syndicate-affiliated theaters (Allen 1983, 177). These companies made use of national distribution circuits developed for theater and vaudeville in the late nineteenth century, circuits already supported by the communications-transportation infrastructure of telegraphy and railroads (Allen 1983, 178). What rapidly became a vast North American circuit was propped on the low costs and almost limitless duplication of prints and the virtually daily conversions of legitimate theaters to movie palaces. By 1923, even towns with populations under 10,000 would commonly have more than one movie theater operating seven days a week (Jowett 1983, 201).

The process of selling your product in this climate was simple: you just put your film under your arm and kept going down 14th Street until one of the film exchanges offered to buy your picture. Until well into the silent period, even the price was standard: ten cents a foot (Balshofer 1989, 38).

By midway through the 1920s, however, independent production of this sort had become virtually impossible. Even earlier in the period, competition had been fierce; spying, sabotage, and straightforward theft were commonplace. With the financial and technological gearing up for sound, the film industry was interpenetrated by big business and organized crime. This new formation of the industry saw the rise of the big studios and the monopoly practice of vertical integration of production, distribution, and exhibition. The exhibition and distribution circuits which remained unaffiliated with studios were rapidly closed down. All of the stalwarts of the silent cinema collapsed along with Shipman—Selig, Biograph, Vitagraph, and Essanay, as well as Solax (Alice Guy Blache's company) and other tiny independents such as Kalem (Spehr 1977, passim). Shipman's cottage-industry mode of production, as Peter Morris points out in his afterword to Shipman's autobiography, was out of step with the new industrialization of Hollywood (Shipman 1987, 216).

Biography—The End of the Story

Bert Van Tuyle's delusions of grandeur were the initial cause of the demise of Nell Shipman Productions. *The Girl from God's Country*, which Van Tuyle produced, went disastrously over budget, and Nell Shipman Productions was never able to recoup the loss. Van Tuyle was also a drunkard. Nell stuck with him through the bankruptcy of the company, but finally let him go. After her production company collapsed and Bert Van Tuyle left, Nell Shipman married artist Charles Ayers and supported herself and her family for the duration of her career as a writer—a place in the industry that remained open to women through Hollywood's classic period. Nell Shipman's career trajectory thus not only parallels the history of the silent cinema itself, but also represents in microcosm the history of women's participation in the industry.

At the personal level, she remained plagued by her disastrous selections of male partners. As Nell pursued her obsessive attempts to revive her career in the film industry, third husband Ayers became afflicted with permanent artist's block, due to the humiliations of being supported by his wife, and began a series of extramarital affairs. She let him go. She married a fourth time to a man who had as many aliases as he had creditors, and bounced around America with him until he too drifted off. She died alone, "broke to the wide," with the manuscript of her autobiography waiting for publication.

History and Theory

Even in a period of transition and transformation, doxas rise up fast and sharp. It is already apparent that there are limited reasons for approaching a historical text. Tom Gunning allows that

analysis of the individual film provides a sort of laboratory for testing the relation between history and theory. It is at the level of the specific film that theory and history converge, setting up the terms of analysis. We could even say that the individual text stands as a challenge to both theoretical and historical discourse, revealing the stress points in each as they attempt to deal with the scandal of the actuality of a single work as opposed to the rationality of a system. (1990, 6)

He suggests further that we should be looking for specific nodal issues: e.g., "the way individual works can *transform* aesthetic norms, not simply actualize them" or in order to "reveal the individual texts as contradictory and dynamic" (1990, 11). He cites Lea Jacobs's work on censorship and *Blonde Venus* as exemplary for its analysis of the conflicting impulses of producers and directors in response to the production code:

An historical textual reading uncovers the conflict still alive and wriggling throughout the film itself, as modes of discourse continue to struggle for dominance in our reception of the film. [Thus] an historical analysis of a text does not simply dissolve it into its positivistically discernable elements . . . but into its processes of production and reception. . . . What [historical readings] undertake is more than a placing of a text into an historical context. The context itself is seen as a field of conflicting discourses and the dynamic of the text derives from this complex genesis. Therefore historical textual analysis demands more than micro-analyses. The analyst must establish the clash of discourses that surround the text. (1990, 11–14)

Feminist Theory and History

Sandy Flitterman-Lewis is equally firm in her notions of what feminist film historiography and a history of feminist film practice would entail. "A feminist cinema must necessarily conceive its challenge textually," she declares. A feminist filmmaker, she goes on, must understand the entire cinematic apparatus, including the fact that the apparatus is designed to produce and maintain its hold on the spectator by mobilizing pleasure through the interlocking systems of narrative, continuity, point of view, and identification (1990, 3). A history of feminist cinema, therefore, will construct that history in terms of textual resistance to the dominant mode (Flitterman-Lewis 1990, 22). Flitterman-Lewis has chosen her exemplary filmmakers wisely: Germaine Dulac, for example, who worked in France during the same period as Shipman was working in America, operated within an intellectual, political, and aesthetic milieu in which she was able to work consciously as a feminist. A writer as well, Dulac theorized in her own terms the necessity to deconstruct the dominant model, emphasizing the materiality of the cinematic signifier vs. the conventions of narrative causality and visual continuity of the traditional cinema. In short, Dulac precisely suits Flitterman-Lewis's historiographical prescription (Flitterman-Lewis 1990, 26). No "negotiated" reading is required here, for we have "the clash of discourses" in full battle mode in these consciously "oppositional" texts.

Old and New Configurations of Femininity

The case of Nell Shipman is not so amenable to such readings. Far from oppositional to the dominant mode, Shipman was scratching her career out of the wilderness, trying her best to compete in that dominant commercial cinema. At fifty miles from the nearest railroad, she was well out of earshot of the clash of discourses. Shipman's is not a cinema that poses the *difference* of women's filmmaking (Flitterman-Lewis 1990, 21) but one which plunks its ample derriere firmly on its generic base. As controller of the discourse, her "attempts to originate the representation of her own desire" (Flitterman-Lewis 1990, 22) map almost exactly onto patriarchal configurations of femininity—complete with pipe-smoking hubby, burbling baby, and great dane on the hearth rug. Finally, Freud's "normal" woman, and loving it.

In Shipman's films we find, a fortiori, a patriarchal, non-oppositional construction of femininity. Shipman's character includes an intuitive rapport with animals and nature which functions as constitutive of feminine subjectivity. It also emphasizes an unproblematized heterosexuality, which features a closeness to and unclaustrophobic comfort in her own body that is displayed with at least moderately exhibitionist gusto. The heterosexual feminine body on display is accompanied perforce with an acknowledgment of her potential victimization due to the spontaneous lust that in such melodramas is constitutive of villainous subjectivity. We even find something approaching hysteria, madness, even stupidity, in the almost pathological femininity of the Shipman character. For my contemporary students, Shipman/Dolores in *Back to God's Country* represents everything that as feminists they deplore in a woman.

Furthermore, she makes absolutely no attempt to "restore the marks of cinematic enunciation so carefully ellided by patriarchal cinema" (Flitterman-Lewis 1990, 22). It's a bit embarrassing, really. Here I find myself identifying with Irit Rogoff's "scholastic mortification" upon finding that her subject, "a woman whom [she] had constructed in [her] mind as an autonomous female artist, a feminized version of the masculine participant in the heroic avant-garde project of the pre-war years," was in fact replete with "thoroughly conventional bourgeois anguish" (Rogoff 1992, 38–39).

What I intend to argue in this chapter is that it is within the terms not only of conventional narrative cinema but also of conventional patriarchal definitions of gender that Nell Shipman's work defines heroic femininity. I contend also that within such a patriarchal construction of femininity we can find definitions of sexual difference which speak from a historical moment in the past directly to feminist concerns of the present.

Femininity and Genre

Shipman's work with animals and the natural settings of her films were among their chief commercial features. As genre, wilderness and adventure stories had topped the literary best-seller lists since the early teens, with Zane Grey and Jack London the leading exponents of the form. T. E. Harre's *The Eternal Maiden* (1913), a tale of feminine virtue in an "Esquimaux" setting, was an early example of the trend toward settings in the Canadian North (Hale 1919, 71). Novels of the Canadian woods took off in popularity around 1914, with authors such as Ralph Connor, Harold Bindloss, H. Footner, Virgie Roe, B. W. Sinclair, and Alice Jones among the top sellers (Hale 1919, 91), although their fame did not rival the lasting prominence of Zane Grey and Jack London. By 1917, "the novel of adventure or mystery . . . [and the] story of the great outdoors still made up a considerable part of the year's fiction," but the genre was beginning to be nudged off the top of the best-seller lists by novels of contemporary everyday life or of exotic romance (Hale 1919, 135). Well into the twenties, however, the wilds of the Canadian Northwest were a "commonplace" setting for popular fiction (Hale 1919, 197), and in cinema the genre of wilderness films remained a minor staple of the film industry, continuing to be made well into the fifties.

Shipman's earliest successes as a star had been in films based on James Oliver Curwood novels or short stories. Curwood had had modest success with the wilderness and local color adventure novels which dominated popular fiction in the first decade of the twentieth century, but with the publication of *Kazan* (1914), a story of an escaped sled-dog who returns to his own wild-wolf kind in the Canadian Far North, his fame had begun to equal that of Jack London's *White Fang* and *Call of the Wild*. *Kazan* was followed in 1915 by *God's Country and the Woman*, a "lively melodrama of the Canadian Northwest" (Hale 1919, 111). *God's Country and the*

Woman, a story of a "love so deep and confident in the breast of the hero that it pierced the curtain of apparent unworthiness in which the heroine had felt it necessary to cloak her own actions," enjoyed great sales and was made into a film which began the partnership between Shipman and Curwood, and which would label Nell Shipman forever as "the girl from God's country." In 1917 Curwood returned to the animal kingdom with *The Grizzly King* and *Baree, Son of Kazan* (1918), the latter of which again starred Nell Shipman in the film version. By the end of the war, James Oliver Curwood had achieved a short-lived position alongside Zane Grey and Jack London as the best-selling authors of wilderness adventure.

Many of Curwood's novels were made into films, including *God's Country and the Woman* (1915), *Baree, Son of Kazan* (1918), *Back to God's Country* (1919), *The Golden Snare* (1921), *Code of the Mounted* (1932), *Red Blood of Courage* (1935), *Call of the Yukon* (1938), *Call of the Klondike* (1950), *Northwest Territory* (1952), *Northern Patrol* (1953), *Yukon Vengeance* (1954), and a remake of *Back to God's Country* starring Rock Hudson (1953). Although among film genres westerns were always reliable as the most popular genre, nevertheless both dog stories dating from *Rescued by Rover* (1903) and adventure films had been staples of the distribution syndicates. With Curwood, Nell Shipman had come to a productive partnership.

As not only the star of the films but the screenwriter/adaptor of the Curwood stories, Shipman routinely shifted the protagonist's position from the dog to the woman, and effected concomitant shifts in the working of the narrative as well. Thus into this circuit of commercial cinema, popular genre, animals, and nature, Shipman inserts the new variable, heroic femininity.

Femininity and Nature

In her autobiography, Shipman offers her down-to-earth, pragmatic analysis of her first encounter with Brownie the Bear:

Big Brownie was my first wild animal encounter on camera unattended by keepers, guns, wire, whips or cages. At Vitagraph I'd handled sled-dogs but now I was acting with a free, large bear who might bite, hug or merely swat. She reared, put an arm about my waist, drew me close, gave me a tentative sniff, then licked my cheek, pushed me gently aside and dropped to the ground at my feet. While I relaxed in her embrace I knew my theory was okay, and that it was a fifty-fifty deal between human and animals. Had there been a seedling of fear in me I would have felt it sprout, recognized alarm or a least a faint quiver of concern. It could lie in the deepest, darkest thought-cell but would communicate. It simply was not there. All about us and within us was serene, untroubled, unquestioned. No personal bravery in this, just a fact of communication. (1987, 80)

Shipman's femininity is in part defined by and through such intuitive natural connections. This was a feature of the Shipman character not only in the Curwood adaptations but in her own independent productions as well. In *Trail of the North Wind* (1923), for example, the construction of feminine subjectivity hinges around communication with animals of all kinds. Dreena the heroine (Shipman) is identified as the "story-girl" because she listens to the tales told by the creatures of the wild and translates them into human language, and the film opens with a montage of alternating comic and lyric wilderness scenes with dogs, ducks, donkeys, and baby skunks. Such montages and tableaux exhibiting the tame animals and Shipman's communication with them are trademarks of her films. William K. Everson complains of *The Grub Stake* (1923) that "Midway through the film, its narrative comes to a virtual halt when Shipman's character discovers a Disneyesque hidden valley, shares a cave with a bear, and communes with nature and wild animals for a reel or two" (1989, 231).

Back to God's Country (1919), for many years the only feature film of Shipman's that was known, includes the most excessive of all the displays of human/animal communication. In an early scene, Dolores (played by Shipman) lolls about in erotic play with Brownie the Bear, nuzzling his snout and tweaking his ears, as skunks, squirrels, raccoons, and baby foxes cavort about her. Such moments of intransitive display are central to the Shipman oeuvre; they become generic elements equivalent to the star turns in Fred Astaire or Gene Kelly musicals, functioning pivotally in the construction of the central persona as ego ideal. And just as in Astaire or Kelly films, the casual and effortless grace which marks the exhibition of the star's extraordinary capabilities indicates that such achievements are not the result of practice, effort, training, or the like, but rather innate, natural, endemic. Indeed, it is such superhuman qualities—displayed with such "natural" insouciance—which justify stardom. In Shipman's case her extraordinary communication with the world of nature is an essential element in the constitution of heroic hyper-femininity. Rather than the narrative coming to a virtual halt, as Everson complains, I would argue on the contrary that the plots of Shipman's films are very often devices constructed precisely to afford such moments of intransitive heroic display.

The Naked Feminine Body

In *Back to God's Country*, the construction of feminine subjectivity operates upon Shipman's intuitive communication with animals and nature, and this natural connection is relayed to a level of heroic defiance of social convention. As a character and as a star, Shipman doffs the fetters of ladylike decorum to cavort not only in nature but au naturel. The famous nude scene, for example, which was fully capitalized upon in advertisements for *Back to God's Country*, cannot be explained away by the usual relations of economic and sexual exploitation that are rebuked by contemporary "no nudity" clauses in the more powerful female stars' contracts. Diegetically and extra-textually, this is one of the scenes which again defines Dolores/Shipman's femininity through a closeness to her body, and through essentialist connections to nature. Those elements are also inextricably linked to a fearless rejection of social hypocrisy that brooks no moral outrage and to Shipman's own control of the cinematic discourse as enunciator.

The scene originally functioned, in Shipman's script, to convey a simple definition of the elements of femininity, situating Dolores firmly within nature as the essentialist landscape of feminine subjectivity. The scene was first shot with Shipman wearing a modest flesh-colored wool bathing costume. After the first take, however, when she saw the wet thick wool bunch and wrinkle about her body, Shipman firmly stepped in, shedding the costume and directing the cinematographer so that the mise-en-scène would invite no prurience while still making her unadorned flesh amply evident (Shipman 1987, 79). For the period, the gesture indicated a sense of easeful corporeal display at a time when melodramatic heroines were marked by Gish-like modesty and nudity appeared in films only in scenes of epic debauchery. Indeed, such a forthright "naturalness" in relation to the naked female body didn't surface again among women until the 1960s.

The historical spectator's readings of the scene, like our own, would be guided by diegetic inscriptions of Dolores's virtue, her "naturalness," and her femininity, sustained diegetically and semiotically from the early scenes of the film. In addition, the movie was advertised with posters which featured a drawing of Shipman pulling a shawl across her evidently naked body as she stood knee-deep in water. In the trade papers, the promotion was even more explicit, featuring a sketch of a naked female body arching lyrically on tiptoe, with this advice to exhibitors: "Don't Book

'Back to God's Country' *unless* You want to prove that the Nude is NOT Rude" (*The Moving Picture World*, July 24, 1920, 42). Thus the historical spectators' readings would also be marked by the interpenetration of the textual by the extra-textual (the promotion and advertising strategies), inviting a reading which not only invoked a provocative challenge to the contraints of contemporary mores about the display of women's bodies, but which also ascribed a forthrightness, fearlessness, and control of the discourse to Shipman herself as enunciator and star.

Feminine/Canine Relations

It is in Dolores's/Shipman's relation with the dog, however, where the connection between conventional definitions of femininity, here heavily inflected with an intuitive rapport with the animal/natural world, are aligned most transparently with courage and heroism.

Back to God's Country is at core a dog story, based on James Oliver Curwood's *Good Housekeeping* short story "Wapi the Walrus" (collected in *The Golden Book of Dog Stories*, ed. Era Zistel—no longer in print). In contrast to the relatively domestic achievements of the dogs in other Shipman films such as *The Bear, the Boy and the Dog* and *Trail of the North Wind, Back to God's Country* presents the dog Wapi (played by matching mastiffs Tresore and brother Rex) in a much more heroic mode. A variation on the bad dog story, *Back to God's Country* features Wapi, a fierce mastiff who responds to the gentle touch of a woman's hand. When the time comes for the inevitable chase and rescue, Wapi is at the woman's side, her salvation and—almost—her heroic lover. Paradoxically, such scenes define Shipman's/Dolores's helpless femininity, her fearless heroism, and her control of the discourse. And they define them as intertwined.

Femininity and Extrasensory Inter-Species Communication

An uncanny extrasensory communication materializes between Wapi and Dolores. Before they even meet, there is a cut from Dolores on ship to Wapi at the trading post, followed by the title, "Like a great winged-bird the Flying Moon [the ship] brings to Wapi a strange and thrilling message from the white man's world of his forefathers." Wapi senses Dolores's presence, although they have not met, and that knowledge is linked (through the intertitle) to an atavistic memory of his forefather the Great Dane Tao, whose Chinese master was murdered by the "white man" in the film's prologue. This intertitle is followed by a close-up of Wapi in vicious-killer mode. Again in the scene in which the villain is trying to get his way with Dolores on ship, her plight is intercut equally with shots of Wapi far away across the ice, straining at his leash at the trading post, and shots of Dolores's helpless husband lying injured in his bed in the next cabin. Wapi, like Dolores's husband, senses her plight. This also occurs before Wapi and Dolores meet for the first time.

In one of the most affecting scenes in the film, the scene in which the woman and the dog finally meet, Dolores's fearlessness and her femininity are marked by her actions and underscored by the intertitles. Dolores/Nell has decided to take matters into her own hands, and she strikes out across the ice and snow to seek help at the trading post, never suspecting that the post is run by a man in cahoots with the villainous ship captain who is plotting Dolores's seduction and her husband's death. Cut to Wapi snarling viciously in close-up, fighting with the other dogs. Blake, his owner, takes a whip to Wapi just as Dolores/Nell approaches. Without hesitation, she flings herself between the whip and the dog. Dolores's fearlessness and her courageous attempt to rescue the abused dog are outlined by Blake's warning of the threat from the dog himself: "Look out! That dog is a devil . . . " (intertitle). But as he speaks, the killer dog miraculously becomes quiet, as the intertitle—by this point in the film virtually synonymous with Shipman's discourse as enunciator—comments "A new miracle of understanding, roused by the touch of a woman's hand."

Whereas the display of inter-species communication in the other films demonstrated that remarkable understanding as idiosyncratically symptomatic of Shipman as persona and star, in *Back to God's Country* the connection between inter-species understanding, femininity, and courageous heroism is made explicit and shown to be essential to the nature of femininity. It is "*a* woman's hand"—not necessarily *this* woman's hand—which promotes the animal's peace; the "miracle of understanding" is explicitly connected to gender. Moreover, in this film, as in most of Shipman's work, she stands for Everywoman, for she is virtually the only female character in an all-male world.

The mutuality of the connection between the dog and the woman is underlined by a scene depicting the dog remembering or desiring: a shot of Wapi chained to a stake dissolves to a matching shot of Dolores at the dog's side, embracing him. That memory or wish triggers the dog's action, for he breaks his chains and follows Dolores's scent to the ship. The scene closes with an iris in on the woman embracing the dog and kissing him on the face. This kiss signals the transformation of the dog into heroic lover, displacing the husband until the closing scenes of the film.

Racial Difference and the Power of Sisterhood

The prologue of *Back to God's Country* gives the dog Wapi a heroic genealogy. Brought by a Chinese man to the North, both dog and immigrant become victims of the white man's racism. The Chinese dog owner is first insulted and then murdered in an episode of callously racist violence, and the noble and gentle dog is subjected to "forty dog-generations" of the white man's abuse, until Wapi the Killer emerges as the result. The rhetorical flourishes of the prologue establish the intertitles as central to the enunciative apparatus of the film, which will soon come to stand for Shipman's authorial voice. These titles do not shirk either moral attitude or affective sympathy as they tell Wapi's tale. At the outset of the film, then, Shipman as enunciator distances herself firmly from those white men, and the marks of that difference are found not only in gender but in attitudes of racism or antiracism.

I will not argue a nonracist purity for Shipman by any means. That would be carrying heroic femininity just too far. The quotidian racism of Shipman's era is evident in the use of phrases such as "yellow man" and "half-breed" and in the comic representation of the soap-eating Inuit women, as well as in the romantic feminizing of the oriental Other, who is immediately assumed to be gentler, more civilized, and more sensitive than the uncivilized white brutes into whose den he stumbles.

Later in the film, however, Shipman once again underlines her antiracist impulses, in the only scene in the film in which Dolores connects with another woman. The sailors on the *Flying Moon* have brought some "eskimo guests" on board, and the quotation marks of the intertitle ironically underscore the white men's racist and sexist designs. When one of the aboriginal women resists a would-be seducer, Shipman/Dolores steps in to assist her. This moment is clearly both antiracist and proto-feminist. As in the prologue, it is Shipman's/Dolores's femininity, marked here as a doubled difference of gender and ideology, with which we can finally identify. But sisterhood is not powerful enough, and both women are overcome. Shipman/Dolores will live to save her own virtue and her husband's life, but she cannot change the Inuit woman's destiny.

In these moments Shipman's patriarchally defined femininity slips from the bonds of mere historical curiosity and bespeaks an antiracist and proto-feminist heroism that reaches out of the past directly into current feminist debates.

Hysteria at the Climax

The climax of the film depends upon a two-step relay of negative and positive elements, hysterical and heroic forms of femininity. Dolores/Shipman is mushing across the arctic landscape, her injured husband laid out in the sled, while the villain is in hot pursuit with his dog team. At one moment, for no earthly reason, Dolores drops the revolver and leaves it behind. The text jeers with an insert: "MCU gun up to its handle in snow." Here we have a moment of the type we used to find with such glee in the classic realist text, that instance of overdetermination when the ideological imperative overcomes narrative plausibility, the text is fissured, and a moment of spectator alienation breaks the hold of narrative continuity. It's the moment when everyone groans. That groan signals a recognition of the discursive pressures upon the woman protagonist to be scatterbrained, incompetent, and stupid, to conform to a patriarchal stereotype of hysterical femininity. And they groan again only a few seconds later when, as if to underline the patriarchal operations of the text, the invalid husband briefly rouses himself to say "Dolores, give me the gun" (intertitle). In close-up, Dolores responds by hanging her head in shame. Here we have the quintessentially feminine moment, the moment beyond language, when words have left her, and her only language is the purely affective language of emotion. It is, as Catherine Clement writes, a "losing song; it is femininity's song" (1988, passim). In Rogoff's terms, Dolores is here "the site of uncertainty, ambiguity, and disorientation" (1992, 61).

In Shipman's text, however, that moment beyond language is simultaneously the woman's moment of shame and the instance of the spectator's recognition of the overdetermining operations of the narrative in the construction of femininity. "Here we can perceive the need for negotiations between contradictory forces, between middle-class bourgeois conventions regarding an appropriate emotional and moral climate for women and the eroding questions being formulated regarding identity and fulfillment for women" (Rogoff 1992, 62). For Gunning, we find that de rigeur clash of discourses, alive and wriggling across the text!

Feminine Heroism

It is at this moment, and out of the very depths of the damages that such an overdetermined femininity has produced, not only upon the character of Dolores but also upon narrative plausibility, that the climax of the film is constructed.

From this point in the tale, Wapi occupies the position of a heroic lover, taking up the traditional melodramatic function of the human male protagonist, who must rescue the imperiled heroine. As the chase begins, a title indicates that Wapi's "hour of destiny is at hand." Close-ups of Wapi are intercut with shots of Dolores worrying and the villain approaching in this high-speed chase by dogsled—a scene rivaled in its quintessential Canadianness only by the canoe chase in Joyce Wieland's *The Far Shore* (1975)—and a title pierces the dog's consciousness: "Sensing the swift approaching menace of the men he hates." Cut to close-up of Wapi. A few minutes after Dolores's moment of shame, a still photo of Wapi in close-up forms the uncharacteristic background to the generic title "Her Last Hope," dramatically marrying signifier and signified in one image underlining the relation of feminine desire to the animal subject.

This rather complex relay of inter-species desire, it must be recalled, is the creation of the woman screenwriter and star. The dog, then, in the expression of its desire, must be seen as the representation of the excessive desire of femininity, a transgressive desire which exceeds the capacity for satisfaction through relations with the woman's human lover/husband.

As Wapi runs off to attack the dogs pulling the villain's sled, an intertitle intones: "Fighting at last the greatest of all his fights—for a Woman." Once again, the enunciative apparatus draws the connection between the feminine and the heroic action; the dog at its most heroic functions merely as the agent of the woman's desire. And once again—thank goodness—we have that welcome clash of discourses: on the one hand, the narrative and specifically generic demands for an action climax overdetermining the woman's helplessness in the scenario and, on the other, the discursive connections that previously have been established between the woman, the animal, and essential femininity, producing her as the controlling agent in the action. It is due to her intrinsic qualities as a woman that she can command the obedience of this heretofore untameable beast. Her hysteria and her helplessness, then, become the masquerade, but such excessive femininity masks not masculinity or its lack (as in Riviere and Doane respectively) but the even more profound (though retrograde) wellsprings of essential femininity.

The rewards of such normative essentialist femininity are made explicit in the denouement. With hubby safely tucked into bed at Fort Confidence, Dolores kisses Wapi in close-up, and the scene ends with a sweet iris in and fade to black. Dog and Woman—together at last. But the iris-out positions

Dolores as replete in the achievement of the totality of excessive feminine desire: she is centered in the frame, with pipe-smoking hubby by her side and former heroic lover Wapi now transformed into devoted nursemaid to the burbling baby on the hearthrug.

Conclusion

In most of her films, Nell Shipman played the leading role, always of the heroic stamp. Husbands or lovers were either absent or incapacitated: they fell ill, were injured, or were simply "artistic." Nell inevitably had to save the day, for what with the travails of the wilderness and the villainy of the antagonists, there was always a day and a life that needed saving. Her Amazonian beauty, the easeful presence of her body (cross-hatched with equal parts of hysteria, display, strength, and bravery), her great sense of moral justice, and the instinctive connection with animals and nature: these are the signs of her essential femininity, and simultaneously the source of the heroism which allows her to resist conventional narrative inscriptions of the woman protagonist as victimized and rescued. These are not simply Meaghan Morris's "imaginary acts of piracy" (1988, 16), but precisely Rogoff's "endless negotiations . . . the circularity of advance and retreat, of point/counterpoint negotiations" which allow historical "parameters to expand while changing [women's] position in relation to [them]" (1992, 62–63).

Out of the uncertainties and failures, out of the negotiations between an essentialist construction of feminine subjectivity and heroism, between generic convention and control of the discourse, between ideological complicity and radical antiracism, finally emerge dramatically different models of femininity played out in a gendered narrative of heroic achievement. The negotiations between contradictory forces are not only endless but immense: between the requirements of genre and transgressions of social mores, between the heroic character which Nell Shipman created as her exemplary persona and her humiliating failure as a producer in the film industry, between her staunch commitment to her work and her own career and her repeated infatuations with male partners who alternatively exploited her and failed her. As Rogoff writes, "Nothing better exemplifies the contradictory nature of modernism—its weaving together of a valorized and radical concept of production with a traditional and unrevised legacy of the symbolic order—than the work of women within it and of their historiographic position in relation to it" (1992, 61).

For Shipman, then, we must recast the old critical model dramatically, from the female spectator to the female adventurer, from the desiring body to the bear, the dog, and the raccoon, from the masquerade to the mukluk. But if we follow in Nell Shipman's snowshoed footsteps, we may make some gains in the recognition of female subjectivities of the heroic stamp, and with them the beginnings of women's cultural traditions in cinema.

Known Nell Shipman Filmography

The Ball of Yarn (scen./star, 1910); *Outwitted by Billy* (scen., Selig Polyscope Co., 1913); *Under the Crescent* (scen./star, 6 two-reel episodes, Universal, 1915); *Under the Crescent* (novel, publ. Grosset and Dunlap, 1915); *God's Country and the Woman* (from James Oliver Curwood short story, co-dir./co-scen./star, 1915); *Baree, Son of Kazan* (from Curwood story, co-dir./co-scen./star, 1917); *Back to God's Country* (dir. David M. Hartford, scen. Nell Shipman, prod. Ernest Shipman, starring Nell Shipman, Canadian Photoplays Production, 1919); *Something New* (scen./co-dir./star, 1920); *The Girl From God's Country* (prod./scen./co-dir./star, Nell Shipman Productions, 1921); *The Boy, the Bear and the Dog* (prod./dir./scen., Nell Shipman Productions, 1921); *The Grub Stake* (prod./co-dir./scen./star, Nell Shipman Productions, 1923); *Trail of the North Wind* (prod./dir./scen./star, Nell Shipman Productions, 1923); *Light on Lookout* (prod./dir./scen./star, Nell Shipman Productions, 1923); *The Golden Yukon* (co-dir./scen./star, Sierra Pictures, 1927); *Wings in the Dark* (scen. Nell Shipman, dir. James Flood, stars Myrna Loy and Cary Grant, Paramount, 1935).

Works Cited

Allen, Jeanne Thomas. "Copyright and Early Theater, Vaudeville, and Film Competition," in John L. Fell, ed., *Film before Griffith*. Berkeley: University of California Press, 1983.

Allen, Robert C. "Motion Picture Exhibition in Manhattan, 1906–1912: Beyond the Nickelodeon," in *Film before Griffith*, op. cit.

Balshofer, Fred. "Going into the Film Business," in Richard Dyer MacCann, ed., *The First Film Makers*. Metuchen: Scarecrow Press, 1989.

Clément, Catherine. *Opera, or the Undoing of Women*. Trans. Betsy Wing. Minneapolis: University of Minnesota Press, 1988.

Doane, Mary Ann. "Masquerade Reconsidered: Further Thoughts on the Female Spectator," *Discourse* 11.1 (Fall-Winter 1988–89).

Everson, William K. "Rediscovery," *Films in Review* (April 1989).

Flitterman-Lewis, Sandy. *To Desire Differently: Feminism and the French Cinema.* Urbana: University of Illinois Press, 1990.

Gunning, Tom. "Film History and Film Analysis: The Individual Film in the Course of Time," *Wide Angle* 12.3 (July 1990).

Hale, Edward Everett. *The American Year Book: Literature and Language Bibliographies from the American Year Book, 1910–1919.*

Jowett, Garth S. "The First Motion Picture Audiences," in *Film before Griffith*, op. cit.

Marchessault, Janine. "Is the Dead Author a Woman?" unpublished paper (1990).

Mellencamp, Patricia. "Taking a Cue from Ariadne," in *Indiscretions: Avant-Garde Film Video Feminism.* Bloomington: Indiana University Press, 1990.

Musser, Charles. *Before the Nickelodeon.* Berkeley: University of California Press, 1991.

Nowell-Smith, Geoffrey. "On History and the Cinema," *Screen* 31.2 (Summer 1990).

Pollock, Griselda. *Old Mistresses.* London: Routledge and Kegan Paul, 1981.

Shipman, Nell. *The Silent Screen and My Talking Heart.* Boise: Boise University Press, 1986.

Slide, Anthony. *Early Women Directors.* New York: Da Capo Press, 1984.

Spehr, Paul C. *The Movies Begin: Making Movies in New Jersey 1887–1920.* Newark: Newark Museum, 1977.

9

STREETWALKING AROUND
PLATO'S CAVE

Giuliana Bruno

Film in the Cityscape: A Topoanalysis

[In Naples] building and action interpenetrate in the courtyards, arcades, and stairways . . . to become a theatre of the new. . . . This is how architecture, the most binding part of the communal rhythm comes into being here, . . . [in] the baroque opening of a heightened public sphere. . . .

What distinguishes Naples from other large cities is [that] . . . each private attitude or act is permeated by streams of communal life.

—Walter Benjamin

In March 1896, at the Salone Margherita, in Naples, cinema entered the world of spectacle. This world was concentrated around the arcade, Galleria Umberto I, a *passage* which faced the Teatro San Carlo opera house, the Royal Palace, and the sea. A local newspaper reported the following about one of the early screenings at the theater in the arcade:

This evening the Salone Margherita will reopen with a completely new program. The Cinématographe Lumière, the most grandiose novelty of this century, will be shown. Then will follow: the Benedetti family, top Icarus-style acrobats coming from Berlin; Vargas Bisaccia, the incredible shrinking couple returning from their Russian, Spanish, and German engagements; the eccentric French star Bloquelle; the German singer Milford; Herman the snake man; Belvalle the music-hall singer—in other words, a great spectacle. (*Il Corriére di Napoli*, April 4, 1896)

From the very beginning, the Naples arcade was a prominent film center. As the home of over twenty film magazines and of a lively film production, the city was in the vanguard of the silent film art's development. Naples established its own style of filmmaking; predating stylistic features of neorealism, it pioneered a realistic representation opposed to the aesthetic of "super-spectacles" then dominant in Italy. Neapolitan cinema, rooted in local cultural traditions, was of the street.

A major force within this cinema was Elvira Notari (1875–1946), Italy's first and most prolific woman filmmaker. Her name and work, excised from historical memory, are today unknown. As head of her own production company, named Dora Film after her daughter, Notari made sixty feature films and over one hundred documentaries and shorts between 1906 and 1930. Her films were shown in America, most particularly in New York City theaters, providing an imaginary voyage of return for Italian American immigrants, who went so far as to sponsor some of Notari's films. Her production, suppressed by the fascist censorship, ended with the advent of sound.

Elvira Notari shot women's stories on location in the *vicoli* (alleyways) of Naples. Her (public) women's melodramas issued from the body of urban popular culture. These films, inscriptions of urban transit and panoramic vision, used documentary sequences of street culture and city views. Their narrative reproduced the metropolitan topography and the cityscape. Notari's melodrama of the street represented *"il ventre di Napoli,"*[1] the "belly" of a metropolis, her *meter-polis*—her mother-city, as the word's Greek root suggests.

This popular cinema, primarily shown at a theater in the arcade, was sustained by a passion for the urban travelogue. The Neapolitan film magazine *L'arte muta* remarked in 1916 that the audience of the arcade's cinema expressed a demand for the panoramic, and expected it to be satisfied by the films it saw there. The success of any given film was predicated upon the fulfillment of the panoramic desire. Notari's popular urban cinema succeeded in providing such pleasure:

> A moving drama where passion blossoms, red as the color of blood, is produced by *Dora Film*, the young Neapolitan production house, whose serious artistic intents are well known. The film was screened at Cinema Vittoria, the movie house of the Galleria Umberto I. The expectation of the public attending this theater has been completely fulfilled: the suggestive drama develops against the enchanting panorama of the city of Naples. (*L'arte muta*, June 15, 1916)

It was, then, the urban matrix of a (plebeian) metropolis that enabled Elvira Notari's cinema, its circulation and reception in the arcade's theater. The Neapolitan arcade, the allegorical emblem of modernity, facilitated the revitalization of an urban popular culture. Naples had traditionally offered the spectacle of movement. Its intermingling of architectural styles create "a baroque opening of a heightened public sphere"; its fusion of dwelling and motion within "a theater of the new" provided a fertile ground for the development of cinema. As film was implanted in the cityscape, the cityscape was implanted within film.

To trace the steps of this implantation of cinema in the cityscape, one best proceeds by "streetwalking" through a topoanalysis. In mapping this microhistorical configuration of events, I wish to explore the terrain of the cinematic apparatus, thereby expanding the range of its theorization, and offering a reading of film pleasure effects, conceived as complementary to a psychoanalytic understanding of the subject. Despite their differences, most psychoanalytic theories (in particular the early Lacanian ones) have tended to view cinema as deriving its main impact from the viewer's identification with the camera's gaze.[2] Through a sort of vision of dominance, along this theoretical path, the spectator has become a motionless subject, enraptured in a state of solitary reverie. Chained in Plato's cave, the spectator/prisoner is fixed in place, his or her gaze unable to really wander. Pleasures other than that of mastery have been obscured; consequently, the diversified dimensions of cinematic desire have been excised. There are modes of pleasure in going to the cinema that precede, traverse, and follow the scopophilia of film-viewing to which most theories of the apparatus have cathected. Unable to account for a collective, nomadic, and historical dimension of reception, they have reached an impasse. I wish to reclaim these pleasures and pursue a theorization of spectatorship opened to motion, the public sphere, and historicity.[3] The spectatorial fascination with cinema—a kinetic "affair"—exceeds the fantasmatic scene of Plato's cave.

Film at the Arcade

> A stranger upon his arrival in so large and celebrated a city as Naples generally makes the public spectacles his first pursuit.
> Neapolitans go to see, not to hear an opera. It is the custom to light the stage only, which renders their spectacles frightfully dark.
>
> —Samuel Sharp, *Letters from Italy, 1765–66*

The implantation of cinema in the arcade was a product of Naples's metropolitan fabric. An ancient city (founded by the Greeks in the ninth century B.C.), Naples was, for centuries, the capital of a kingdom that extended throughout the southern part of Italy, a position that made it, in the seventeenth century, under Spanish domination, the second largest city in Europe after Paris and an important artistic center, particularly notable for its baroque painting and architecture. In the eighteenth century, Naples was renowned for its artistic and musical life; it was still the largest Italian city and the fourth largest city in Europe after London, Paris, and Istanbul. Intense urbanization brought with it a great disparity between the city's infrastructures, its potential, and an increasing population. During this period, Naples developed its characteristic "persona," so aptly defined by Pier Paolo Pasolini as that of a "plebeian metropolis" (17): extremes of wealth and poverty, a rich intellectual life and illiteracy, the coexistence of high and popular culture. On the eve of cinema's advent, the 1861 unification of Italy transformed the ancient capital into a regional metropolis, fully participatory in nineteenth-century culture. Naples housed the first Italian railway line (the Napoli-Portici), and it played a prominent role in the rise of the motion-picture industry. Cinema found a home in the city's arcade.

Film programs became an everyday attraction in the theater Salone Margherita of Naples's main arcade, the Galleria Umberto I, from 1896 to 1898. Next to the theater, at the very entrance of the arcade, there were open-air film screenings. Films were projected onto a very large screen and were visible from the street. These public filmic events were sponsored by the arcade's department store. At the same time, in the Galleria, the first movie theater was opened by an Italian Jewish businessman, Mario Recanati. For the newly formed arcade audience, he conceived an entrance to the cinematic imaginary derived from American dream machinery: Recanati's lobby was a Neapolitan interpretation of Broadway-like devices.[4]

In the early days of Neapolitan cinema, the Galleria Umberto I served not only as the center of film exhibition but also as the main location for the film business. All cinematographic activities were at first concentrated around the Galleria Umberto I. Neapolitan cinema was produced within the arcade's network of transactions: as a commercial, artistic, and social center, the arcade became a catalyst for ventures in film production and trade.

Elvira Notari's cinema was deeply involved in these developments, as her films were regularly screened at the Cinema Vittoria, in the Galleria Umberto I, as well as at the Cinema Monte Maiella, located in the Galleria Principe di Napoli, Naples's other, if lesser, arcade. According to a magazine of the time:

> Mrs. Elvira Notari shows in Naples the strong impact that the new cinematographic art may have on the people. Mrs. Notari has been writing great dramas, vibrating with emotions, aimed at elevating the popular soul and showing its inner virtues. The Cinema Vittoria is always overflowing

with the public for many evenings, a public which exits moved and in a better frame of mind. (Fossataro)

Dora Film screenings at the Vittoria, which could accommodate 360 people, usually lasted for a period of one or two weeks, and drew, on the average, an audience of fifty thousand people. Even the publicity material for U.S. distribution emphasizes the fact that films were successfully shown at the arcade. The most notable of these arcade screenings was that of 'A legge (The Law), or 'O festino e 'a legge (The Feast and the Law), a "Bakhtinian" film, whose story was suspended between "the feast and the law," desire and punishment, deviance and rules. Due to popular demand, 'A legge was screened continuously for over a month at the Vittoria, from 10 A.M. to late at night, in both sections of the movie theater. About six thousand people saw this film in Naples's arcade every day.

Cinema's implantation in the arcade is illuminated by Benedetto Croce's two-volume history of Neapolitan theater. A contemporary of Elvira Notari, Croce lived in Naples all his life. His theater history was published in 1891, a few years before the entrance of cinema into the world of spectacle. Croce's study was conceived as a response to traditional literary and philosophical scholarship, which demonstrated no interest in spectacle. Writing a history of theater not simply reduced to a history of plays, Croce mapped out the city's theatrical geography. His account discussed as well the difficulties traditionally encountered by women in theater, who, like the prostitutes, were forced to live outside the city limits, in accordance with eighteenth-century laws (Croce, 306–23). "Almost all women associated with the theater and spectacles were affected by those laws. . . . They were not considered honest as their profession carried with it the hard necessity to deal with many men, musicians, poets, and lovers of music" (310–12).

Exploring the sites of spectacle, Croce shows that popular spectacles and temporary theaters were set right in the area of the Teatro San Carlo, the oldest Italian opera house, from the time of its construction in 1737. This area, located in the vicinity of the harbor, was a site where, traditionally, popular spectacles and high forms of theater and music were juxtaposed. It was here, between 1887 and 1890, that the Galleria Umberto I was built and cinema was soon implanted.

The dedication of the Galleria Umberto I took place on November 10, 1892, with an exhibition of artistically ambitious industrial products. The arcade immediately "became *the* social center of the city as it was the privileged meeting point of journalists and writers and housed commercial

activities as well as theaters, *cafés chantants*, clubs, etc." (De Seta, 276).
Naples's arcade was a modern covered forum:

> The Galleria Umberto I . . . is the largest public space in the entire city. It
> is gigantic in its dimensions, is protected from both rain and sun, and is
> cooled by the sea wind which blows through it. . . . The entrances are per-
> pendicular to the lines of the street. One strolls unsuspectingly along Via
> Roma. A chance glance to the left, and the eye is overcome by the sudden
> revelation of the existence of this huge, hidden space. The passerby does
> not have to be of a special religion or have a ticket to enter. The arcade
> belongs to everyone. It is the monumental expression of this most charac-
> teristic achievement of the nineteenth century, the public sphere. (Geist,
> 428–37)

The Galleria extended the function of the *piazza* (forum), the Italian
urban site of meeting and *passeggiata* (promenade), social events and transitory activities. It represented the coalescence and transformation of this
public life, typically and traditionally set in the urban *piazza*, into modern
terms. Cinema, housed in the arcade, was thus grounded in a locus of spectacle and circulation of people and goods, in the metropolitan site of diverse social configurations—from those of a social elite and the intelli-
gentsia to that of the underworld. A Neapolitan journalist, protesting
against the presence of the underworld in the elegant arcade, in 1902
wrote:

> The arcade has become the attraction of beggars, pimps, street urchins,
> idlers. . . . It should not be allowed that a beautiful and elegant meeting
> place, such as our arcade, continue to be the refuge of the filthiest derelicts
> of our Neapolitan life. Those people must be pushed back into the dark-
> ness where they belong. (*Il pungolo*, October 14–15, 1902)

It was the darkness of the movie theater that welcomed them, and the arcade became a terrain for the reproduction of the city's popular culture.

Genealogical Travelogue: Cinema, Arcades, and Trains

In John Horne Burns's novel *The Gallery* (1947), the Galleria Umberto I
is the geographical center of action. The site is described as resembling the
railway:

> The Galleria Umberto I in Naples is a large arcade, a cross between the
> hall of a train and the nave of a church. . . . Everyone in Naples went to the
> Galleria. . . . The arcade . . . was secretive . . . ; it seemed like being inside
> a Baroque Underground station. (432)

Investigation of the sites of exhibition in Naples establishes that another area of the city that favored the rise and concentration of cinematographic activities was indeed the neighborhood of the railway terminal.
In 1899, Menotti Cattaneo began public screenings there. Other theaters
were soon opened; among them was Sala Eglé of Roberto Troncone, who
was, as well, the founder of one of the first Neapolitan production houses.[5]

The railway was a major place for the circulation of Neapolitan film
culture. *La Cinefono,* a local film magazine, continually advertised the
magazine's sale at the train station's bookstore and regularly listed the
bookstores and newsstands of the area. A typical advertisement, charting
the route of the film magazine itself, ran as follows:

> Our magazine is for sale at the bookstore of the train station and in all the
> most important newsstands in Naples, in Italy's major cities and in Trip-
> oli. (February 1917)

In the January 29, 1908, issue of the film magazine *La lanterna,* a curious item appeared. Entitled "Even Cinema on the Train," it discussed the
possibility of film screenings on trains. Thus the notion of cinema on
trains preceded that of film on airplanes. The idea was to have "*vagoni-cin-
ema,*" cinema-cars, just like the "*vagoni-ristorante,*" the restaurant-cars
on trains. The oral nature of pleasure in cinema was likened in this imaginary assimilation to eating.[6] Literalizing the assimilation, this Neapolitan
utopia suggests that the absorption of images is also an absorption of the
subject in the image—an oral urge, positioned on the threshold of inte-
rior/exterior, figured as a movement of swallowing/swallowed, eating/be-
ing eaten. Oral pleasure and the pleasure of the mobilized gaze were thus
to be joined in the form of a cinematic apparatus traveling on a train.

Neapolitan film exhibition and production of this early period, as it was
concentrated around the arcade and developing around the train station,
leads one to consider the geography of cinema's genealogy and the historicity of the cinematic apparatus. The arcade represented the nineteenth-century transition of architecture into urban itineraries.[7] A structure built of
iron and glass, it opened up the urban space and exploded the division in-
terior/exterior in favor of a fluid light space. The arcade was not an isolated
phenomenon. Iron was the "structural" mark of railroad stations, bridges,
and exhibition halls. All were sites of transit, signifiers of a new notion of
space and mobility, signs of an industrial era which generated the "motion
picture." The genesis of cinema in Naples took place within this new perceptual geography, in the urban site of transit, between interior and exte-

rior. Located in the arcade and around the railway, the seventh art of motion pictures, which was to become the medium of "unconscious optics" (Benjamin 1969, 235–37), found in the cityscape its appropriate home. In Gaston Bachelards phrase, "the unconscious is housed" (10).

Urban and Spectatorial *Flânerie*

Naples's arcade, completed just a few years before cinema's implantation there, became the home of wanderers, the host for those whose daily activity was to gather, stroll, or look around. It welcomed the *flâneur*, described nostalgically by Walter Benjamin, who witnessed his replacement by the more modern "man of the crowd":

> The *flâneur* goes botanizing on the asphalt. But . . . strolling could hardly have assumed the importance it did without the arcades. . . . "An arcade is a city, even a world in miniature." It is in this world that the *flâneur* is at home; he provides "the favorite sojourn of the strollers and the smokers, the stamping ground of all sorts of little *métiers*, with its chronicler and its philosopher. . . . " The street becomes a dwelling for the *flâneur*; he is as much at home among the facades of houses as a citizen in his four walls.
> (Benjamin 1983, 36–37)

Edoardo Notari, Elvira's son, an actor in all his mother's films coined a Benjaminian expression, *ombrello de pirucchi*, which in Neapolitan dialect means "umbrella for idlers," to define the Neapolitan arcade, and called attention to the Galleria's function in the genesis and implantation of film activities. According to him, *strascinafacende* (a Neapolitan name for *flâneurs*) inhabited the arcade, strolled and gathered under its umbrella, and, following the contemplative trail of urban wandering, would be attracted to the cinema. *Strascinafacende* would cruise the cafés around the arcade, talking of pictures, eventually ending up at the Cinema Vittoria for a movie. Neapolitan idlers also discussed and even got involved in aspects of film production, developed ideas for films, provided the new *métier* with its chroniclers and philosophers.[8]

The overall deployment of our Neapolitan micro-history suggests that arcades and cinemas are to be understood as forms of optical consumption by a mobile collectivity.[9] Topoi of modernity, they share a fantasmatic dimension in their function of site/sight. Cinema, a space of the gaze, is to be placed within a discourse of circulation and the desire therein inscribed. Let us then proceed in this direction.

Wandering around Plato's Cave

In defining the nomadic dimension of cinematic fascination, one first returns to Roland Barthes's notes upon going to the cinema. Barthes suggests that:

> One goes to the movies as a response to idleness, leisure, free time. . . .
> Vacancy, inoccupation, lethargy; it is not in front of the film that one dreams—it is without knowing it, even before one becomes a spectator. . . .
> The darkness of the theater is prefigured by the "twilight *rêverie*" . . . which precedes it and leads the subject from street to street, from poster to poster, finally burying oneself into a dim, anonymous, indifferent cube.
> . . . The "noir" of the cinema . . . is also the color of a diffused eroticism;
> by its human condensation, by its absense of *mondanité*, . . . by the relaxation of postures, . . . the movie house (ordinary model) is a site of availability, and it is the availability, the inoccupation of bodies . . . which best defines modern eroticism— . . . that of the big city.[10]

Idleness, leisure, and the inoccupation of bodies describe the "cinema situation." A step in the erratic trail that takes one from street to street, cinema inhabits *flânerie*. And, grounded in seeing, the idler's way of loitering reminds us of the film spectator:

> To the idler who strolls the streets, things appear divorced from the history of their production, and their fortuitous juxtaposition suggests mysterious and mystical connections. Time becomes "a dream web where the most ancient occurrences are attached to those of today." Meanings are read on the surface of things: "The phantasmagoria of the *flâneur*: reading profession, origins and character from faces."[11]

As perceptual modes, *flânerie* and cinema share the montage of images, the spatiotemporal juxtaposition, the obscuring of the mode of production, and the "physiognomic" impact—the spectatorial reading of bodily signs. The "dream web" of film reception, with its geographical implantation, embodies *flânerie*'s mode of watching, and its public dimension.

The genealogy of spectatorship reveals it as grafted upon the terrain of public "leisure pleasure," in Italy termed *"dolce far niente"*—an urban erotics where "the joy of watching is triumphant."[12] A revealing passage in Baudelaire's writings foreshadows in the *flâneur*'s joy the genesis of the film spectator:

> For the perfect *flâneur*, for the passionate spectator, it is an immense joy to set up house in the heart of the multitude, amid the ebb and flow of

movement, in the midst of the fugitive and the infinite. To be away from home and yet to feel oneself everywhere at home; to see the world, to be at the center of the world, and yet to remain hidden from the world—such are a few of the slightest pleasures of those independent, passionate, impartial natures. . . . The spectator is a *prince* who everywhere rejoices in his incognito. . . . [He] enters into the crowd as if it were an immense reservoir of electrical energy. Or we might liken him to a mirror as vast as the crowd itself; or to a kaleidoscope gifted with consciousness, responding to each one of the movements and reproducing the multiplicity of life and the flickering grace of all the elements of life. He is an "I" with an insatiable appetite for the "non-I" at every instant rendering and explaining it in pictures more living than life itself, which is always unstable and fugitive. (9–10)

As if recognizing "the site of traces left by the future," Baudelaire describes here a *flâneur*-to-be, the film spectator. The *flâneur* is someone who sets up house amid the multitude, as a spectator at home within the theater's crowd. Like the *flâneur*, the film spectator sees without being seen, rejoicing in his incognito: seeing the world, at the center of the world, he is, nonetheless, hidden from it. Baudelaire's pictures are more living than life itself, fugitive and unattainable like the filmic text; his metaphor of the kaleidoscope, his scenario of the mirror—the "I" with an insatiable appetite for the "non-I"—akin to the Lacanian mirror-stage, are paradigms often invoked to describe the effects of the cinematic apparatus. The perfect *flâneur* is the passionate spectator, Baudelaire states. The wandering urban spectator, historically eclipsed by the life of the big modern city, is transformed, reinvented, and reinscribed in the figure of the film spectator. The modern *flâneur* is the film spectator. The perfect *flâneur* is the passionate film spectator.

Undergoing historical changes, *flânerie* "travels." And, along the way, the terms of a relation between interior and exterior shift as, in its various configurations, the street turns into an interior and the latter, in turn, becomes a street (Benjamin 1983, 54), ending in the film spectatorial reincarnation. Cinema's spatio-visuality physically enforces this dynamic, as well as issuing fantasmatic shifts between inside and outside. Founded on the physical/emotional experience of both intimacy and collectivity, film spectatorship dwells on the borders of interior/exterior. It offers "an imaginary private sphere from the vantage point of public space" (Mayne, 81). As a tactile appropriation of space, in a site of public architecture, film reception is related once more to the perception and reception of arcades and their cafés, to railway terminals and their arriving trains.

Streetwalker

In his study of travel in the nineteenth century, Wolfgang Schivelbusch, who first formulated the relation between train and cinema, showed that these new technologies profoundly affect perception: as they condense time and space, they introduce a "panoramic vision."[13] The railway effect, similarly generated by the glass architecture of the arcades, is also produced by that other "light-space"—film. This new visuality, grounded in a panoramic gaze, heir of the panorama painting and the diorama, results in a new geography.

A voyage is produced by an apparatus of vision, as the spectator travels through and along sites, in a perceptual machine ensemble. In a movie theater, as in a train, one is alone with others, and travels in time and space, viewing panoramically from a still-sitting position through a framed image in motion. Hence the train can be seen as "the mechanical double for the cinematic apparatus. . . . The very term 'tracking shot' is a compelling index of the permeation of filmmaking practice by the language of the railroad."[14]

Contributing to a growing theoretical interest in train and film, Mary Ann Doane has argued that, given these two machines of vision, a despatialization of subjectivity occurs, and this in turn has sexualized Schivelbusch's panoramic perception, which had linked the cinema not only with the railroad but also with the department store. Speaking of the "consumption" of cinema, she states:

> If the film frame is a kind of display window and spectatorship consequently a form of window-shopping, the intimate association of looking and buying does indeed suggest that the prototype of the spectator-consumer is female. (1987, 27)

Here is a point of departure for the articulation of the public "panoramic" dimension of nineteenth-century technologies and inquiry into issues of gender. For it is here that we confront a central question about space and desire: Is the mobile gaze male? In the literature of modernity, the most significant female figure inhabiting the arcade is the whore.[15] Still today, we find prostitution identified as the female version of *flânerie*: a male loiterer is a *flâneur*; the female version is a "streetwalker." The Italian term for *prostitute* is *"passeggiatrice."* And the Neapolitan *"peripatetica"* is equally indicative of the "impossibility" of female *flânerie*, an impossibility semiotically established,[16] for the adjective "peripatetic," when indicating a woman, is not the attribute of a Greek philosopher but the mark of prostitution. Woman cannot wander. The figure of the *flâneur* is traditionally male. A female equivalent was made difficult by a division of sexual realms that restricted female mobility and confined woman into the space of the private. As a result, the "peripatetic" gaze of the *flâneur* is a position that a woman has had to struggle to acquire and to liberate from its connotations of social ostracism and danger. It is not by chance that one of the first acts of Italian feminism was for women to "streetwalk" together through the city at night.

Cinema plays an important role in this process. The "institution" of cinema (that is, the act of going to the movies and its viewing space) historically legitimized for the female subject the denied possibility of public pleasure in leisure time. Cinema provided a form of access to public space, an occasion to socialize and get out of the house. Going to the cinema triggered a liberation of the woman's gaze, enabling her to renegotiate, on a new terrain of intersubjectivity, the configuration of private/public. Moreover, the cinema situation made it possible for the female to experience a form of *flânerie*, as film, triggered by a desire of loitering, offered the joy of watching while traveling. The female spectator could thus enter the world of the *flâneur* and derive its pleasures through filmic motions. We may see film spectatorship as providing access to an erotics denied the female subject; she could enjoy the pleasures of darkness and (urban) wandering. Mobilizing the gaze—the "panoramic" feature of cinematic language—implied the appropriation of territories and the freedom of "streetwalking." Textually and contextually, literally and figuratively, historically and fantasmatically, the female subject's encounter with the cinema constructs a new geography, gives license to venturing. In its embodiment of fantasy, female spectatorship maps out the spaces of the gaze as sites to traverse and trespass.

Female spectatorship triggers, and participates in, women's conquest of the sphere of spatial mobility as pleasure. The full expansion of woman's territorial horizons is, however, a journey in slow motion. Female spectatorship itself involves a long, reluctant process of historical affirmation of female *flânerie*. In Italy, it was not until the 1950s that going to the cinema gained definitive acceptance as a group activity for women unaccompanied by men. Attendance undisturbed at a movie theater by a woman alone is still not always assured.[17] The female *flâneur*, suspected of selling rather than buying pleasure, is implicated, as "streetwalker," within the sphere of the commodity. Female spectatorship originates in a shift from privatization toward urban circulation and public leisure that is closely related to consumption,[18] understood as both selling (one's body), "streetwalking," and buying. Urban wandering was historically legitimized for the female in the form of shopping trips. Given the analogy between film-viewing and window-shopping, the question of *flânerie* takes us, as Anne Friedberg has claimed, all the way to its contemporary incarnation in the modern mall and its inscription in mall-cinema, where we may encounter a *"flâneuse du ma(l)l"* (419–31). The female *flâneur* thus wanders across history, establishing her identity and desire in a space of consumption (of images).

The Neapolitan implantation of a cinema analogous to "the display window," in the arcade, the site of "window-shopping," points to the overlapping terrains of urban and spectatorial modes which provide, for the female subject, a way to pleasure. Through access to cinema, a female sense of the space of desire comes into play, and travels. "Mapping" this terrain of fantasy means wandering toward a female desire of our own, for "what is experientially female is the association of desire with a space" (Jessica Benjamin, 97). One more step toward acquiring the right to be, positively, an (urban) *voyeuse*, a *"flâneuse,"* a streetwalker—in other words, a female spectator.

At issue is the practice of *trans*gressive spaces. In this respect, the model of panoramic, mobilized perception, transposed from the glass architecture of the arcade and the railway to the cinema, offers yet another possibility of theorizing female spectatorship in terms of spatial desire. As Lynne Kirby suggests, the railway and the cinema are both a "motor force of desire bringing together different social-sexual types in a public space of forced juxtaposition, a space of substitution and deception in general" (3). As deterritorialized spaces, trains, cinemas, and, we may add, arcades traverse and break up the formerly closed notion of the milieu. In these sites of pervasive eroticism "consumed" by the collectivity, individuals from different backgrounds, classes, venues, and genders are transgressively put in close "touch," share a temporary intimacy, in fleeting encounters. Triggering desire, the loci of modernity alter the dichotomy of private/public, for, despite providing for social events, they also house various private behavioral modes.

An article entitled "The Cinema's Public," published in 1908 in the Italian film magazine *Rivista fono-cinematografica*, points to its sociosexual dynamics and clarifies the historical situation relative to modes of access to the cinema for women at the time of Elvira Notari. It was mostly women, as well as workers and marginals, who were subject of, and subjected to, the shocking change of modernity—mobility:

> New discoveries create new environments. . . . Just as tearing down certain old sections of town to make boulevards creates new ways of cohabiting and abolishes traditional habits . . . the cinema has created new habits. . . .
>
> The public of the movie theater is composed mostly of workers, women, and young people . . . social classes that are entering society with new attitudes and mores. . . . One finds the worker and the elegant lady sitting close to each other, the spoiled bourgeois kid next to the old man, the social classes mixed together.
>
> A little democracy is entering into our mores. Rather it is the new habit, the new invention, which is triggering the democratic spirit. The same . . . was true for the public of the streetcar.
>
> When it is already dark, there comes a group of dressmakers. . . . The passersby look, and someone lured by all that flesh decides to spend twenty cents to find himself in the middle of it, in the dark, for a good half-hour. . . .
>
> Erotic adventures occur. Can you see that young lady, accompanied by her maid, who . . . suggests they enter for a moment just to rest a little? A young man . . . will find a way to sit next to her in the movie theater, and in the darkness the two of them, who pretended not to know each other, will touch hands and maybe exchange long and passionate letters. It is so easy in the dark! . . .
>
> There is also a public of idlers, one which attends the movie theater by chance or casually. Who has not had this experience, after wandering around the city, or in between errands, of entering a movie theater . . . ? The movie theater lures you . . . ends up persuading you, and you enter. . . .
>
> As for streetwalkers: . . . a sample is always at the movies.[19]

This description approaches the terms of our "mobile" spectatorship. An Italian film produced in 1913 by Cines confirms this view. *Tragedia al cinematografo* comically narrates a tragedy at the movie theater. A woman leaves the house to go to the movies. Her jealous husband, suspecting that she is meeting her lover, follows her. Parading a gun, he is about to enter the theater. But a movie clerk attempts to save the woman by warning the spectators that an enraged husband is coming into the movie house to unmask his wife's infidelity. At the announcement, the entire audience gets up and escapes.

Cinema is a response to (popular) leisure time. A place of urban relaxation, a catalyst for the loitering of passersby, a stop on the idler's *passeggiata*, the movie theater is a site of pervasive eroticism, a space of darkness where sociosexual mores might be transgressed. Women gain access to the public sphere and/as the erotic sphere. Dressmakers, servants, streetwalkers, as well as upper-class ladies accompanied by maids, may inhabit this public space, mix together, and plunge into erotic journeys of the gaze.

The implantation of cinema in the cityscape, the constitution of spectatorship, gave the female subject access to the dream-*rêverie* of *flânerie*, and the erotic exchange that, within the space of public sites, takes place.

Metropolis and Film

A new form of urban spatial desire, film was a product of the era of the metropolis. In turn, inhabiting the metropolis changed perception in ways that approach the "cinema situation." In a paradigmatic article, written in 1903, Georg Simmel discussed city life in terms that almost literally describe film reception: in the metropolis one is exposed to a "fast telescoping of changing images" and sensations; in this continuous shift of interior/exterior, the space itself is constantly being composed and recomposed, by way of difference within the field of single-glance perception, and the unexpected juxtaposition of violent stimuli. Writing in such a way about the metropolis, at the very moment of the rise of cinema, Simmel's very phraseology speaks the language of motion pictures, although he does not acknowledge it. Later on, Benjamin will recognize the parallel between metropolis and film, and will articulate it in terms of perceptual shocks:

> The camera gave the moment a posthumous shock . . . such as that supplied by the . . . big city. . . . In a film perception in the form of shocks was established as a formal principle [and] . . . is the basis of the rhythm of reception. ("On Some Motifs in Baudelaire," 132)

Cinema expresses the perceptual changes of modernity—changes that are also embodied in the city:

> The film corresponds to profound changes in the apperceptive apparatus—changes that are experienced on an individual scale by the man in the street in big-city traffic, on a historical scale by every present-day citizen. ("On Some Motifs in Baudelaire," 132)

At the turn of the century, a threshold between the metropolitan experience and the cinema was being built both historically and epistemologically.[20] In 1910, the Italian futurist Umberto Boccioni painted *Rissa in galleria* (*Riot in the Arcade*). In a "cinematic" representation, Boccioni envisaged the arcade as a site of the city's dynamism and tension, and wrote: "A figure is never stable in front of us but is incessantly appearing and disappearing. Because images persist on the retina, things in movement multiply, change form, follow one upon the other like vibrations within the space they traverse" (Coen, 93).

Futurism, the art that epitomized modern motion, was connected in Naples to forms of popular culture. Naples's most distinguished futurist artist, Francesco Cangiullo (1884–1977), favored such topoi as street crowds and the train.[21] As stated in his writings as well as evident in his creative expression, Cangiullo believed that futurist and pre-dadaist elements were engrained in the popular culture of Naples, a city in constant motion. He therefore chose to work the threshold between futurist experimentation and traditional popular expressions.

Among Cangiullo's favored subjects was the "Piedigrotta," a popular Neapolitan street festival, a theme that was also a favorite of Elvira Notari, the filmmaker of city films, for whom popular festivals, street crowds, and city views were an integral part of the fictional flow. And in the movie house of the arcade, these "motion" pictures, whose text(ure) ingrained the city's imaginary, were returned to urban crowds. Spectators of Notari's films who attended the movie theater in the arcade could experience the pleasure of the urban travelogue in a mirroring effect. The panoramic vision was reflected in the glass architecture of the arcade, where they traveled as *flâneurs*, on their way to the cinema. It was then reproduced in, as well as by, the perceptual mechanism of the cinematic apparatus. In the films themselves, such vision was textually articulated. Finally, this visual pleasure was offered back to the film audiences of the arcade, for cinema, itself an extension of panoramic geography, when housed in a metropolitan *passage*, offered a *mise-en-abîme* of spatial pleasures.

The Neapolitan case was not an isolated phenomenon, as early cinema was generally speaking an urban affair.[22] A medium primarily addressed to urban audiences, it fed on the city's *imaginaire* and expressed a definite urban viewpoint. In Paris and New York, as in Rome or Berlin, films were often shown in major sites of metropolitan entertainment. Cinema was an integral part of the metropolitan experience, its "unconscious optics" a participant in the metropolitan unconscious.

The Unconscious Is Housed:
Heterotopias and *Transitorial* Architectures

Dwelling on the experiential relation between traversing sites and the cinema, the surrealist movement offers an exemplary case. The surrealists, who loved going to the arcade, and to the movies, established a practice of film reception based on urban nomadism and transitory pleasure.[23] Constantly wandering from theater to theater, continually entering and exiting from the film itself, they affirmed a nomadic reception and constructed an itinerant montage of filmic experiences. This practice suggests dimensions of pleasure to be found in the cinematic apparatus that go beyond the motionless subject conventionally advocated as the prerequisite of cinematic pleasure. The surrealists' use of the cinematic space, their very fascination with the medium, epitomizes its pleasure understood as a part of the mental space of the metropolis, its motion and transit.

Thrown into the rhythm of the metropolis, a field of forces in motion, the body is affected. As a result of the flow of impressions, the optical montage, and the fluctuating nature of the metropolitan space, the unity of the body disintegrates. The subject becomes a body in space, a fragmented body, a "desiring machine." When a nomadic dynamic prevails, within a transitory space of traversing sites, one does not end where the body ends.

I ultimately argue that it is such a metropolitan *body* that incarnates in film spectatorship, thus extending the venue of "touristic" ventures. My argument throughout is sustained by the notion of *"transito"* (untranslatable in English in one word) theorized by the Italian philosopher Mario Perniola. Revealing the spatial component of desire, Perniola defines *transito* as a wide-ranging and multifaceted notion of circulation. *Transito* connotes many levels of desire as inscribed in both physical and mental motion: it includes *"passages,"* traversing, transitions, transitory states, and erotic circulation, and it incorporates a linguistic reference to transit. It is such a traversing of desire that is called upon here to account for spectatorial fascination. If we believe that "whatever its particular fiction, the film produces a pleasure akin to that of the travelogue" (Doane 1985, 42), we can go further and assert that cinematic pleasure is more than the unique product of a textuality produced in the enclosed darkness of the apparatus—Plato's cave; it literally belongs to a wider territory. Breaking out of the cave, film theory should acknowledge that forms of *transito* lie at the root of cinematic pleasures, and place these pleasures in the context of journeys of the gaze through geographies. In such a way, we should theorize the inscription of the apparatus in space, and consider the historical trajectories of film architectures.

Cinematic pleasure stems from *"curiositas,"* the desire to explore mapped on the "lust of the eyes."[24] It belongs to the range of those erotic pleasures of the nomadic gaze first known to the traveler and the *flâneur* and then embodied, by way of panoramic spatio-visuality, in the modes of inhabiting space of *transito*rial architectures. Suggesting this historic aspect of the fascination of the apparatus, and highlighting its fantasmatic connection to travel and landscaping, one looks back to early cinema, but also "back to the future." This view offers numerous developments for future studies. One can place the art of "unconscious optics" in the context of contemporary forms of intercultural traveling, and sites of spatiotemporal tourism, of which airplane-cinema is the ultimate metonymy. For, if "the unconscious is housed," it is also "moving."

Embodying the dynamics of journey, cinema maps a heterotopic topography.[25] The heterotopic fascination of cinema is to be understood as the attraction to, and habitation of, a site without a geography, a space capable of juxtaposing in a single real place several possibly incompatible sites as well as times, a site whose system of opening and closing both isolates it and makes it penetrable, as it forms a type of elsewhere/nowhere, where "we calmly and adventurously go traveling." Thus we, female spectators, in the midst of the "far-flung ruins and debris" of our old enclosed prison-world, may go traveling.[26] As we move through filmic architectures, as in "streetwalking" through the *meter-polis*, our own mother-city, we reclaim forbidden pleasures—wandering through erotic geographies.

Notes

A version of this chapter has been published in my book *Streetwalking on a Ruined Map: Cultural Theory and the City Films of Elvira Notari* (Princeton: Princeton University Press, 1993).

1. The commonly used expression *"il ventre di Napoli"* derives from a book by the female novelist and journalist Matilde Serao, a contemporary of Notari. See Matilde Serao, *Il ventre di Napoli* (Naples, 1884).

2. For the antecedents of the ongoing discourse on the cinematic apparatus, see Christian Metz, *The Imaginary Signifier* (Bloomington: Indiana University Press, 1981); and Jean-Louis Baudry, "The Apparatus: Metapsychological Approaches to the Impression of Reality in the Cinema," in Philip Rosen, ed., *Narrative, Apparatus, Ideology* (New York: Columbia University Press, 1986).

3. Current work on spectatorship in the the U.S. shows a growing concern for a theorization of history, a concern which is increasingly directed to silent cinema. As it regards the interaction of historicity and public, see, among others, Miriam Hansen, *Babel and Babylon: Spectatorship in American Silent Film* (Cambridge, MA: Harvard University Press, 1991); Hansen, "Early Silent Cinema: Whose Public Sphere," *New German Critique*, no. 29 (Winter 1983): 147–84; and Judith Mayne, *Private Novels. Public Films* (Athens: University of Georgia Press, 1988).

4. Outdoor film screenings were taking place, at the time, also in Paris and New York, mostly for publicity purposes.
On film exhibition in Naples, see Vittorio Paliotti and Enzo Grano, *Napoli nel cin-*

ema (Napoli: Azienda Autonoma Cura Soggiorno e Turismo, 1969); Aldo Bernardini, *Cinema muto italiano*, 3 vols. (Bari : Laterza, 1980–82) (in particular vol. 1, chapters 2, 3, 5, and vol. 2, chapters 2, 4); Vittorio Martinelli, "Sotto il sole di Napoli," in *Cinema e film*, vol. 1, ed. Gian Piero Brunetta and Davide Turconi (Rome: Armando Curcio Editore, 1987); Claudio Rubino, "Cinematografo a Napoli: Appunti sulle origini, 1896–1899," *Immagine*, vol. 2, no. 2 (June-September 1982): 21–24; and S. Pappalardi, "I primi cinema napoletani," *Cinema*, Rome, no. 66, March 25, 1939. Bernardini's data are most accurate.

5. By 1906, there were at least seven steady movie houses in the area of Naples's train station, one had opened at the Galleria Principe di Napoli, and film exhibition had spread from the Galleria Umberto I to the surrounding neighborhood, where fifteen theaters were reported to be functioning. By the teens, the number of theaters in the Galleria Umberto I had gone up to six.

6. That filmic desire is rooted in orality is suggested by Jean-Louis Baudry, only tentatively, in a footnote to his essay "The Apparatus," pp. 317–18.

7. For a treatment of the arcade in this framework, see, among others, Siegfried Giedion, *Space, Time and Architecture* (Cambridge, MA: Harvard University Press, 1962).

8. See Martinelli, "Sotto il sole di Napoli," p. 369; Martinelli, "Due o tre cose che so di Gustavo," in Guido Barlozzetti, Stefania Parigi, Angela Prudenzi, and Claver Salizzato, eds., *Modi di produzione del cinema italiano: la Titanus*, Di Giacomo Editore, 1986; and Edoardo Notari's interview, in Annabella Miscuglio and Rony Daopoulo, eds., in collaboration with Judita Hribar, *Kinomata*, Bari: Dedalo, 1980.

9. Though not necessarily in direct connection, the arcade and the cinema are discussed in similar terms by Benjamin, who very early recognized the importance of cinema in the cultural modification of space and perception, and also recognized the importance of the arcade along the same lines, in his fragmentary and unfinished book *Das Passagen-Werk*. See vol. 5 of Benjamin, *Gesammelte Schriften*, ed. Rolf Tiedemann (Frankfurt am Main: Suhrkamp Verlag, 1982).

10. The translation of this quotation by Roland Barthes has been slightly modified according to the original French.

11. Susan Buck-Morss, *The Dialectics of Seeing: Walter Benjamin and the Arcades Project* (Cambridge, MA: M.I.T. Press, 1989), p. 106. Several reincarnations of this figure have been suggested, including the urban writer as *flâneur*, proposed by Benjamin himself. Adorno pointed to radio listening as a kind of aural *flânerie*. Though Buck-Morss herself sees television as a modern extension of *flânerie*, the very way in which she describes the *flâneur* suggests that, although overlooked, a parallel with cinema is appropriate, on the basis of the public nature of the space where watching takes place, and the dynamics of the exchange *interieur/exterieur* therein embodied.

12. Benjamin mentions that "in the *flâneur* the joy of watching is triumphant" in his *Charles Baudelaire*, p. 69. "*Dolce far niente*" literally means "sweet doing nothing," hence referring to the pleasure of loitering.

13. Wolfgang Schivelbusch, *The Railway Journey: Trains and Travel in the Nineteenth Century* (New York: Urizen Books, 1979). Schivelbusch derives the notion of "panoramic" perception from Dolf Sternberg, who developed it in his discussion of panorama painting. See Dolf Sternberg, "Panorama of the 19th Century," *October*, no. 4 (Fall 1977): 3–20.

14. Lynne Kirby, "Male Hysteria and Early Cinema," *Camera Obscura*, no. 17 (May

1988): 113. On the relation between the train and the cinema, see also Charles Musser, "The Travel Genre in 1903–04: Moving toward Fictional Narrative," *Iris*, vol. 2, no. 1 (1984): 47–60; Mary Ann Doane, " ' . . . when the direction of the force acting on the body is changed': The Moving Image," *Wide Angle*, vol. 7, nos. 1–2 (1985): 42–58; Kirby, "Romances of the Rail in Early Cinema," unpublished paper, Society of Cinema Studies Conference, Montreal, May 1987; Kirby, *The Railroad and the Cinema, 1895–1929: Institutions, Aesthetics and Gender*, Ph.D. dissertation, University of California, Los Angeles, 1989; and Annette Michelson, "Track Records, Trains of Events: The Limits of Cinematic Representation," in *Junction and Journey: Trains and Film* (New York: The Museum of Modern Art, exhibition catalog, 1991).

15. See Buck-Morss, "The *Flâneur*, the Sandwichman and the Whore: The Politics of Loitering," *New German Critique*, no. 39 (Fall 1986): 99–140; and Janet Wolff, "The Invisible *Flâneuse*: Women and the Literature of Modernity," *Theory, Culture & Society*, vol. 2, no. 3 (1985): 37–46. The literature of modernity produced by male authors, in general, fails to acknowledge women's experience of modernity.

16. Alongside the Italian examples (including "*battere il marciapiede*" for "streetwalking"), the French "*faire le trottoir*" and "*péripatéticienne*" and similar expressions in other languages, such as German and Spanish, also indicate the semiotic "impossibility" of female *flânerie*.

17. For a historical account of women's access to and attendance at the cinema in Italy, see Giovanna Grignaffini, "Female Identity and Italian Cinema of the 1950s," in Giuliana Bruno and Maria Nadotti, eds., *Off Screen: Women and Film in Italy* (London: Routledge, 1988); Piera Detassis, "Una sala vissuta pericolosamente," *Ciak* (April 1989); 65–68; and Gian Piero Brunetta, *Buio in sala* (Venice: Marsilio, 1989).

18. Cf., among others, Rosalind H. Williams, *Dream Worlds: Mass Consumption in Late Nineteenth Century France* (Berkeley: University of California Press, 1982); Kathy Peiss, *Cheap Amusements: Working Women and Leisure in Turn-of-the-Century New York* (Philadelphia: Temple University Press, 1986); Judith Mayne, "Immigrants and Spectators," *Wide Angle*, vol. 5, no. 2 (1982): 32–40; and Hansen, *Babel and Babylon*. For further research work on the subject, see Lynn Spigel and Denise Mann, "Women and Consumer Culture, a Selective Bibliography," *Quarterly Review of Film and Video*, vol. 11, no. 1 (1989): 85–106.

19. The passages quoted have been selected from "Il pubblico del cinematografo," *Rivista fono-cinematografica*, no. 11 (February 1908), reprinted in Mostra Internazionale del Nuovo Cinema, eds., *Tra un film e l'altro. Materiali sul cinema italiano 1907–1920* (Venezia: Marsilio, 1980) pp. 43–45.

20. On the subject of spatiotemporal changes as experienced by urban populations, see Stephen Kern, *The Culture of Time and Space 1880–1918* (Cambridge, MA: Harvard University Press, 1983).

21. Cangiullo was an eclectic Neapolitan artist who produced paintings, drawings, and graphics and wrote literary and poetic texts. His interest in motion included a drawing called *Il treno sul ponte* (*The Train on the Bridge*): Cangiullo composed a visual picture of a train using the letters of the linguistic sign *treno* (train). Among the artist's written works, see Francesco Cangiullo, *Piedigrotta* (Milan: Edizioni di "Poesia," 1916); *Caffé concerto-Alfabeto a sorpresa* (Milan: Edizioni di "Poesia," 1918); *Il debutto del sole* (Naples: L'Editrice Italiana, 1919) (with a critical piece by Marinetti; *Teatro della sorpresa* (Milan: Il Futurismo, 1922) (co-authored with Marinetti; *Le vie della città* (Naples: Pironti, 1937); and *Il golfo di Napoli* (Naples: Rispoli, 1938).

On Futurist art in Naples, see Luciano Caruso, *Francesco Cangiullo e il futurismo a Napoli* (Florence: Spes-Salimbeni, 1979); Luciano Caruso, ed., *Futurismo a Napoli (1933–35). Documenti inediti* (Naples: Colonnese, 1977); and Mariantonietta Picone Petrusa, ed., *In margine. Artisti napoletani tra tradizione e opposizione. 1909–23* (Milan: Fabbri Editori, 1986).

22. See Tom Gunning, "The Book That Refuses to Be Read: Images of the City in Early Cinema," unpublished paper, presented at the Society for Cinema Studies Conference, University of Iowa, Iowa City, April 1989. As Gunning shows, the transfer to film allowed the city street to become another form of spectacle, one mediated by an apparatus, as early motion pictures insistently portray the urban masses, and are offered for viewing to an urban public.

As for the female spectator in modernity and the city, see: on German cinema, Patrice Petro's *Joyless Streets: Women and Melodramatic Representation in Weimar Germany* (Princeton: Princeton University Press, 1989); on American film, see Hansen's *Babel and Babylon*. On urban mode of film perception, see also Lynne Kirby, "The Urban Spectator and the Crowd in Early American Train Films," *Iris*, no. 11 (Summer 1990) 49–62, and Annette Michelson, "Dr. Crase and Mr. Clair," *October*, no. 11 (Winter 1979): 31–53.

23. For a good treatment of this topic see Paul Hammond, ed., *The Shadow and Its Shadow: Surrealist Writings on Cinema* (London: British Film Institute, 1978); and Rudolph E. Kuenzli, ed., *Dada and Surrealist Film* (New York: Locker and Owens, 1987).

24. St. Augustine included "*curiositas*" (curiosity) as one of the "lust of eyes" leading to the formation of, and fascination for, spectacle. (St. Augustine, *The Confessions* [New York: New American Library, 1963]). Tom Gunning claims that early cinema's "aesthetics of attraction" developed precisely out of this *curiositas*. See his "An Aesthetic of Astonishment: Early Film and the (In)credulous Spectator," *Art & Text*, no. 34 (Spring 1989): 31–45.

25. The concept of heterotopia was the subject of a lecture given by Michel Foucault in March 1967, published as "Des espaces autres," in the French journal *Architectures-Movement-Continuité*, in October 1984. The text has been translated into English with a less effective title ("Of Other Spaces," *Diacritics*, vol. 16, no. 1 [1986]). Speaking of cinema as an "heterotopia," Michel Foucault related it to other sites of contemporary relaxation, such as trains, cafés, and beaches. Heterotopia is a place without a place, which exists by itself but is also infinitely open, and as such establishes and modifies the relation to all spaces around it, as well as serving a social function. Heterotopias are all linked to each other and often contradict all other sites. Spatial dimensions, they also establish a relation to slices of time, to "heterocronies," to indefinitely accumulating time and/or fleetingly transitory aspects of time.

An intriguing contemporary filmic example of the heterotopic space of cinema is offered by Raoul Ruiz's film *Life Is a Dream* (1986). The film takes place in a movie theater, conceived as a site of continual spatiotemporal motion. While the protagonist dreams his past through filmic images, a number of narrative events take place around him. Spectators-passersby continually walk in and out of the movie theater, and act out their stories. A woman periodically wanders in, people chase and shoot each other, children play, chickens wander about, while a mechanical train runs underneath the spectators' seats.

26. I am paraphrasing, in the gender feminine, Benjamin's well-known passage on film in "The Work of Art," p. 236.

Works Cited

L'arte muta. vol.I, no. 1 (June 15, 1916).

Bachelard, Gaston. *The Poetics of Space*. Boston: Beacon Press, 1969.

Barthes, Roland. "Leaving the Movie Theatre," in *The Rustle of Language*. New York: Hill and Wang, 1986.

Baudelaire, Charles. *The Painter of Modern Life and Other Essays*. New York: Garland, 1978.

Benjamin, Jessica. "A Desire of One's Own: Psychoanalytic Feminism and Intersubjective Space," in Teresa de Lauretis, ed., *Feminist Studies/Critical Studies*. Bloomington: Indiana University Press, 1986.

Benjamin, Walter. *Illuminations*. New York: Schocken Books, 1969.

———. "The *Flâneur*," in *Charles Baudelaire: A Lyric Poet in the Era of High Capitalism*. London: Verso, 1983.

Buck-Morss, Susan. *The Dialectics of Seeing: Walter Benjamin and the Arcades Project*. Cambridge, MA: M.I.T. Press, 1989.

Burns, John Horne. *The Gallery* in Geist.

La cinefono (February 1917).

Coen, Ester, ed. "Futurist Painting: Technical Manifesto" (April 11, 1910), in *Umberto Boccioni*, exhibition catalog. New York: Metropolitan Museum of Art, 1988.

Il Corriere di Napoli. Naples, April 4, 1896.

Croce, Benedetto. *Il teatro di Napoli*. 2 vols. Naples: Giannini, 1891.

De Seta, Cesare. *Le città nella storia d'Italia: Napoli*. Bari: Laterza, 1987.

Doane, Mary Ann. *The Desire to Desire*. Bloomington: Indiana University Press, 1987.

———. "The Moving Image," *Wide Angle*. Vol.7, nos. 1–2 (1985).

Fossataro, Giuseppe. *La frusta*. November 30, 1920.

Friedberg, Anne. "Les *Flâneurs* du Mal(l): Cinema and the Postmodern Condition," *PMLA*, vol. 106, no.3 (May 1991).

Geist, Johann Friedrich. *Arcades: The History of a Building Type*. Cambridge, MA: M.I.T. Press, 1983.

Kirby, Lynne. "Romances of the Rail in Early Cinema." Unpublished paper, Society of Cinema Studies Conference, Montreal, May 1987.

Mayne, Judith. *Private Novels, Public Films*. Athens: University of Georgia Press, 1988.

Pasolini, Pier Paolo. *Lettere luterane*. Turin: Einaudi, 1976.

Perniola, Mario. *Transiti. Come si va dallo stesso allo stesso*. Bologna: Cappelli, 1985.

Il pungolo. Naples, October 14–15, 1902.

Schivelbusch, Wolfgang. *The Railway Journey: Trains and Travel in the Nineteenth Century*. New York: Urizen Books, 1979.

Simmel, Georg. "The Metropolis and Mental Life." In Donald Levine, ed., *Georg Simmel: On Individuality and Social Forms*. Chicago: Chicago University Press, 1971.

IO

AN/OTHER VIEW OF
NEW LATIN AMERICAN CINEMA

B. Ruby Rich

I.

Everyday events proceed now in another way. The image of revolution has become ordinary, familiar. In some ways we're achieving transformations even more profound than earlier ones, but ones that aren't so "apparent" now, not immediately visible to the observer. . . . Thus we find it no longer sufficient just to take cameras out in the street and capture fragments of that reality. . . . The filmmaker is immersed in a complex milieu, the profound significance of which does not lie on the surface.

—Tomás Gutiérrez Alea,
"The Viewer's Dialectic"[1]

The critics of our movement see it with eyes that do not comprehend what is going on in our movement. Anything that doesn't correspond to the old formulas, they don't recognize as being genuine New Latin American Cinema. In other words, they're trying to impose a model on us which is alien.

—Ruy Guerra & Fernando Birri,
Park City, Utah, 1989[2]

The films and filmmakers of the New Latin American Cinema movement have in recent years become the victim of a stereotype, in that the entire history of New Latin American Cinema has come to be judged by the yardstick of its early classics—as though history were static, as though the relationship of aesthetics to politics, once fixed, must remain in that same equation forever. Because Latin American cinema was able to penetrate North American and European consciousness and markets with its own particular style and set of concerns, the terms of that debut have continued to set the standard governing the interpretation of all the work that has followed.

In fact, the 1980s have seen a profound transformation of that history and a marked change in what the "new" New Latin American Cinema may be seen to represent, in the people who are creating it, and in the context within which its works are now being produced and exhibited.[3] Of course, history has never really been a matter of linear progress marching ever more efficiently and homogenously toward the horizon. There are refinements, reversals, denials, rebellions, leaps forward, regressions, revivals, and wholly new developments that appear to hold no echo of the past whatsoever.

Before assessing the present, a return to the past is in order. The New Latin American Cinema had a beginning far more complex than usually acknowledged and a development that has in fact been less hegemonic than perceived. The starting point is the 1950s, the post-World War II moment in our global cultural history. It is in part an anti-hegemonic moment, in that it signified a rupture both with previous balances of power and with previous modes of representation in cinema (with causes at once economic, philosophical, political, and technological). At the very least, it predated the U.S. global ascendancy that would last for some thirty years, right up to the 1980s. Significantly, this postwar period gave rise, in Italy, to neorealism, which would cross over to Latin America in three steps.

The first crossing was made from Europe to Mexico, when Luis Buñuel went there to live and work, and ended up making, among other films, *Los olvidados*. Given its emphasis on the dispossessed, the "real" life of the Third World, on pictures not pretty enough to have made it into the movies before and a camera style fluid enough to match, the film is a portent of things to come. But Buñuel wasn't Mexican. Despite the shared language between Mexico and Spain, Buñuel's film was not aimed at evolving a national identity or a Latin American aesthetic. It was, however, a forceful announcement, in 1950, that neorealism had arrived (though Buñuel, of course, was himself pre-neorealist in his aesthetic strategies) and could have a role to play in Latin American cinema.

The second crossing was a roundtrip. During 1952–55, four young Latin Americans traveled to Italy to study at the legendary Centro Sperimentale (Center for Experimental Cinematography) at the University of Rome: Tomás Gutiérrez Alea, Fernando Birri, Julio García Espinosa, and Gabriel García Márquez. When Birri returned to Argentina, he founded the Film School of Santa Fe, now legendary for the generation of filmmakers he trained there. When Tomás Gutiérrez Alea and Julio García Espinosa returned to Cuba, they collaborated on *El megano*. This first work of the new Cuban cinema was completed in 1954 and banned by Batista. In the insurgency period, García Espinosa became the head of "Cine rebelde."[4] Both thus became key participants in the fashioning of a cinema that would attempt to fuse new subjects with new forms and in so doing set a standard for the New Latin American Cinema movement. Though Gabriel García Márquez, the would-be screenwriter, first turned to literature, in the past few years he has become a singular influence upon Latin American film-making: through his role as head of the FNCL (New Latin American Cinema Foundation) which oversees the film school established in 1986 in Cuba to train young filmmakers; through the screen adaptations of his writings and his own screenplays; and, in 1987, through the screenplays for the *Amores difíciles* series of six co-productions with Latin American or Spanish filmmakers for Spanish television, all based on García Márquez stories or ideas.

Finally, the third step illustrates that the influence of Italian neorealism was not limited to those who physically journeyed to the mecca of Rome to study with its masters. Nelson Pereira dos Santos, back in Brazil, was part of a circle that recognized the import of this aesthetic and political strategy for Brazilian cinema. This circle was stimulated by the arrival of Alberto Cavalcanti, who exposed the young cinephiles to neorealist cinema. Pereira dos Santos's first short film, *Juventude*, was made at the same time as Buñuel's Mexican debut (produced for the Brazilian Communist party, it was lost when sent to a European festival) and his first feature, *Rio 40 Degrees*, built on the neorealist example to become the founding work of *cinema novo* in 1955. Pereira dos Santos recalls:

> Without neorealism, we would have never started, and I think no country with a weak film economy could have made self-portraying films, were it not for that precedent.[5]

The influence of Italian neorealism coincided with political shifts in Latin America: then, as now, aesthetics and politics could not be sequestered into separate arenas. In Brazil, Pereira dos Santos's stance was part of a larger position articulated through two key film industry conferences (of 1952 and 1953). The growth of a cinema defined by its national position, in turn, was made possible by the nationalistic government of Getúlio Vargas (1937–45 and 1951–54), nurtured by the atmosphere of increasing democratization under the elected government of Juscelino Kubitschek in 1955, and stunted by the military coup that overthrew João Goulart in 1964.[6] Then, the coup within a coup of 1968 greatly eroded the cultural zones of tolerance, and led to the emphasis in Brazilian cinema of this period upon metaphor and symbolic allusion. The establishment of Embrafilme in Brazil in 1969, ironically, provided an ambiguous freedom of expression for filmmakers during the years of military rule: Embrafilme itself was notable for its lack of censorship, but the produced films were frequently censored by the government.[7]

The political stage was never incidental. Fernando Birri could return to Argentina in 1956 because of the ouster of Perón; the film school which he established upon his return could flourish in part due to the democratic Frondizi government (which fell in 1962, the beginning of Birri's long exile). Fernando Solanas and Octavio Getino's *La hora de los hornos* has been long acknowledged for its cinematic rupture of the preexisting spectator/film relationship. Less acknowledged has been the explicit political agenda that led to the creation of the third part of the trilogy (so clearly Peronist that it was largely omitted from screening after Perón's disastrous return to power in 1973) or to Getino's service as head of the film censorship board under Perón.

In Cuba, extraordinary films could be made not simply because of a particularly inspired generation, but because of the massive change in social, economic, political, and—yes—aesthetic relations caused by the Revolution in 1959. Because of the promising conjunctural relations (and of the new cinema that might be created within a revolutionary context) Fidel Castro's government, as one of its first official acts, founded ICAIC, the Cuban Film Institute. It is no coincidence that *La batalla de Chile* was shot during the period of Allende's presidency in Chile (though finished, of course, tragically, after), nor that Allende's brief term as president coincided with a film renaissance in Chile as filmmakers sought to implement the ideals of his government at an aesthetic level. After the coup of September 11, 1973, the military immediately destroyed the university's film equipment and banned all the films made by Chile Films in the preceding three years.[8]

In sum, the emergence of the New Latin American Cinema cannot be separated from the political events during the period of its "uneven development" in the distinct regions that make up Latin America, nor can its different direction today be separated from the political circumstances of our decade.[9] For a (North American and European) critical perspective that tends always toward some form of auteurism, toward a celebration of individualism and heroic genius, the fundamentally political preconditions of cinematic achievement in Latin America may seem beside the point. But they have been very much the point throughout the history of the New Latin American Cinema movement, and continue to be today. Just as Latin American culture is a nexus between nationalism and regional coherence, and the New Latin American Cinema a crossroads of aesthetic innovation and ideological motivation, so too have politically committed filmmakers positioned themselves between individualism and identification with the popular sectors.

II.

The early years of the New Latin American Cinema were characterized by a neorealist style adapted to meet Latin American needs and realities. Objecting to the long-dominant Hollywood style of studio shooting and seamlessly composed narratives, the artists of the New Latin American Cinema immersed themselves in the opposite. Freeing the camera from its confinement and isolation, the eye of this political movement roamed the streets. Instead of the customary replication of the Hollywood studio system, nonprofessional actors replaced the stars. The preoccupations of a leisure class, and the presentation of a sanitized history, were replaced by the here-and-now, historical reclamations, the lives of a class that had not seen itself reflected in the cinema. It was an oppositional cinema at every level, self-consciously searching out new forms for the new sentiments of a Latin American reality just being recovered. It was a cinema dedicated to decolonialization, at every level including, frequently, that of cinematic language. A cinema of necessity, it was different things in different countries: in Cuba, an "imperfect cinema"; in Brazil, an "aesthetics of hunger"; in Argentina, a "third cinema."

As the first films appeared on U.S. and European screens, their image was imprinted on the critics who, just discovering Latin American cinema, would name them classics. Even in the beginning, however, the New Latin American Cinema was more complex than such a unilateral model would indicate. In Brazil, for example, the eloquent grittiness of the neorealist cinema was paralleled by the baroque mysticism of Glauber Rocha (to take just one example). In Cuba, Tomás Gutiérrez Alea was to make *Memorias de subdesarrollo*, but he had also made *Las doce sillas*, a madcap comedy, six years earlier. Only one year after *La hora de los hornos* was made in Argentina, Brazilian director Joaquim Pedro de Andrade made *Macunaíma*, a film which drew on a Brazilian visionary Modernist novel to create a film that was anti-rational, anarchistic, and fantastical in its mix of folkloric and pop-culture iconography.

Were this not enough, consider the example of Fernando Birri. For years, the legendary film *Tire dié* was considered the prime example of the New Latin American Cinema movement due to its unprecedented portrayal of marginal life among the trash-pickers of Santa Fe and the boys who ran along the train trestles, risking or suffering an early death for a few pennies tossed by wealthier travelers from the comfort of their railroad cars. Birri's reputation and the birthright of New Latin American Cinema rested on this work. Shortly after making *Tire dié*, however, Birri made another film: *Los inundados*.[10] The railroad motif reappears, inverted, because this time around Birri made a comedy—a comedy about the homeless and dispossessed. *Los inundados* is important because it establishes an initial parallel development internal to New Latin American Cinema that would be unacknowledged in the First World reception to the movement's new film strategies and aesthetic evolutions. It testifies to the *joie de vivre* of a cinematic movement that became more acceptable (perhaps more marketable) when it could be packaged as the testimony of victims or the exoticism of underdevelopment.

III.

Suggesting a redefinition of appropriate subject and style for the New Latin American Cinema of today, Latin American filmmakers rightly contend that "there is no aesthetics without politics." I would argue that the reverse is also true: each political moment demands a specific aesthetic strategy. The 1980s have been very different from the 1960s, and so are the films. Current concerns and strategies are visible in a trio of key films from the past (specifically *La negra Angustias* from Mexico in 1949, *Los inundados* from Argentina in 1962, and *De cierta manera* from Cuba in 1974). Each film was an anomaly, particularly since two of the filmmakers were women, a startling amendment to the virtually all-male pantheon of the New Latin American Cinema. Clearly, the project of this article is the construction of a revisionist history.

In 1949, the Mexican director Matilde Landeta made her second feature film, *La negra Angustias*.[11] This was a contradictory period for women in Mexico: the Cárdenas presidency (1934–1940) was a time of immense progressive movement, land reform, an opening up of society—and the denial of the vote to women, due to Cárdenas's fear that women would represent a reactionary force and vote against him. It would be 1953 before women obtained the right to vote in Mexico.[12]

Landeta created a film in which the daughter of a famous revolutionary is ostracized for her refusal to marry and her insistence on maintaining her manly *marimacho* attributes long past adolescence. After the death of her father, she becomes a revolutionary in her own right. Yet the film turns the codes of revolutionary cinema upside down: the scenes of heroic action turn out not to fit so naturally with a woman protagonist, and the true passion and drama of the film increasingly occur, not between revolutionary fighters and a corrupt government, but in the battles between men and women.

The film's most notable battle occurs in two parts: a would-be rapist's assault on Angustias, and her later revenge when she captures him and has him castrated (off-screen). The greatest struggle takes place, not on a battlefield, but on the field of emotions, as Angustias struggles to differentiate her role as a woman from that of a leader of men, and seeks to find a way out of the trap in which her purportedly female heart has landed her. Thus, the film's dramatic line is drawn consistently along the ground of sexuality, as Angustias seeks over and over to reconcile competing gender identities and demands.

Apart from its prescient attention to race and gender, roles and contradictions, *La negra Angustias* is unusual for its ending, which leaves Angustias strong, active, and fighting still after her momentary surrender to the subjugation of romantic love. In an era when Mexican cinema routinely relegated women to positions of subservience—if not throughout the film, then certainly in its final scenes—this was a radical break. If, as Jean Franco has suggested, films such as these (made by El Indio Fernández et al.) were key to a national agenda for a family model within which women were subservient, then Landeta's film has a landmark political importance. She laid the groundwork for the Latin American women's films of the 1980s, which began to incorporate women's struggles for identity and autonomy as a necessary part of a truly contemporary New Latin American Cinema.

In Argentina in 1962, when Fernando Birri was installed in what was in retrospect a temporary bastion, his film school of Santa Fe, he conceived *Los inundados*, mentioned above. The film's most striking feature is Birri's insistence on joy, his emphasis on the vital subjectivities that characterized the squatter colony and the family's buoyant responses to its sequence of reversals. Equally important is the film's creation of particularized characters who do not so much as stand in for "types," let alone archetypes, but rather manifest marked identities, an expansion of individualism rather than a denial of it. With this film, Birri shifted the terms in which the downtrodden of society had been viewed, exchanging the singular term of "the people" for the third-person plural, persons, so seldom used rhetorically. In this sense, Birri created the preconditions necessary for the attention to subjectivity characteristic of the New Latin American Cinema of the 1980s.

Moving as did Birri from documentary to fiction, but in quite a different context, Cuban director Sara Gómez made *De cierta manera* in 1974 (due to her death during post-production and damage to the negative, the film wasn't released until 1978).[13] The film makes its points formally and ideologically, using documentary and fiction against each other, interrupting its own melodrama to insert an intertitle introducing "a real person in this movie" or intercutting a social worker's smug summations with documentary footage to delegitimate her. Its story of a love affair between Yolanda and Mario becomes the story of the couple's sociocultural formations and deformations in terms of the differences between the bourgeois class and marginal class, blacks and whites, men and women, official prescriptions and subcultural traditions—a story, in short, of unresolved contradictions. In the end, Yolanda must learn how to deal respectfully with the children and mothers in the "marginal" neighborhood where she's teaching, while Mario must decide whether to expose an unregenerate friend who has cut out of his factory job to shack up with a girlfriend, claiming to be at his mother's hospital bedside.

Long exemplary for its formal innovations, *De cierta manera* becomes important, in the context of this overall history, for its challenge—posed in both psychological and experiential terms—to ideological and sociological assumptions. Gómez systematically refutes Revolutionary platitudes and politically correct analyses in favor of depicting the full scope of life in the black and "lumpen" neighborhoods she knew so well. Virtually the only woman ever to direct a feature film in Cuba, she offers clear critiques of *machismo* and the consequences of male pride.

Combining humor with documentary-like exposé, Gómez repeats Birri's achievement in claiming the strengths of both. Focusing on both race and gender, she follows Landeta's success in initiating a narrative examination of both. Perhaps *De cierta manera*, in its assessment of problems neither caused by nor cured by the Revolution, but fast becoming endemic to its existence, is the first "post-Revolutionary" Cuban film. In this sense, it demonstrates an early awareness of a potential disjunction between the portrayal of the individual and that of society, with an influential demonstration that new aesthetic alternatives would have to be investigated for this trajectory to continue.

All three films—*La negra Angustias, Los inundados, De cierta manera*—share a refusal to attribute "otherness" to subjects formerly marked as such, accompanied by a commitment to the narrative inscription of an "other" selfhood, identity, and subjectivity. In this sense, all three share a contemporaneity with our current concerns that lift them even further out of the historical moment of their making, in which, at any rate, they were so anomalous, each in its own very different national and historical context.

If the period of the early New Latin American Cinema movement was strongly identified with the reclaiming of the dispossessed and with the portrayal of the sweep of history, in both ideological and folkloric terms— and if exceptions to this tendency, like the three mentioned here, were either written out of the histories or perceived as solitary exceptions— then it is fitting that the current phase of the New Latin American Cinema should follow the lead of these films, turning away from the epic toward the chronicle, a record of a time in which no spectacular events occur but in which the extraordinary nature of the everyday is allowed to surface. Its films mark a shift from "exteriority" to "interiority." In place of the explicitly and predictably political, at the level of labor or agrarian struggles or mass mobilization, we often find an attention to the implicitly political, at the level of banality, fantasy, and desire, and a corresponding shift in aesthetic strategies. Such a shift has also, not coincidentally, opened up the field to women.

The move from exteriority to interiority holds implications for our sense of individualism and collectivity. The new films advance a reclaiming of the individual (which can hold either progressive or reactionary consequences, as the very concept and practice of individualism carries the potential for either direction). In today's New Latin American Cinema, the old phrase "the personal is political" can almost be heard, murmuring below the surface. Its expression, however, is not a privatized one at all but very much social, political, public.

The films of the New Latin American Cinema of the 1980s are engaged in the creation, in cinematic terms, of what I would term a "collective subjectivity." They are concerned, nearly obsessed, with a new form of looking inward that offers the possibility of a radical break with the past, with an approach that can put on the screen, now for the first time, the interior world of persons whose lives first reached these same screens, in their stage of struggle, more than thirty years ago.

And the reasons for such a redirection? Just as the earlier development of the movement had its roots in the political climates of the distinct nation-states that pass for a single entity under the misleading term of Latin America, and which do nevertheless have a common unity in spite of their different cultures and histories, so too do the films of the 1980s reflect the political circumstances of the continent at the time of their making. The early 1980s were a time of sweeping change for a number of Latin American countries. In Cuba, the Mariel exodus led to changes and reassessments. In Argentina, the defeat of the military in the Malvinas led to an end of military rule and a new elected government. In Brazil, the military surrendered power through a national process instituting a constitutional government. In Uruguay, too, the years of dictatorship came to an end. And in Venezuela, the end of the oil boom shifted society from largesse to shortfall.

To be sure, the democracies that have superseded military rule in Argentina, Brazil, and Uruguay may well be pseudo-democracies, unstable and vulnerable to both military and economic pressures. Many in the hemisphere are rightly suspicious of the U.S. agenda behind the election panacea. Even more to the point, the crisis in Latin America today is more apt to center on the economic than the governmental, as the foreign debt becomes a sinister updated name for imperialism. Even so, the 1980s were indisputably different from the 1960s, and filmmakers—even those veterans who continued to work and produce films throughout this brief history of the New Latin American Cinema—demonstrated in their narrative strategies that they knew the difference.

IV.

When a dictatorship falls, the people become great devourers of culture. They need to exorcise the horror.
—Beatriz Guido[14]

As political frameworks change, from anti-fascist to post-fascist, for example, an oppositional cinema inherits the same obligation to change as do the oppositional parties in the electoral sector. In this new environment, a cinema which turns inward and which begins to enable viewers to construct an alternate relationship—not only with their government but with an authentic sense of self—is an indispensable element in the evolution of a new sociopolitical environment. Slogans, pamphlets, and organizing have been key to political change; character, identity, empathy, and, most important, a sense of personal agency now are of equal importance to political evolution.

It could perhaps be argued that the democratic (or pseudo-democratic) process has itself become the foremost aesthetic influence on contemporary New Latin American Cinema, given its shift in emphasis from the "revolutionary" to the "revelatory." Just as oppositional political action demanded one kind of cinema, so does the individual's open participation in a newly legitimatized form of government demand another. To quote a young Brazilian critic, Joao Carlos Velho, from the *Jornal do Brasil*: the "aesthetics of hunger" of *cinema novo* has given way to a "hunger for aesthetics."[15] Similarly, an Argentine actress at the women's symposium of the International Festival of New Latin American Cinema in Havana in 1986 told of the explosion of new body workshops and body-therapy classes then taking place, as people tried to discharge the years of repression literally, physically, from their bodies. In this same period, an article appeared in the *New York Times* detailing the therapy methods being employed to ease the pain of the children of the disappeared, concluding that the most effective therapeutic intervention thus far had been the coming of democracy, because it allowed the telling of secrets necessary to drain the political—and emotional—wounds.

The telling of secrets is an important theme in recent works of the New Latin American Cinema. In Argentina in 1987, the young filmmaker Carlos Echeverría used the documentary form to try to dig up secrets that were no longer welcome in a society more intent on creating a picture of so-called normalization. His *Juan: Como si nada hubiera sucedido* set out to investigate the case of one disappeared youth. In the film, a young radio journalist, alter ego to the disappeared youth, fronts for the filmmaker as they journey through Argentine society like the most dogged of detectives, interviewing on camera all the surviving principals of the original scenario. The film's grim lesson is that secrets are liberating only to the extent that they imply some action, to the extent that they are examined and not just buried once again. In this film, however, there is no happy ending, no "truth" to be uncovered, only a persistent trail of deception and subterfuge leading up to the *punto final* ruling that ensured future immunity for the military.

Similarly, Eduardo Coutinho's *Twenty Years After* (*Cabra Marcado Para morrer*, 1984) could not function without the telling of a major secret: the identity of a legendary figure in the history of labor struggles (the widow of a martyred union leader who has been in hiding under an assumed identity for twenty years), whom Coutinho and his camera crew track down. Coutinho pushes his unearthing of secrets from the publicly political to the familial, finally tracking down her children and investigating the emotional consequences of the military repression that fractured the family.

The film was the hit of the first Rio film festival in 1984, and was awarded a standing ovation just at the moment of the transition to democracy. Significantly, Coutinho makes the telling of private secrets as important as the public ones and, in so doing, reflects the increased emphasis on the personal that is so central a feature of the current wave of New Latin American Cinema.

Raúl Tosso's *Gerónima* mixes documentary with fiction to expose another kind of secret: the survival of Indians despite the official proclamation in Argentina of their extinction. By describing in visceral detail the incarceration and interrogation of Gerónima and her children in a hospital for the singular sin of living a non-assimilationist life marked by Indian customs, Tosso makes his point that ethnocide is as bad as genocide. He inscribes the private as a sphere of struggle, particularly since all that is meant by "cultural" is sequestered within the unstable receptacle of individual identity. The point is made particularly chilling by two aspects of the film: first, the role of Gerónima Sande is played by an actress who is herself a member and activist of the same tribe (the Mapuches) to which Gerónima belonged; and second, the soundtrack is composed predominantly of Gerónima's voice, taped during her interrogation sessions by the hospital personnel. Here, then, psychic alienation is equated with, and leads to, death.

The uncovering of secrets in these films is one aspect of the move toward "interiority," but it is carried further away from the concrete and into the imaginary by the fiction films of the decade. In the recent Busi Cortés feature, *El secreto de Romelia*, the secret turns out to be a quintessentially feminine one: virginity itself. Based on a Corín Tellado story, the film charts the costly collision (for the woman, of course) between the cult of female virginity and the cult of male honor. Cortés demonstrates to what extent women filmmakers can rework/imagine even the classic scenarios of family, purity, and revenge.

It is in the arena of fiction that the influence of women directors and feminist ideas regarding behavior, gesture, and pacing is most pronounced. Interiority in this sense is not a retreat from society, but an altered formal engagement. New social orders mandate a narrative cinema that constructs a new spectator, both through deploying processes of identification and through the structuring of new formal strategies; while the first has been more widespread than the second, both may be found represented in the New Latin American Cinema of the 1980s.

From this perspective, Suzana Amaral's *Hora da estrela* is a key work.

Her subject may be classically oppositional (story of a downtrodden north-easterner who comes to the big city and has the life smashed out of her) but her treatment owes nothing to historical or sociological perspectives:

> What's important is what's behind people, the interior life (. . .) The facts may be important, but what's more important is what's behind the facts. (. . .) My film shows that poor people also have fantasies, that they, too, dream and want to be stars.[16]

Her central character in the film, Macabea, is a regendered update and revision of the above-mentioned *Macunaíma:* her inchoate self becomes both a metaphor and a concrete representation of Brazil. For Macabea isn't just an anti-hero, she's virtually an anti-character in a film that Amaral has termed "anti-melodrama." Macabea has a terrible job that she performs terribly; marginal or exploitative relationships with her co-workers, roommates, and boyfriend; a terror, awe, attraction, and repulsion of/to men; and a fearsome faith in the detritus of modern consumer culture.

Amaral explicitly critiques the role of mass culture in the lives of the disenfranchised, showing, for example, the rush of Macabea and her roommates to watch the daily *telenovela* through the window of a neighbor's adjoining apartment. Similarly, she represents the reality of lumpen consciousness through its mass-media determinant: Radio Reloj, a station that constantly broadcasts meaningless information which Macabea, its devoted listener, repeats throughout the film. Amaral uses the film's ending (Macabea's hallucination of herself at the moment of her death—as a *telenovela* heroine) to summarize the effects of underdevelopment, neo-colonialism, and the mass media. Macabea embraces this pop-culture fantasy as her last will and desire, but because of its very origins, such a fantasy can be nothing other than obscene . . . and fatal.

One scene in the film signifies most unambiguously the distance traveled emotionally and ideologically from the early years to the present: it is the one in which Macabea orchestrates a moment alone in her room, illicitly, during the day. Locking herself in, she turns up her beloved radio, swings the sheet off her bed, and begins to dance around the room. It is her first moment of solitude, probably unlikely to recur for a hundred years, and it's represented with all the desperate urgency of a commodity. It is also Macabea's first moment of experiencing the self, the person who had never had the luxury of taking shape before. In her alternation between feeling and seeing (herself in the mirror), listening and luxuriating, she presents the audience with a scene of victory every bit as glorious, as liberating in its implications, as heroic in its triumph, as those reflected in the films of the 1960s. This moment of self-identification and self-definition, in a space that feels at first like a vacuum for its removal from the domain of pseudo-information that has permeated Macabea's environment, is emblematic of the new cinematic direction that is becoming so marked, yet still so unremarked, by First World critics or audiences.

Other films made by Latin American women directors in the 1980s further strengthen the case for seeing emotional life as a site of struggle and identity equal to those more traditional sites by which the New Latin American Cinema was once, and continues to be, defined. Tizuka Yamasaki is an interesting case in point, for her *Patriamada* (1985) tries mixing documentary with fiction to get at the emotions behind events.[17] Filming at the time that all of Brazil was debating its transition to a civilian government, Yamasaki took three actors along on all her shoots of mass public events and historic meetings, and managed to insert her own melodrama into the proceedings. Her film, which illustrates just how contradictory the codes of fiction and documentary can be from one another, insists upon the equality of private and public, man and woman, the sexual and the political. Taking this insistence to the extreme, the film posits the planning of a baby and the planning of a government as mutually metaphoric.

Thus, it may be no accident that María Luisa Bemberg was filming *Camila* as democracy came to Argentina in mid-shoot. *Camila* pointedly redefined the site of political struggle as the sexual, in her interpretation of the famous story of an aristocratic young woman and a priest, whose love affair presented the ultimate challenge to the repressive patriarchalism of their day and whose ultimate murder proved the equation between sexuality and liberation inherent in the narrative. By seeing the sexual struggle as one on an equal plane with other kinds of ideological struggle, Bemberg was able to include women in the ranks of heroes and freedom-fighters without falling prey to the contradictions with which the character of Angustias, years earlier, in Mexico, had to contend. In this case, the radical shift in the area of inquiry was not accompanied by a parallel formal shift but rather by a dedication to creating seamless art cinema (lush, transparent, and perfect periodicity) in the service of a new idea.

Similarly, Bemberg's *Miss Mary* (1986) situated rebellion in the realm of sexuality, both for the children of the aristocrats that a governess (played by Julie Christie) is brought to oversee and for the repressed British governess herself. The plot concerns the self-realization of the governess and the coming of age of her charges, set within the world of wealthy Anglophile Argentines on the eve of World War II. The elaboration of the girls' sexual identity and the patriarchal modes of its repression are explicitly made parallel to the rise of Peronism by Bemberg's intercutting of archival footage in the midst of otherwise flawless art-direction. For Bemberg, women are the lynchpin in the ongoing battle between repression and liberation, a battle which she views atomistically as launched inside the family to explode throughout society. In this film, then, menstruation is trauma, sexual acts involve psychic risk, and Peronism is built in the bedrooms of the nation.

In Mexico at a time when there was as yet no sign on the horizon of any fracture in the endless fortification of PRI, the party seemingly sworn to rule the country forever, Paul Leduc fractured cinematic traditions with *Frida* (1985). The film emerged from this very traditional national film-making tradition to call into question its comfortable assumptions, both cinematic and ideological. Leduc's film was inspired by the life of Frida Kahlo, an artist whose reputation today is an accurate index of the difference made by recent feminist scholarship and the reevaluation of art history hierarchies. This difference, precisely that between the public and private, parallels exactly the shift being described herein from the early days of the New Latin American Cinema movement to the present and is echoed interestingly by Leduc's own evolution from the public canvas of *Reed: México insurgente* (1971) to the private one of *Frida*.

Frida Kahlo is now known for a variety of reasons: revered painter, wife of Diego Rivera, victim of physical disabilities caused by accident, intimate of Leon Trotsky, supporter of the Communist party, wearer of Indian costume, collector of folk art, lover of her own sex. Leduc chose to eschew none of this and to subordinate no one part to the demands of the other. He followed the lead taken by so many historians of submerged "others" and relied, not on the obfuscating texts but, rather, on what he termed "the history of gossip" to compose the details of her life. Even more radically, he chose to reprise Kahlo's commitment to the visual, basing his film in image, color, gesture, and sensuality instead of the relentless dialogue more common to Mexican cinema.

Probably the most formally daring of the recent films here enumerated, *Frida* as a project carries a particular ideological importance as well. Kahlo's paintings were long ignored or undervalued precisely because they represented woman, the body, a gendered pain, a psychic split. At a time when politically correct art pictured workers (not braces or babies) and when the acceptable scale was massive and public (that is, murals) not small and enclosed, the paintings of Frida Kahlo were doomed to be dismissed as an eccentric avocation, the irrelevant pastime of an otherwise politically committed person who, alas, was born female. Given the evolution from exteriority to interiority that this article seeks to describe, Paul Leduc could hardly have chosen a more relevant subject. He is aware of the implications of his choice: "Frida was closed up in her body, in her house, in her studio. In the midst of all these *noises* of her time (the politics, the demonstrations, in which she also took part), there was her expressive silence. Of images."[18] By according Frida Kahlo's journey inward a place in history equal to that of John Reed's journey outward, Leduc cast his hat into the ring of a bold revisionism committed to replacing the epic with the chronicle and to synthesizing a new sense of pleasure with the pain that has been present all along.

Jorge Toledo's *Vera*, made in Brazil later (1987) in the democratization process than Bemberg's films, fits well onto the trajectory pioneered by Leduc since it carries the examination of sexual identity as political act even further. Taking as its starting point the release of a young woman from an orphanage/reform school, Toledo's film traces Vera's life backward and forward as she attempts to unravel her particular riddle of gender and reinvent herself, literally, as a man. Her ambition survives the sadistic prison administrator's attempt to humiliate her and her kind: "I'm concerned about this butch-girl business. . . . Okay, you're so butch, let's see your pricks." He tries to topple the standards by setting up dances with a brother institution, importing real boys to dance with the femmes. Meanwhile, the girls discuss among themselves the ambiguity of life outside the joint, where guaranteed butch-girls have been known to get knocked up.

In her total isolation, self-invention, alienation, and hopelessness, the character of Vera (based in part upon an actual woman who came out of a similar joint, wrote poetry and the story of her life, and killed herself) has much in common with the everywoman figure of Macabea. Taking antihero as heroine, Toledo anchors his tragedy in the details of gender identity and sexual structuring. It is a drama that is specifically, achingly, female. It is a drama that is concerned most fundamentally, not with action, but with language itself: at the keyboard of the word processor, Vera meets a defeat as total as she met in the bed. Yet, nonetheless, Toledo never quite abandons metaphor, the possibility that Vera represents not only a woman, not exactly a lesbian, not just a woman who wants to be a man, but perhaps Brazil itself—the country that emerged so recently from prison, unsure of its identity, formed and deformed by its captivity, cast so adrift in the land of object-choice that its own desires are opaque, unspoken, transgressive but unattainable. *Vera* orchestrates its erotic tension so successfully that finally the struggle for gender definition seems to the viewer as worthy of respect as any other fight in the Latin American struggle for self-determination.

V.

We fought for the people to have a right to education, a right to housing, a right to food, but forgot that people also have el derecho a la alegria, the right to joy.

—Ruy Guerra[19]

If Paul Leduc can be seen to have made a film that is nearly the opposite of the one that first established him in the canon of the New Latin American Cinema, how much more so Fernando E. Solanas, *auteur* of the classic of Third World revolutionary theory, *La hora de los hornos,* who went on to make, of all things, musicals: *Tangos: El exilio de Gardel* (1985) and the recent *Sur* (1987). In *Sur,* as in Toledo's film, prison plays a central role. This time, however, in a thematic strategy that would seem to invert Solanas's early tenets, he posits as the central drama not the released man's political re-engagement but how and whether he'll be able to reclaim his emotional life by forgiving his wife her infidelity during his years in jail. It is the private life which is assigned priority; now the emotions demand as much commitment, engagement, and action as events did a few decades earlier.

Solanas thus takes the notion of interiority and transforms it into an aesthetic. The urban landscape of Buenos Aires is made artificial, its streets a cityscape of the soul, a theatrical space in which memories and longings can be enacted. The film's drama is an interior one made exterior, as the protagonist passes his long first night of freedom debating the figures of his imagination on street corners suffused with the mysterious smoke and fog of memory.

After years of exile, Solanas was able to return at last to Argentina to continue his filmmaking. Back at the time of *La hora de los hornos,* it would have been the spirit of Che or Perón that presided over Argentina. Now, with *Sur,* it is the spirit of Carlos Gardel—redolent of nostalgia, romance, feeling—that Solanas chooses to enshrine. The time in jail was matched to the political activity that preceded it; the future is tied to acts of emotional restoration that can activate the feelings shut down during years of military rule.

Ruy Guerra, the Brazilian director who like Solanas is identified with the early golden age of New Latin American Cinema and in his case specifically the foundations of *cinema novo*, also returned from long exile to make a musical. His *Opera do Malandro* mixes romance and rebellion, this time in the unlikely setting of Brecht's *Threepenny Opera*, rescripted for the underworld of Rio on the eve of World War II and rescored by Chico Buarque. Ruy Guerra defends his move from post-neorealism to musical: "opera is a political form." The late Manuel Octavio Gómez would agree. His penultimate film, and Cuba's first musical, *Patakín*, paid homage to the subcultural powers of *santería* with ritual characters who acted out the oldest struggles of all: man versus woman, good versus bad, industry versus sloth, all coded to signify commentary on the state of the Cuban revolution in the 1980s.

The contemporary search for the meaning of pleasure and the pleasure of meaning in a post-fascist or post-revolutionary or post-economic boom society reaches a suggestive apotheosis in *Best Wishes*, a recent film by Brazilian director Teresa Trautman. Here, numerous themes already activated by other Latin American directors take an even more surprising form than the recyling of the musical: melodrama, nearly soap opera, reclaimed. Like many of her fellow filmmakers, Trautman concerns herself with the telling of secrets, the breaking of prohibition, the speaking of the unspeakable. Like fellow Brazilian Toledo, she situates sexual construction at the center of political life.

Best Wishes takes a formulaic pace and structure—an artistocratic family gathering at its summer estate for one last weekend before mother sells it off, complete with a long cathartic night in which secrets are revealed and couples realigned—and sneaks ideological meaning into the mix. She makes explicit her insistence upon challenging the old order of political priorities with a new gender agenda which combines a transgressively female comic sense with an ephiphanic revelation that disrupts the previous patriarchal order. The film's central family is dedicated to the memory of its favorite son, a *desaparecido* who vanished during the years of military rule. When the daughter of the lifelong family groundskeeper, drunk and panicked over where she and her aged father and adolescent daughter will live after this last night, finally reveals the identity of her daughter's father—he turns out to be this very same beloved son, who had raped her, those many years ago. This is dangerous stuff, mixing political messages into the genre of sex comedy, but it suggests how far the New Latin American Cinema has come in reconsidering its own issues and history from new perspectives.

Certainly the presence of women directors where almost none had ever tread is a factor in this reconsideration. If *Best Wishes* took the figure of the *desaparecido* and insisted on a revision of his idealization from a gendered perspective, then a recent dramatic documentary can be seen to take a related step—the gendering of assassination and torture, through the testimony of women survivors.

In *Que Bom Te Ver Viva* (1989), Brazilian director Lúcia Murat focuses upon a figure that must itself embody a contradiction in the Latin American context: the figure (in sense of the representative as well as the body itself) of the woman guerilla fighter who survives martyrdom to speak.[20] And speak she does, as the director interviews a number of women, former militants in the armed struggle against the military dictatorship, who'd been captured, jailed, tortured, and managed to survive "without going crazy." The documentary mixes direct interview footage, usually conducted on videotape, with footage of the women contextualized within their daily lives, older footage of their lives in the period of the dictatorship (sometimes limited to newspaper headlines of their capture), home movies of one of the women in jail, and the women's reflections both on that period and on contemporary attitudes toward them in post-military Brazil.

Ironically, this explicit attempt to write gender into the survival narratives is the one that fails: the use of an actress to address the camera which is, variously, torturer, lover, friend, or audience, and to speak the unspoken. The unspoken turns out to be, as one survivor puts it during her interview, not the mechanics of torture, which are by now so well known, but rather the emotional mechanics of survival, the literal subjectivity of the tortured. It is the riskier testimony of love, sex, intimacy, and social nicety that director Murat, in a gesture no doubt of emotional identification with her subjects, puts into the mouth of a well-known actress to present to the audience, thereby avoiding the added disapproval that would have met such pronouncements by any nonfictional woman.

Perhaps it is the acting style (overwrought, stagey, arch-ironic) that dooms the strategy, but it is just as likely that the very taboos that Murat sought to bypass return nonetheless to sabotage the detour. For if the figure of the woman fighter is always, in patriarchal societies, an oxymoron, then the fact of any woman's survival (not, Tania-style, her martyrdom) becomes a triple contradiction when she is converted into the mother and, in fact, bases her claim to sanity and survival upon that same motherhood.

As Murat tries to demolish the very constructions of myth that have been the habitual last resort of reaction to such figures, she occasionally founders. Nevertheless, the testimony of her subjects speaking almost transparently to the audience across a wide range of devices of attempted distanciation moves the viewer with long-dormant inspiration. *Que Bom Te Ver Viva* re-genders the *guerrillera* and, in the process, poses a series of retroactive questions to the historical construction of the male hero.

VI.

An idea about the cinema that reigned when we began on this road is today dead. . . . We need to look collectively toward the future. As cinema becomes an extinct dinosaur, lizards and salamanders appear that survive the catastrophe. Today, facing reconversion and crisis, the response must be to include the species. It must derive from collective action and solidarity. . . . We have a lot to do. To survive. Yes. To survive not only as filmmakers or videomakers, but as cultures, as exemplars of national dignity.

—Paul Leduc[21]

In the 1980s, national debt is the biggest problem. . . . It would seem we've gone backwards, as though we haven't made any progress. It may seem that the 1960s were radical, and the 1980s regressive. . . . The danger now is an attempt to make a "more perfect" cinema to try to attract a public. It's a danger because politics cannot regress, but cinema can.

—Julio García Espinosa[22]

The conference in Bellagio which occasioned this chapter had hardly begun before we participants were spending our spare time, huddled in the library, trying to translate from the Italian papers the news of the food riots that had broken out in Venezuela. In Venezuela! It shattered all the fondest stereotypes of Latin American stability. So much for the vaunted promise of democracy, when faced with the international pincers of economic shortfall and IMF negotiations. Notions of self-determination had already been crushed, anyway, with PRI's theft of the Mexican election just months before. Soon after the Venezuela debacle, Brazil witnessed the murder of Chico Mendes and the intensification of the Amazon crisis, Cuba underwent the disaster of the Ochoa revelations (and the ongoing, equally serious, challenge of its government's seige-like response to *perestroika* and *glasnost*), and Argentina suffered its own food riots, an unimaginable inflation rate, and the election of Menem, its contemporary

Peronist president. The last year of the decade turned out to be a costly one for the continent. Within each country, the economics confronting film production are disastrous: local markets that can no longer return the investment necessary for late-1980s budgets, plans that require international stars and co-production money to get off the ground, movie theaters that are closing down by the hundreds as a combination of videocassette distribution and operating costs make them unprofitable.

The 1980s were a time for optimism regarding the revision and re-invention of the New Latin American Cinema in a contemporary guise. The breaking of taboo and prohibition, the freeing of the imagination to fantasy, a respect for the mundane and everyday, the introduction of humor and music, the construction of new narrative strategies, and the reconsideration of the relationship to the audience have all contributed to what I've identified as the monumental task of forging a new "collective subjectivity." While I've chosen to interpret these tendencies optimistically, I could also make another point about the less salutary effects of a certain kind of individualism at the level of *auteur*.

In tracing the kind of strategies that have become necessary in the wake of the declining film economies of Latin America and the loss of self-sufficiency they have brought about, I would identify as significant the recent alliance between a traditional, essentially conservative, form of authorship and a traditional, international form of co-production. The *Amores difíciles* was a series, mentioned earlier, based upon ideas or scripts by Gabriel García Márquez, utilizing the talents of notable Latin American or Spanish filmmakers, and produced by and for Spanish television. The deal, jokingly referred to as the "return of the conquistadors,"[23] got terrific ratings on its Spanish broadcast, and has won limited festival inclusion as well as theatrical and public television release (with video release pending).

Some of the films are excellent, but there are numerous problems with the series, not least of which is the absence of a single woman director in the lineup of filmmakers.[24] The very real danger of such a series is that it tends to remove any political specificity from the works that comprise it. Packaged as a Gabriel García Márquez commodity, it falls easily into the co-production pattern: the novelist is just slotted into the attraction slot in place of a famous actor. Just so are the qualities of individual national cinemas subordinated to the creation of a homogenous product, one that often (and predictably, given its *raison d'être*) valorizes the novelistic qualities of cinema by valuing the screenplay over all other elements. Obscuring questions of intentionality and urgency, *Amores difíciles* sells itself as a product on the marketable *don Gabo*. Meanwhile, the dependence of the entire package upon García Márquez's participation gives him inordinate control over the contracting of principals and the handling of the treatments.[25]

The threat of such packaging under the sign of a single personality is that, should its success and the concomitant lack of financial alternatives lead to a proliferation, the New Latin American Cinema could enter a baroque phase: historical subjects would no longer be chosen for their particular ideological implications for a particular country at this juncture, contemporary fictional themes would no longer arise out of the specificity of an identifiable set of national circumstances, documentary would be decisively marginalized and no longer inhabit any place at all, and the very real heterogeneity that has always made "Latin America" itself such a near-fictional construct would vanish under the homogeneity of brandname magic realism flying a multinational banner.[26] Still, given economic forces arrayed against cinema (and life itself, sheer survival) in most of Latin America, it is not surprising that most filmmakers are grateful that Gabriel García Márquez is committed to film production and that Spanish television has seen fit to bankroll his film ideas. With Spanish television recently poised to expand this entry into a large-scale agenda of co-productions, similar fears regarding the influence of such European input must again be weighed against the necessity for just such marketing and financing strategies if the New Latin American Cinema is to survive to the turn of the century (at least Spanish money doesn't demand English as the production language).

Meanwhile, the influence of the political and economic situation in each Latin American country continues to affect its cinema far more forcefully and decisively than any co-production deal could ever dream of. In Argentina, on the eve of Menem's election, not a single film was in production thanks to the hyper-inflation ravaging the economy. In Chile, on the other hand, in the wake of the "no" vote in favor of ending Pinochet's reign, the strength of its recent cinema is starting to attract notice at film festivals internationally. The school established by Birri and García Márquez in Cuba already has its own victories and problems, its own student insurrections, and the energy of a new generation of filmmakers from throughout Latin America.

Such a constantly evolving situation demands an improvisational rigor from Latin American filmmakers, but equally demands that critics and audiences outside of Latin America give up their attachment to outmoded scales of value in assessing the cinemas that emerge from such conditions.

La lucha continúa, the struggle continues, but the site of the battle and the choice of weapons changes by the decade. The New Latin American Cinema is dead, long live the New Latin American Cinema.

Notes

A previous version of this chapter was commissioned for the conference "High Culture/Popular Culture: Media Representation of the Other" held at the Rockefeller Foundation's Bellagio Study and Conference Center in Bellagio, Italy, February 27 to March 4, 1989. The proceedings of the conference are published in the book *Other Representations: Cross-Cultural Media Theory,* ed. by John G. Hanhardt and Steven D. Levine.

The original inspiration for the chapter was the massive retrospective "The Winds of Change," organized by the Toronto Festival of Festivals in September 1986, and the women's symposium at the International Festival of New Latin American Cinema in Havana, December 1986. A preliminary version appeared as "After the Revolutions: The New New Latin American Cinema," in the *Village Voice,* February 10, 1987.

My thanks to my fellow participants in the Bellagio conference for their responses to the version of this chapter delivered there from notes, in particular to Tomás Gutiérrez Alea, Julio García Espinosa, Nelson Pereira dos Santos, Jean Franco, Juan Downey, Trinh T. Minh-ha, and Lourdes Portillo. Thanks to Paul Lenti for his subsequent careful reading and helpful suggestions. Finally, thanks to Norma Iglesias Prieto, co-organizer of the conference "Cruzando Fronteras/Crossing Borders," held in November 1990 at the Colegio de la Frontera Norte in Tijuana, Mexico, for creating a forum for this work there; and to my co-participants, especially Rosa Linda Fregoso, Sonia Fritz, Carmen Huaco-Nuzum, Lillian Jímenez, Lillian Liberman, and Patricia Vega, for their support and encouragement.

1. Tomás Gutiérrez Alea, "The Viewer's Dialectic" in *Reviewing Histories: Selections From the New Latin American Cinema,* ed. Coco Fusco (Buffalo, NY: Hallwalls, 1987), p. 179.

2. Panel on New Latin American Cinema, moderated by author, U.S. Film Festival, Park City, Utah, January 26, 1989.

3. Recent writing has begun to take note of this evolution. See, for example: the special "Nuevo Cine Latinoamericano" issue of *Areito* (ed. Lisa Davis and Sonia Rivera), Volume X No. 37, 1984; Pat Aufderheide, "Awake Argentina," *Film Comment,* April 1986, pp. 51–55, and "Cultural Democracy: Non-Commercial Film Distribution in Latin America" *Afterimage,* November 1986, pp. 12ff; Julianne Burton, *Cinema and Social Change in Latin America: Conversations with Filmmakers* (Austin: University of Texas Press, 1986); my own "New Argentine Cinema" essay in the U.S. Film Festival catalog, Park City, Utah, 1988; and most recently, *Latin American Visions* (ed. Pat Aufderheide and Lois Fishman), catalog commissioned for the Latin American Visions retrospective organized by Linda Blackaby and Beatriz Vieira of the Neighborhood Film/Video Project of International House, Philadelphia.

4. Julianne Burton, *Cinema and Social Change in Latin America*, chapters 9 and 19.

5. Luis Elbert, "Neorealism," in *Latin American Visions*, p. 27.

6. Randal Johnson, *Cinema Novo X 5* (Austin: University of Texas Press, 1984), p. 2.

7. For descriptions of this period, see Guillermo Zapiola, "Cinema under Dictatorship" in *Latin American Visions*, pp. 38–39, and Richard Peña, "The Legacy of Cinema Novo: An Interview with Nelson Pereira Dos Santos" in *Reviewing Histories: Selections from New Latin American Cinema*, pp. 51–52.

8. E. Bradford Burns, *Latin American Cinema* (L.A.: UCLA Latin American Center, 1975), p. 27.

9. Similarly, the development of Latin American Cinema in the postwar period cannot be separated from the U.S. embargo of Argentina during World War II, part of then Secretary of State Cordell Hull's overall agenda for overthrowing the Argentine government. In 1942, allegedly punishing Argentina for its neutrality in the war, the U.S. placed an embargo on the shipment of raw film stock to the country, a policy initiated by Nelson Rockefeller's Office for the Coordination of Inter-American Affairs (CIAA) and its Motion Picture Division. At the same time, U.S. interests (including Rockefeller) began investing capital rapidly in Mexico instead. This tactic led to the decline of Argentina as the preeminent film producer to the continent and to the rise of Mexico as its market competitor. See Tim Barnard, "Popular Cinema and Populist Politics" in Barnard (ed.), *Argentine Cinema* (Toronto: Nightwood Editions, 1986), pp. 32–39, and John King, "The Social and Cultural Context" in *The Gardens of Forking Paths: Argentine Cinema* (ed. John King and Nissa Torrents, The British Film Institute, 1987), pp. 1–15.

10. Long unseen and lacking any North American distribution, *Los inundados* was shown for the first time ever with English subtitles at the Toronto Festival of Festivals and Pacific Film Archive in 1986. A 16mm print was struck for the Latin American Visions series by the Neighborhood Film/Video Project, and will be distributed by the Museum of Modern Art Circulating Film Department after its initial tour.

11. Born in 1913, Matilde Landeta was unknown in the U.S. and long ignored in Mexico until "rediscovered" when she came to Havana to attend the women's symposium of 1986, bringing this film under her arm. For a full theoretical discussion of the film itself, as well as the history of its making and of Landeta's career, see: Carmen Huaco-Nuzum, "Matilde Landeta: An Introduction to the Work of a Pioneer Mexican Filmmaker," *Screen*, Volume 28 No. 4, Autumn 1987, p. 96–105. The unsubtitled film was shown for the first time in the U.S. in the "Corrective Cinema" series curated by Yvonne Rainer and Berenice Reynaud at the Collective for Living Cinema in 1988. Marcela Fernández Violante directed a film on Landeta's life for Mexican television in 1983, and subsequently published "Mexican Women Film Directors" in *Voices of Mexico*, No. 6, Dec. 1987–Feb. 1988 (Universidad Nacional Autónoma de México, México City).

12. See Jean Franco's *Plotting Women: Gender and Representation in Mexico* (New York, Columbia UP, 1989) for further discussion of Mexico in this period.

13. The film was completed by Tomás Gutiérrez Alea, who had been Gómez's mentor and has been the most dedicated champion of her memory and her example.

14. Nissa Torrents, "An Interview with Beatriz Guido" in *The Garden of Forking Paths*, op. cit., p. 47.

15. Thanks to Joao Luis Vieira for this citation.

16. Personal interview with author, Toronto Festival of Festivals, September 1986.

17. For an in-depth analysis of both this film and the Coutinho film, see: Julianne Burton, "Transitional States: Creative Complicities with the Real in *Man Marked to Die: Twenty Years Later* and *Patriamada*," *Studies in Latin American Popular Culture*, Volume 7, 1988, pp. 139–55.

18. Personal interview with author, Toronto Festival of Festivals, September 1986.

19. Personal interview with author, Toronto Festival of Festivals, September 1986.

20. The film premiered at the International Festival of New Latin American Cinema in Havana, December 1989, where it received a jury prize; its U.S. premiere took place in spring 1990 at the San Francisco Film Festival.

21. Paul Leduc, "Dinosaurs and Lizards" in *Latin American Visions*, p. 59.

22. Statement in response to this chapter, Bellagio, Italy, 1989, author's notes.

23. "The return of the conquistadors" is taken from comments to me by Helga Stephenson, director of the Toronto Festival of Festivals, as published in my article on the series in the *N.Y. Times* in August 1989.

24. The Venezuelan film *Un domingo feliz (A Happy Sunday)* was originally slated for direction by Fina Torres, who dropped out of the picture, reportedly after irreconcilable differences with García Márquez.

25. This threat is heightened by García Márquez's role as the presiding patriarch of the *Fundación*, which, with offices in Havana and Mexico City, has become the prime hope of Latin American filmmakers in search of production and co-production monies.

26. I'd argue that it's not just coincidence that makes *Milagro en Roma (Miracle in Rome)* the very best of the series. In part due to the extraordinary talent of director Lisandro Duque, its success may also be ascribed to its being the only Colombian production in the series and thus benefiting from a grounding in the specificity of García Márquez's own culture.

IV.

FEMINIST FILM READINGS: PERSONAL POLITICS/SOCIAL POLITICS

A PARALLAX VIEW OF LESBIAN AUTHORSHIP

Judith Mayne

DIANE KURYS'S 1983 film *Coup de foudre* (*Entre Nous*) has a devoted following among many lesbians, despite—or perhaps also because of—the fact that the allusions to lesbianism occur from within the securely defined boundaries of female bonding and friendship.[1] Two women, Léna (played by Isabelle Huppert) and Madeleine (played by Miou-Miou), living in post–World War II provincial France discover an attraction for each other (an attraction that is definitely erotic though never explicitly sexual) and eventually leave their husbands to live together. As was widely publicized at the time of the film's release, the friendship of the two women has a strong autobiographical significance, for it corresponds to the experience of Kurys's own mother. At the conclusion of the film, when Léna (Kurys's mother) asks Michel (Kurys's father, played by Guy Marchand) to leave, their daughter—i.e., the fictional representation of Kurys herself—is seen watching them. Over the final shot of the film, of Madeleine walking with the children on the beach, a title appears, a very literal authorial signature: "My father left at dawn. He never saw my mother again. It's now been two years since Madeleine died. I dedicate this film to the three of them."[2]

The sudden appearance of the author's signature, within the child's point of view, situates the enigma of the women's relationship in the ambiguous world of childish perception. All of Kurys's films are marked by the connection between story telling and a female bond that wavers between the homosocial and the homoerotic. Somewhat surprisingly, perhaps, that connection is most strongly marked and articulated in what appears to be, on the surface, the film that departs the most sharply from the distinctly female world central to Kurys's first three films (*Diablo Menthe* [*Peppermint Soda*], *Coctail Molotov*, and *Entre Nous*). In *A Man in Love* (*Un Homme amoureux*) (1987), the plot centers upon a young actress, Jane (played by Greta Scacchi), whose affair with a narcissistic American movie star, Steve Elliot (played by Peter Coyote), is interwoven with her relationship with her mother (played by Claudia Cardinale), who suffers from and eventually dies of cancer.

While the film follows Jane as its central protagonist, it is not until approximately two-thirds of the way through the film that her voice emerges, quite literally, as the voice of the film, through voice-over commentary. The voice-over is the major component of the film's self-mirroring quality; in the concluding scenes, Jane begins writing a text entitled "A Man in Love." The first appearance of the voice-over occurs immediately after a scene in which Jane, in bed with her lover Steve, speaks—seemingly at his request—a fantasy of lesbian lovemaking. Hence, the conditions of the emergence of the female narrator's voice are bound up, narratively, with the lesbian fantasy, a fantasy which offers, within the logic of the film, the possibility of combining two spheres otherwise separate—heterosexual passion, on the one hand, and the mother-daughter bond, on the other.

Some aspects of Kurys's films offer significant revisions of the components of narrative cinema—such as the rewriting of the boys'-school scenario (central to two classics of French film history, Jean Vigo's *Zéro de conduite* and François Truffaut's *The 400 Blows*) in her first feature film, *Peppermint Soda*, or the exchange of looks between the two women in *Entre Nous*. The self-representation of Kurys (in *Peppermint Soda* and *Entre Nous* in particular) and the representation of female authorship are far more problematic in the present context, for they consistently evoke and dispel lesbianism simultaneously. Put another way, the "lesbianism" affiliated with Kurys's signature is so framed by the duality of heterosexuality on the one hand and the maternal bond on the other that female authorship is foregrounded but not significantly reframed or retheorized outside of that duality.

However, if the popular reception of Kurys's *Entre Nous* by lesbian audiences is any indication, then the film lends itself to the same kind of reading as Barbara Smith offered of *Sula*, a reading based, that is, on the permeable boundaries between female bonding and lesbianism (Smith 1977). This is not to say that *Entre Nous* has been defined in any simple way as a "lesbian film." Indeed, whether Kurys's film is appropriately described as a "lesbian film"—permeable boundaries notwithstanding—has been a matter of some debate among lesbians. In a letter to the editors of *Gossip*, a British lesbian-feminist journal, Lynette Mitchell criticizes two essays published in the journal which represent *Entre Nous* as "an unequivocally lesbian film" (Grundberg n.d.; Whitelaw n.d.). Mitchell notes that in the film, "the two women are shown admiring each other's bodies and at one point in the film they exchange a swift kiss, but this could just as easily be an expression of deep physical affection as erotic desire" (Mitchell n.d., 11–13). In any case, if *A Man in Love* offers the theory (and *Entre Nous* the practice), then the lesbianism evoked in Kurys's work is not only fully compatible with but also fully dependent upon heterosexual fantasy and maternal connections. Put another way, lesbianism is simultaneously a limit and a horizon of female narration and authorship.

In some oddly similar ways, lesbianism is also a limit and a horizon for contemporary feminist work on the female subject. Two of the most common and persistent threads of this work have been, first, the theorizing of a double position for women, as both inside and outside of patriarchal culture, and, second, a staging of what is by now a classic fixture of feminist theory, the encounter between so-called American empiricism and French theory. While feminist theories of the subject and of subjectivity are often criticized by lesbians and women of color for being inattentive to the difference that marginalities make, it's not altogether accurate, at least not in the case of lesbianism, to describe the apparent indifference as an absence.

Consider, for example, the by-now notorious dismissal in Toril Moi's *Sexual/Textual Politics* of American black or lesbian feminist criticism: "Some feminists might wonder why I have said nothing about black or lesbian (or black-lesbian) feminist criticism in America in this survey. The answer is simple: this book purports to deal with the theoretical aspects of feminist criticism" (1985, 86). Moi proceeds to explain that black and lesbian literary critics are as controlled by the limits of empirical criticism as their straight white sisters; while they may have *political* importance, their work is theoretically, well, theoretically retarded. Moi does note, however, that these " 'marginal feminisms' ought to prevent white middle-class First-World feminists from defining their own preoccupations as *universal* female (or feminist) problems" (86). By the conclusion of her own book, even this vapid concession—from which the term "heterosexual" is, in any case, conspicuously absent—is forgotten. That lesbian criticism doesn't have too much importance—political or otherwise—is demonstrated by Moi's elevation of Julia Kristeva as a model of theoretical feminism, with no mention of the extent to which Kristeva's theorizing establishes the lesbian as bad object, and no consideration that this might be a problem for her feminist usefulness (Butler 1989; de Lauretis 1987; Grosz 1989; Silverman 1988).

This isn't to say that Moi is representative of all feminist explorations of the French-American encounter and the contradictory status of the female subject. Nancy K. Miller, for instance, has noted that Moi "manages to collapse each side of the American/French divide with an astonishing lack of concern for the bodies (and positions) under erasure" (Miller 1988, 21n16). Indeed, Miller's own work is far less invested in the simple dualities of simpleminded American feminism versus smart French theory. But here, lesbianism also acquires an implicit function, one defined far more in terms of the pole of attraction (in contrast to the pole of repulsion in Moi's account). In the introduction to her book *Subject to Change*, Miller notes that "[i]t may also be that the difference of another coming to writing requires an outside to heterosexual economies" (10). While the term *lesbian* is not used to describe the utopian female communities which figure so prominently in Miller's analyses of women's fiction, the language used is quite evocative of much lesbian writing, and Miller's own reading of Adrienne Rich with Roland Barthes can be read as an attempt both to acknowledge lesbian writing and to redefine the intersections between homosexuality and feminism. Thus, while Miller's avoidance of the term *lesbian* has more to do with the desire to avoid a perilous opposition of "lesbian" and "heterosexual" than to dismiss lesbian possibilities, one is left with a conception of female space with distinct, yet distinctly unspecified, lesbian contours.

Moi dismisses while Miller is more inclusive. However, if the specter of lesbianism does not necessarily haunt feminist theories of the subject, lesbianism has had a signifying function by virtue of its very status as "other"—whether untheoretical other, in Moi, or utopian other, in Miller. It is commonly assumed—and frequently euphemized through phrases like "radical feminism"—that a politically informed lesbian subjectivity participates in the naive affirmation of self, the unproblematic articulation of agency, and—the most common refrain of all—essentialism, taken to be characteristic of "American feminism."

Many lesbian filmmakers have engaged with the redefinition and reconceptualization of the cinema, and in so doing have challenged the implicit oxymoron of "lesbian theory" that haunts so many feminist explorations of the subject. But why, one might ask, define these projects in terms of *authorship*, particularly given the suspicious reputation it has acquired—much like lesbianism itself, one might add—for harboring idealized, untheorized defenses of the fictions of identity? Furthermore, within the context of cinema studies, the very notion of authorship is far more evocative of traditional, patriarchal film criticism than even is the case in literary studies, for instance. To be sure, throughout the history of contemporary film studies, there have been calls to rethink and retheorize authorship, from Claire Johnston's insistence in 1973 that *auteurism* and feminism could function compatibly, to Kaja Silverman's recent critique of feminist film theorists whose ostensible dismissal of the film author is accompanied by the return of a desire for unproblematized agency (209). Nonetheless, the revision of the concept of authorship has not been a high priority in film studies.

The need to bring authorship into a discussion of lesbian representation is evidenced by a significant body of films in which the filmmaker herself is written into the text, although not in ways that match the common, easy equation between authorial presence and the fictions of identity. There are some lesbian films where this does occur as an affirmative and self-revelatory gesture—Barbara Hammer's celebrations of lesbian love come immediately to mind. But a far more provocative feature of contemporary lesbian filmmaking is the articulation of lesbian authorship as a critical exploration of the very components of subjectivity: self/other relations, desire, and—where lesbianism provides the most crucial challenge to theories of the subject—the relationship between the paradigms of gender and agency, e.g., the presumed identity between activity and masculinity, passivity and femininity. Chantal Akerman's 1974 film *Je tu il elle*, for instance, is saturated with an authorial presence that explores the possible alignments of the pronouns of its title, and Akerman attempts nothing less than the rewriting of the cinematic scenario that prescribes formulaic relations between those terms along the lines of heterosexual symmetry. Or, to take a related but different example, Ulrike Ottinger has written herself into her films as cameo performances. From the flashback appearance as the dead lover, Orlando, of the title character of *Madame X* to a drunken passerby in *Ticket of No Return*, these appearances revise substantially the assumed equation between authorial fictions and heterosexual Oedipal narratives.[3]

Midi Onodera's *Ten Cents a Dance (Parallax)* (1985) is a short (thirty minutes) film, divided into three sections (in the catalog of *Women Make Movies*, the film is described as a kind of "*Je tu il elle* in miniature"). Like other explorations of lesbian representation, *Ten Cents a Dance* is less concerned with affirmative representations of lesbian experience than with explorations of the simultaneous ambivalence and pressure of lesbianism with regard to the polarities of agency and gender. This could of course be taken to mean that the film is, because less "explicitly" lesbian in its focus, less lesbian, period. Indeed, the status of *Ten Cents a Dance* as a "lesbian film" has been crucial to its reception.

For *Ten Cents a Dance* has had a controversial reception history. At the Tenth Annual Lesbian/Gay Film Festival in San Francisco in 1986, for instance, Onodera's film was shown last on a program entitled "Lesbian Shorts," with four other films. By all accounts, the film precipitated something close to a riot, with a considerable portion of the audience booing the film and demanding its money back. If the letters devoted to the screening which later appeared in *Coming Up!*—a San Francisco gay/lesbian newspaper—are representative of the controversy, then *Ten Cents a Dance* was indicative of—to borrow a phrase from B. Ruby Rich—a crisis of naming in lesbian filmmaking (Rich 1980). For how could this film, two-thirds of which is devoted to the representation of gay men and heterosexuals, possibly be called a "lesbian film," and advertised as such? More specific criticisms were made as well—that unsafe sex was depicted between the two men, for instance, and that the lesbian scene included a heterosexual woman. The board of directors of Frameline, the organizers of the festival, responded that *Ten Cents a Dance* " . . . was not only by a lesbian, but was strongly pro-lesbian, despite a scene of two gay men and a straight couple having sex [*sic*]" (5). The exhibition context required the charge of "not a lesbian film" to be countered with "not only a lesbian film, but a pro-lesbian film." But the reception of the film speaks to a larger issue about lesbian representation, concerning precisely the relationship between lesbianism and the contradictory subject theorized within contemporary feminist theory.

Each section of *Ten Cents a Dance* is concerned with a different configuration of sexual desire and language. A split screen is used throughout, so that the two players in every scene are divided from each other. In the first section, two women, while waiting for (or just having finished) dinner in a Japanese restaurant, discuss whether or not they will have a sexual relationship. In the second section, shot from a high angle, two men have sex with each other in a public restroom. And in the final section, a man and a woman engage in phone sex. The use of the split screen creates a wide-angle effect, since the top and bottom of the frame are masked, and the two screens appear as if "projected" against a black background, with a dividing line between them. Each scene in Onodera's film captures a sense both of pleasurable duration—depending, of course, upon how you define "pleasure"—and of uncomfortable pauses.

The title of Onodera's film cites the Rodgers and Hart song about a hostess at the Palace Ballroom who sells dances to "Fighters and sailors and bow-legged tailors . . . butchers and barbers and rats from the harbor." The song is a cynical lament, full of bitter resignation and desperation. The most obvious "match" to the song is the third section of the film, and it would be easy to argue that Onodera equates heterosexual sex with the pathos of sex for sale. But in this respect, *Ten Cents a Dance* has an ambiguous quality—it suggests simultaneously the difference and the analogy between different sexualities. For all of the participants in the film enact rituals of erotic connection and distance.

In any case, the title of the film also reminds us that "Ten Cents a Dance" is not to be taken so literally: the addition of "Parallax" in parentheses, over the right screen, can be read in relationship not only to each of the participants in the respective couples but in relationship to the distinction between straight and gay, gay and lesbian, male and female as well. If the difference between two points of view allows the "apparent displacement of an observed object" (as the dictionary says), then the "parallax" of Onodera's title refers quite obviously to the way in which lesbian and gay readings take citation and replacement as central strategies. More specifically, the "parallax" view of *Ten Cents a Dance* is evocative of Joan Nestle's insistence—speaking of the difference between "replication" and "resistance" in the appropriation of butch and fem styles—that lesbians "should be mistresses of discrepancies, knowing that resistance lies in the change of context" (Nestle 1984, 236).

Undoubtedly the doubled screen is the most striking visual figure of discrepancy in *Ten Cents a Dance*. The split screen suggests a number of cinematic precedents, such as the stereoscope card—a doubled image which, when viewed at the proper distance, creates the illusion of depth. Other uses of the split screen come to mind as well. In *Pillow Talk* (1959), for instance, split screens are used extensively to juxtapose the telephone conversations of Doris Day and Rock Hudson, frequently with contrasting pink and blue color schemes—which Onodera adapts in her red and blue portrayal of heterosexual phone contact. If the third section of the film is the one most obviously informed by classical Hollywood conventions, all three sections play upon the edges of the frame, particularly in their contrasting functions of reiterating the markers separating the two women (the rose) and rendering oblique the restroom wall and glory hole that separate and connect the two men.

In all three instances, the two views are juxtaposed to disrupt the seamless fit between the participants in sexual dramas. The relationship between the two screens in each section acquires the contours of simultaneous connection and separation. The screen surfaces are figures of permeability and division at the same time. Far from serving as the unproblematized ground for the image, the screen in *Ten Cents a Dance* becomes a site of tension. This occurs by the doubling of the screens, and by the relationship between the two edges that never quite touch. In addition, the interplay of screen and frame makes the film's representation of sexuality more a question of what is screened, in both senses of the term, than what is unproblematically visible. In the first and last sections of the film, of course, sexual talk obscures the sexual act, but even in the second section of the film, it is the threshold between the two men which is foregrounded far more than sexual acts themselves.

In her recent essay on lesbian representation and Sheila McLaughlin's film *She Must Be Seeing Things*, Teresa de Lauretis distinguishes films like McLaughlin's, which produce "modes of representing that effectively alter the standard frame of reference and visibility, the conditions of the visible, what *can* be seen and represented" (a description which obviously applies to *Ten Cents a Dance*), from those which provide "sympathetic accounts . . . without necessarily producing new ways of seeing or a new inscription of the social subject in representation" (de Lauretis 1989, 2). In the latter category, de Lauretis includes films like *Desert Hearts* and *Lianna*. Mandy Merck has described *Desert Hearts* as "steeped in the heterosexual tradition of the active pursuit of the reluctant woman," and goes on to cite a series of rigid dichotomies which structure the film—those of class and geography, for instance (Merck 1987, 16).

Such dichotomies have more than a passing relationship with *Ten Cents a Dance*, particularly insofar as the first section of the film is concerned. Merck notes that in *Desert Hearts*, the "brunette is to blonde as active is to passive" dichotomy appears as a stock feature of the genre of the lesbian romance. Dark-haired Onodera casts herself in the role of the "experienced lesbian" having relationship talk with a blonde woman whom she had considered "essentially straight" (the experienced lesbian versus the experimenting heterosexual is another typical opposition described by Merck). Yet Onodera cites the dichotomies in order to disrupt them and suspend them simultaneously. For by casting herself, an Asian woman, in the role of the active pursuer, Onodera reverses one of the most common Western representations of Asians, male or female, as passive and obedient. But that such a reversal cannot function in any simple way as an alternative is made clear in the last section of the film, where the woman assumes the active role, but one which reinforces her own position as sexual commodity. More crucially, the oppositions thus cited never attain narrative or sexual resolution—or rather, only attain resolution by displacement and suspension.

But this displacement and suspension engages a risk, for, by focusing on two women talking, *Ten Cents a Dance* could be seen as affirming the popular stereotype that lesbians talk about relationships while men have sex—whether with women or with each other. In other words, *Ten Cents a Dance* could be read as affirming lesbianism as, if not asexual, then at least presexual, or, in the language of much contemporary psychoanalytic theory, as pre-Oedipal, as a recreation of the mother-child bond. However, what seems to me most crucial in this representation of lesbian sexuality is the way it is framed—not so much in terms of the scene itself, but rather in relationship to the sexual rituals that surround it.

In the essay mentioned above, Teresa de Lauretis is critical of the tendency, in much writing about lesbianism and feminism and the female subject, to conflate identification and desire. The so-called pre-Oedipal, mother/daughter bond can be regarded as the foundation for lesbianism only if the desire *for* another woman is subsumed to the desire to be (like) a woman. As de Lauretis puts it, there is a "sweeping of lesbian sexuality and desire under the rug of sisterhood, female friendship, and the now popular theme of 'the mother-daughter bond' " (31). Implicit in such accounts is a definition of heterosexuality as mature, adult, and symbolic, whether such accounts are "straight" or symptomatic—i.e., really the ways things are, or really the ways things are under patriarchy. And heterosexual intercourse becomes the norm against which other sexualities are classified as deviant.

In Onodera's film, the possessors of the most explicit (though not completely visible) *sex* are not the heterosexuals but the gay men, and the closest thing to a sexual referent in the film is oral sex, not intercourse. Indeed, orality is one of the sexual common denominators of the film, whether through conversation, cigarette smoking, or sexual acts. Heterosexual intercourse is thus displaced from its status as the standard of sexuality against which all others are compared. The three sections of the film become, rather, sexual configurations in which orality—so long considered a major attribute of the regressive, narcissistic, homosexually inclined individual (male or female)—figures across the dividing lines of different sexualities.

As de Lauretis suggests, the conflation of desire and identification, and the attendant relegation of lesbianism to the presexual stage, serves to reinforce what are ultimately homophobic definitions. At the same time, however, the definition of lesbianism as an extension of female bonding or mother love is one to which many lesbians have been drawn. Within contemporary lesbianism, there are competing definitions of what lesbianism is, from the most intense form of female and feminist bonding (as theorized by Adrienne Rich in her controversial lesbian continuum), to a sexuality that is distinctly different from heterosexuality, whether practiced by men or women. The ironic signature which Midi Onodera brings to her performance—understood here both in terms of her role and the entire film—suggests both of these simultaneously.

In the first section of the film, Onodera is both the "experienced" lesbian discussing the possibility of an intimate relationship with a woman and an Asian Canadian having dinner in one of the most popularized Western clichés of Asia, a restaurant. In other words, she appears to occupy a position of some authority. But Onodera defines authorship so as to expose its fictions as well as its desires. For the position that she occupies, on the right side of the screen, is taken up by a gay man engaging in anonymous sex in the next section and a woman offering phone sex in the last part of the film. Given the extent to which anonymity and sex for sale are defined, in much lesbian writing, as symptomatic of either male sexuality or heterosexuality, the affiliation between Onodera's position and those of the man and the woman in the subsequent scenes brackets any simple notion of lesbian desire as isolated from other forms of sexual desire.

At the same time, of course, the lesbian scene *is* different than the other two, with more emphasis on conversation and the erotics of the look—the latter serving a particularly ironic function, given the extent to which the look has been defined in much feminist film theory as the province of the heterosexual male's possession of the woman. Onodera's ambiguous role in the film, as both author and actor, and as both like and unlike gay men and heterosexuals, thus suggests that the lesbian author is defined as both complicit in and resistant to the sexual fictions of patriarchal culture, and that lesbian irony holds competing definitions of lesbianism up to each other, while refusing to collapse one into the other.

Notes

1. Thanks to Chris Lymbertos, who provided me with information about the reception of *Ten Cents a Dance*; and Laura George, Lucretia Knapp, and Terry Moore, who read this essay at various stages and offered encouragement.
2. "Mon père est parti au petit jour. Il n'a plus jamais revu ma mère. Madeleine est morte il y a maintenant deux ans. A eux trois, je dédie ce film."

3. I discuss at length Akerman's *Je tu il elle* and Ottinger's *Ticket of No Return* in chapter 4 of my book *The Woman at the Keyhole: Feminism and Women's Cinema*.

Works Cited

Butler, Judith. 1989. *Gender Trouble*. New York and London: Routledge.

de Lauretis, Teresa. 1989. "Film and the Visible." Paper given at the *How Do I Look?* Conference, New York City, October.

———. 1987. "The Female Body and Heterosexual Presumption." *Semiotica* 67, nos. 3–4.

Grosz, Elizabeth. 1989. *Sexual Subversions: Three French Feminists*. Winchester, Massachusetts: Unwin Hyman.

Grundberg, Sibyl. n.d. "Deserted Hearts: Lesbians Making It in the Movies." *Gossip*, no. 4, 27–39.

Johnston, Claire. 1973, rpt. 1975. "Women's Cinema as Counter-Cinema." In Claire Johnston, ed., *Notes on Women's Cinema*. London: British Film Institute.

N. A. 1986. "Lesbian (?) Short Raises Storm of Controversy at Lesbian/Gay Film Festival." *Coming Up!* 7, no. 11 (August): 4–5.

Mayne, Judith. 1990. *The Woman at the Keyhole: Feminism and Women's Cinema*. Bloomington: Indiana University Press.

Merck, Mandy. 1987. "Desert Hearts." *The Independent* 10, no. 6, 15–18.

———. 1986. "*Lianna* and the Lesbians of Art Cinema." In Charlotte Brunsdon, ed., *Films for Women*. London: British Film Institute.

Miller, Nancy K. 1988. *Subject to Change: Reading Feminist Writing*. New York: Columbia University Press.

Mitchell, Lynette. n.d. "Letter." *Gossip*, no. 6, 11–13.

Moi, Toril. 1985. *Sexual/Textual Politics*. London and New York: Methuen.

Nestle, Joan. 1984. "The Fem Question." In Carole S. Vance, ed., *Pleasure and Danger: Exploring Female Sexuality*. Boston: Routledge and Kegan Paul.

Rich, B. Ruby. 1980. "In the Name of Feminist Film Criticism." *Heresies* 3, no. 1 (Issue 9): 74–81.

Silverman, Kaja. 1988. *The Acoustic Mirror: The Female Voice in Psychoanalysis and Cinema*. Bloomington: Indiana University Press.

Smith, Barbara. 1977. "Toward a Black Feminist Criticism." *Conditions*, no. 2, 25–44.

Whitelaw, Lis. n.d. "Lesbians of the Mainscreen." *Gossip*, no. 5, 37–46.

12

SIGNIFYING THE HOLOCAUST
Liliana Cavani's *Portiere di notte*

Marguerite Waller

THERE ARE many subtexts to this paper, some of which I am probably not
even aware of. One of them I am aware of is an ongoing project of analysis
and art-making by a women's art-making collective to which I belong. We
call ourselves Las Comadres (the Godmothers), and we work in the San
Diego/Tijuana border region. In the fall of 1990, we created an installation
called "La Vecindad/The Neighborhood," in which we begin the task of
unpacking the particular form of racism that seems to power the debates
over the immigration of undocumented workers into southern California.
Here are a few sentences from a piece of hate mail sent to Roberto Mar-
tinez, an undocumented workers' advocate, by "The Holy Church of the
White Fighting Machine of the Cross":

> The cops are going to start shooting you Mexicans wholesale soon, and
> there will be nothing you can do about it. Go back to T. J. [Tijuana] and
> watch the mule fuck the whore that will be better for you. . . . Stop criti-
> cizing the border patrol and the whites who are trying to save our white
> country from the Jews and the Goy stooges in the government who will
> not act in behalf of the white Aryan race.

(In our installation, we stenciled a blow-up of the text on a 10' x 6' piece
of fabric, which we used as a rug that museum-goers had to walk on or
consciously avoid to get from one part of the installation to another.) What
interests me here is the conflation of Mexican agricultural workers with
Jews, and the introduction into the equation of sexuality, fantasized as
somehow miscegenating, sterile, bestial, heterosexual, and misogynistic
all at the same time.

The Holocaust as a Feminist Issue

In the first volume of his book *Male Fantasies*, Klaus Theweleit ob-
serves, "The argument that a social democrat is not a communist, a com-

munist not an anarchist, and that none of these categories has anything to do with Jews, has never had much effect. The fascist unconscious perceives an essential sameness in all of the categories (and in the many others that made the spectrum of concentration-camp prisoners so diverse . . .)" (383–84). Topping the list of threatening not-quite-others is woman, according to Theweleit's provocative study of the diaries, poems, and novels of proto-Nazi German Freikorpsmen. A sexual woman is a whore is a proletarian is a Communist is a Jew—or vice versa—regardless of the gender of the person in question (383). In fifteenth-century Ferrara, archival and secondary sources suggest, female prostitutes and male Jews had to contend together in a seminude footrace in the ruling family's annual *palio* (Shemek 5, 10, 24). Red-light districts and Jewish ghettos seem to have come into existence at about the same time in several Italian cities, and Jews and prostitutes were legally required to conform to similar dress codes (Shemek 24).[1] In Hungary, newly liberated from Soviet and domestic Communist domination, the foreign minister, a member of the ruling nationalistic Democratic Forum party, declared in public, in September 1990, that the Hungarian Jews, who make up some of the membership of the more liberal Free Democratic party, are not authentically Hungarian and should not be taken to represent the interests of real Hungarians. Is it coincidental that another of Democratic Forum's initiatives is the illegalization of abortion, a transparently misogynistic approach, it seems to some, to the problem of Hungary's declining population, which seems pretty obviously keyed, not to the dangers of female autonomy, but to the lack of available housing.

Except for Theweilet, and a handful of American feminists—including Susan Griffin in *Pornography and Silence* (168–201) and Elly Bulkin, Minnie Bruce Pratt, and Barbara Smith, whose book *Yours in Struggle: Three Feminist Perspectives on Anti-Semitism and Racism* also makes the connection—commentators have not generally approached anti-Semitism as a feminist issue, nor, conversely, have misogyny and male dominance been a central concern, as far as I know, of historians and analysts of European anti-Semitism. In fact, both Liliana Cavani's *The Night Porter* and Lina Wertmuller's *Seven Beauties* have been vehemently criticized by eminent male Holocaust survivors for muddying our understanding of the "truth" with their sexual allegories of concentration-camp power relations. In *The Drowned and the Saved*, Primo Levi criticizes Cavani's film for confusing murderers and victims, beclouding "our need for justice" (49). In his long *New Yorker* essay, "Surviving," published in 1976, Bruno Bettelheim objected to, among other things, the comedy of *Seven Beauties*, which he complained, "neutralizes the horror" (31). Both men, though, themselves deploy sexual imagery to elaborate their points. Characterizing Cavani's film as "beautiful and false," an exemplification of a "moral disease," Levi speaks of the terrain it explores, what he calls the "gray zone ... of prisoners who in some measure, perhaps with good intentions, collaborated with authority" (20), as not "virgin." "On the contrary it is a badly plowed field, trampled and torn up" (48). Bettelheim, too, is concerned with keeping the horror pure, and the moral issues clear, while, like Levi, he construes the woman filmmaker's intervention in the field as allied with prostitution or pornography: "I must express my disgust that the abomination of genocide and the tortures and degradations of the concentration camp are used as a special, uniquely macabre titillation to enhance its [the film's] effectiveness. . . . [T]his depiction of the survivor . . . robs survivorship of all meaning. It makes seeing the film an experience that degrades" (31, 34).

Let me hasten to say that I in no way wish to discredit the historical and emotional accuracy of these witnesses. On the contrary, the metaphorical structures of their own arguments have heightened my curiosity about the relevance of a feminist or gender-centered approach to the Holocaust and to the questions of national and individual identity with which anti-Semitism seems historically and conceptually linked. As fascist emotions are fanned by recession in North America and, in Central and Eastern Europe, by the formerly Communist bloc's efforts to resurrect and reclaim pre–World War II national and ethnic identities, films like *The Night Porter* and *Seven Beauties* seem particularly prescient. Not attempting the kind of mimetic or documentary representation of what happened favored by Levi, Bettelheim, or *Shoah*'s Claude Lanzmann, these films pointedly approach the questions of what happened, how it happened, why it happened, and what changes need to occur in order for it not to happen again through *non-Jewish* principle characters, unrealistic mise-en-scène and plotting, and, not coincidentally, exhaustive explorations of what might seem the peripheral issue of the constructedness of genders and sexualities. They both begin, that is, from the assumption that fascism cannot be subverted from within the moral and ethnic categories through which the world has come to know it historically. Whether one agrees or not with the analysis that each film, in its own way, performs—and, as I will argue elsewhere, I think Wertmuller's film already takes issue with and revises certain aspects of Cavani's—I would urge that together they constitute a richly suggestive feminist revision of this chapter in modern European history. Here I will comment on Cavani's film, in a reading which, as feminist film theory has already so effectively taught us to do, will take into account not only what is shown but how it is shown, not only the relations enacted between characters on screen but also the relations played out between the screen and the audience. I will return, then, to Levi and Bettelheim, to see whether, reread through the lens provided by Cavani, the terms of their criticism begin to make a different kind of sense.

Constructing a Subject

The spectator's relation to Cavani's Max, the impeccable, ex-Nazi night porter, played by Dirk Bogarde, is as problematic visually as it is morally; or, rather, a major reason for our uneasy relationship with Max is the unstable relation between what the camera seems to be showing us and what we learn from the film's action and dialogue. It would be relatively comfortable were we first seduced by Max, then gradually or shockingly disabused of our sympathy, as happens, for instance, in Costa Gavras's recent film, *The Music Box*. There the retired American factory worker and devoted family man turns out *really* to be the sadistic rapist/murderer of the infamous Hungarian Arrow Cross. The Costa Gavras film refuses, in other words, to entertain the problematics of subjectivity, to question the ontology (including the continuity and stability) of identity, in spite of the obviousness with which such material invites investigation. Throughout *The Night Porter*, on the other hand, the camera insists that we continually be reseduced by Max. Lingering shots of his soulful brown eyes, his exquisite gestures while poring tea, his vulnerability in the presence of his wartime cronies—of a complex range of mannerisms and expressions imperfectly masked by his nearly identical SS and night porter's uniforms—magnetically draw attention to Max as a sensuous, emotionally responsive figure whose next move is as unpredictable as it is eagerly anticipated. We are drawn to him, that is, *at the same time* that his career as a sadistic, murderous, phony camp doctor, only one of whose patients, Lucia, has survived, is also being unfolded.

As I have just intimated, though, Max's attraction differs from that of the stereotypical Hollywood male, who, as film theorists Laura Mulvey and Mary Ann Doane have persuasively argued, is visually portrayed as a kind of ego ideal. Visually Max is as often as not "feminized." (My reasons for putting the word in quotation marks will become apparent momentarily.) Like the classic Mulvey and Doane woman, he is shot in close-up, often centered on the screen, isolated from his context, and delivered up for voyeuristic scrutiny, even in sequences and individual shots where he is simultaneously portrayed, like the classic Mulvey and Doane man, as the origin and owner of the gaze (Mulvey 19–20; Doane 28–31). For example, when we see Max with a movie camera aggressively filming Lucia's thin, naked body amid a crowd of other naked, newly arrived camp prisoners, or, elsewhere, Max training a spotlight on Bert, the virtuosic, homosexual ballet dancer, it is also the image and performance of Max, on screen almost as long as the images and performances his gaze frames, with which the film fascinates us.[2] Lucia, especially in the latter part of the film, is, in these terms, often "masculinized." Though observed by Max, she is shown framed in profile, placed at the edge of the frame, her face partly shadowed, signifying, relative to the "feminine" position described in feminist film theory, that she is also an agent—not only seen but seeing, not only acted upon but initiating and guiding the action (Mulvey 22–23; Doane 28).[3] As if to underscore this strategy, Cavani shows her smoking a pipe in one sequence in which Max, framed in the center of the screen, unpacks groceries and tells her he has quit his job. But, as the film's mixing of conventions also implies, these categories—"masculine" and "feminine"—do not inhere in the people they describe. The bodies and faces of both figures become the site of a dissonant and denaturalized visual language that, across the disturbing story of their past and present relationship, denaturalizes the legibility of sex and gender.[4]

There is good reason for anyone interested in "truth," clearly and morally represented, to be troubled by this twofold instability and multiplicity of Max's and Lucia's subject positions. Gender theorist Judith Butler suggestively describes the kind of signifying practice through which a substantive, knowing "I," which is to say a subject situated in opposition to a knowable and recoverable Other, can appear, in terms which seem equally useful for describing the subversion of such an "I" enacted by *The Night Porter*'s signifying practices. "Such appearances," like all subject positions in Butler's argument, "are rule generated identities, ones which rely on the consistent and repeated invocation of rules that condition and restrict culturally . . . intelligible practices of identity" (145). In ways that can and have been described both historically and philosophically, sex and gender have been among the most thoroughly naturalized, taken-for-granted, of the intelligible identity practices—practices which stabilize no less than they are stabilized by the position or practice of the knowing "I." By proliferating sex and gender configurations on screen, Cavani's film, then, strikes at the heart of the rules that allow mutually constitutive identity *practices* to appear as what Butler scornfully terms "inert substantives" to a global subject (144). As we struggle to organize the slippery images on screen, we are prevented from mistaking ourselves for such a global subject, whose imperializing point of view and substantializing effects are, by contrast, vigorously maintained by Hollywood's consistent and unambiguous language of male and female, weak and strong, good guys and villains.[5] Instead, insistently ambiguous and open, the film offers too many possible readings of figures, actions, images, and sequences. The film as Other is not knowable and recoverable, and the more we try to dig into a position of voyeuristic domination, the less comfortable, intellectually and morally, this position becomes. As many feminist viewers have commented, a lot of this film is "hard to watch" (Stone 41). My point is that this may have as much to do with the way we are watching it as with what is on screen. To give one example, if we assume that everything is as it seems when we see a close-up of Lucia, with her hands chained above and behind her head, approached by Max, who grasps her torso, we may (many viewers do) find the images unbearable (Stone 42, 44). Especially if her enigmatic passivity is read as acceptance or even pleasure, then viewers may find themselves wishing they were not watching, wishing the filmmaker were not showing us this, wishing Lucia would let us off the hook by appearing to suffer more.[6] Why should the film work this way? What do the political stakes of the subject matter—the Holocaust and its aftermath—have to do with how we conceptualize and experience identity? Or, to turn the question around, what cognitive, political, and psychological ends are served when we insist that identities be grounded in bodies and that those identities and bodies be understood as ontological essences? What *new* political possibilities emerge when we experience sexual, ethnic, and national identities—ours included—not as the grounded but rather as an effect of the signifying situations through which they are articulated?

Let me interject here a corollary whose implications will be important for the rest of my argument. This global subject position, as I think Mulvey's work with Hollywood film codes aptly illustrates, is gendered male, whoever happens to occupy it. Truth, knowledge, and thus the very notion of identity are constituted *and* threatened by falsehood, ignorance, and impurity, which are consistently gendered female. To make a long story short, the subject whom Cavani's film will not let us be is implicitly misogynistic. It is also potentially anti-Semitic and racist, since it must see as wrong (to guarantee truth) anything it sees as different. Misogyny and anti-Semitism are, if you will, different vectors of the same kind of identity formation. But what other kind of subject is there?

To begin with, there is Max. Max, who is said to have "imagination," does not want to *be* anybody, but is drawn instead to playing roles and wearing costumes. We see him as a "documentary" filmmaker, an image that quickly becomes itself complexly polyvalent. The images Max has made with his cameras are never presented as ideologically neutral, but the potential arguments embedded in them also change radically with the circumstances and the viewer. His nude photographs of Lucia, for example, can, and at first do, signify Max's power over her, but, later, in the hands of the ex-Nazis, the same photographs come to signify Lucia's power to expose Max. Max's images, then, might caution us against ontologizing Cavani's images as well.[7]

Max is also said to have had fun playing doctor during the war, and before that to have served in the entourage of a count. He accommodates both Bert, the insomniac ex-Nazi and closet homosexual, and Erika, the appetitive countess, in their elaborate psychosexual rituals. But most of all he revels in a relationship with one of his victims in whom he creates or discovers another avid role player. It is interesting to speculate on how or why Lucia responds to Max, though I would interject the caveat that, with both Max and Lucia, I am indulging in a kind of explanation that the film itself problematizes as it reconfigures the notion of identity that produces the appearance of individual histories and psychologies. For this viewer, at least, the film does *not* offer "realistic" portrayals of character, and I see it full of traps and obstructions that discourage the impulse to translate the interaction between Max and Lucia into individual, psychological terms. I propose merely heuristically, then—the better to see where it takes us and what problems it presents us with—the following scenario: As mad Max's "little girl," Lucia, referred to and treated by everyone else as either "the daughter of the socialist" or "the wife of the American conductor," is not locked into the usual heterosexual conventions, the male-centered sociosexual identities, reserved for her in prewar Vienna or postwar North America. Ironically, it is from the hyper-masculinist Nazi power structure that Max derives the power over Lucia that evokes and/or provokes—"legitimates" and/or enforces—her polymorphous, indeterminately active and passive, "male" and "female," masochistic and sadistic sexuality. Already, you will note, my narrative is in trouble. There is no appropriate verb to describe this interaction, since the way one would characterize it depends upon the relative positions of two subjects whose bond has to do very largely with the thrill they experience in constantly renegotiating their subject positions. And I say "ironic" of Max's point of departure because these renegotiations between Max and Lucia subvert the sexual and gender identity principles that are among the most basic of the rigid binaries, taken for absolutes, upon which Nazi (and other fascist) organizations of power and knowledge are founded.[8] Lucia's particular mode of collaboration, one might say, allows Max a respite from, and ultimately a way out of, the untenable role of absolute masculine authority—a role which cannot be a role if it is absolute and cannot be absolute if it is a role, and which is, paradoxically, a kind of passivity, culturally speaking. (This is a way out, it is intriguing to note, not available to poor Bert, the gay Nazi, who is trapped in the closet, as well as in the past, by his own fascist homophobia. In an instance of Cavani's little-remarked, deadpan playfulness, Bert is costumed and made up to resemble a movie vampire, one of the living dead. He comes brilliantly alive when he dances, I presume, because it is there that he *can* role-play. As a dancer he can "move" in several senses of the word.) The denaturalization of Max's position, then, allows Lucia a respite from and a way out of the subordinate and objectified position in which her role as prisoner—and perhaps as woman—places her. (Does her self-absorbed orchestra-conductor husband, a kind of authoritarian by profession, lock her into her perfect performance as bourgeois wife by his "unimaginative" performance as husband?)

I am not saying, nor do I think the film suggests, that Nazis and survivors are therefore the same. Indeed, in this film not all *Nazis* are the same, nor, for that matter, are characters themselves self-identical. It is precisely the point that they occupy different positions simultaneously, as well as over time, in relation to different people, and even in relation to the same person, and that these positions are all contingent, frequently self-contradictory, and always in the process of being renegotiated. I am suggesting, on the contrary, that to distinguish ontologically between "guiltless victims" and "murderers," to try to cement the moral purity of these categories, is itself to deny difference, in a way that, paradoxically, undermines the moral, and, I would argue, political, position of the "victim." As feminist theorists have discovered in their attempts to extend visibility and legitimacy to women, treating a term like *women* as a stable category presumes and fixes the unfavorable status of the very "subjects" that they hope to represent and support. The legitimation of such "subjects" within a system that defines them as inferior and other then involves them in more of the same oppositional logic that produced them. Recall that the two male survivors, Levi and Bettelheim, unself-consciously express their acceptance of the basic dichotomy they have been victimized by in misogynist terms. Like Theweleit's fascist unconscious, their discourse represents diverse categories of difference as essentially the same, as sexual, impure, and disorderly. If binary logic itself and the subjects it produces remain in place, then "Jews" as well as "Nazis," women as well as men, remain burdened with the task of having to represent their positions as stable, coherent, and correct, a task that cannot help but involve them in further representations of difference as opposition and threat.

Signifying the Holocaust

How does Cavani signify the Holocaust, then, if not through binary logic? In the limited space of this paper, I cannot begin to answer that question with the fullness that it deserves. But, as an example, I will conclude by "reading" part of the remarkable sequence, fairly near the film's beginning, that interweaves the reestablishment of Lucia's and Max's relationship in the present, flashbacks to their past in the camp, and a passage from Mozart's opera *The Magic Flute*. As this sequence opens Max takes his seat several rows behind Lucia in the Viennese opera house as Pamina and Papageno on stage sing their duet about the joys of married life and Lucia's husband conducts the orchestra. Max and Lucia make eye contact, and Lucia has a flashback to her experience in the concentration camp where Max was the "doctor" and her lover.[9]

In the first fourteen shots of the sequence virtually every image is destabilized rather than stabilized by its relation to the others. This is accomplished, in part, by the triple focus itself. Mozart's problematic opera, about a woman, Pamina, who first seems to be imprisoned and later "saved" within a rigidly hierarchical masculinist regime, becomes associated, through the complex intercutting of sound and image, with *both* of Lucia's relationships—with her past *and* her present. These three-way associations undo the binary interpretation that, at this point in the film, we are strongly tempted to make. Surely a clean-cut American conductor is good, an uptight ex-Nazi torturer night porter is bad. But Papageno and Pamina sing the praises of heterosexual, compassionate marriage right through the scene of a male prisoner being raped by a male guard on the bed next to Lucia's in the concentration-camp barracks. A spectral group of prisoners helplessly watching the rape is set up visually, by the rhyming of camera movements and framings, as the reverse shot of the Viennese audience watching the Mozart performance. The gorgeously sung phrase— "Nothing is nobler than to be man and wife. Man and wife together attain godliness"—are "married," as a sound mixer would say, with the rhythmic humping of the barely visible prisoner by the beefy guard. It may also be relevant that Papageno and Pamina sing their duet in praise of marriage just after the attempted rape of Pamina by a "Black Moor." The race of this character will eventually serve to distinguish the Moor's attempted rape from the right of the white male power structure, personified by the sorceror Zarastro, to use Pamina's sexuality for its own ends. Having abducted her from her mother, Zarastro will offer her, as a reward, to the hero Tamino, once both Tamino and Pamina have successfully weathered a rigorous, not to say sado-masochistic, set of initiation rituals, designed to indoctrinate them thoroughly in the ideology of male-dominant heterosexuality. Along the way Pamina's mother and the Moor are thoroughly discredited as disorderly and untrustworthy, and women in particular are blamed for abusing "true" language by their useless but seductive chattering. Though the opera's representation of marriage could be read as a contrast to the rape enacted on screen, then, I think the film also suggests a certain congruence between the abuse we see and the familiar heterosexuality being celebrated (or exposed—depending on how you look at it) in the opera—a heterosexuality whose misogynist and racist foundations are at least made more obvious by the comparison.[10] If the Viennese opera house and the concentration camp are seen as reverse images of each other, then it becomes more difficult simply to oppose Lucia's husband to Max. Lucia's husband is, in his own way, reproducing and naturalizing the white or Aryan male subject position that nazism, the epitome of the patriarchal repression of women and "non-Aryans," tried to solidify to an absurd extent. The sexuality and the organization of power that we see in the camp are, in a fundamental sense, continuous with what we see in the eighteenth-century opera, as well as in the postwar culture for whom the opera remains a signficant ruling-class ritual.[11]

The introduction of the third historical moment, the late eighteenth century when *The Magic Flute* was written, makes it equally difficult to indulge in binary historiography, to condemn a "bad" past from the perspective of a "good" present, or vice versa, as Klaus and the other ex-Nazis want to do. As cinema can so powerfully suggest, and does here with its constant reframings of characters, actions, and contexts, what we think we see, with its consequences for who and where we think we are, is an effect of a complex web of relationships with no particular point of origin and no necessary endpoint. The extent to which our readings of even these few images can proliferate over the course of a few moments offers some idea of how much the linear understanding of time produced by binary thinking limits historical understanding, concealing possibilities that could otherwise become visible and articulable.

One final observation: The continual reframings of characters—Max with others in the audience, Lucia with others in the audience and behind the conductor's hands, the audience with the figures on stage, Max the only one in focus, Lucia the only one in focus, etc.—are performed by a camera that does not purport to be objective. It pans and tracks, zooms, pulls focus—a conspicuous, haunting figure in its own right, which seems to want us never to mistake for mimetic representations its "signifying" plays on the images it gives us. Representation, in the sense that one position or effect can stand for another (whereby, for example, Lucia could stand for women, who could stand for victims, who could stand for Jews), would require the inert, monocular vision enforced by binary logic that produces a kind of "truth" in which people and events appear to stay put.[12] (Another of Cavani's visual jokes or puns, like Bert's resemblance to Dracula, is Klaus's monocle, visually literalizing the one-point perspective of fascist logic.) In Cavani's film, positionality is relative and cannot be fixed or "clarified." The camera's restless comparison of every position with every other is among the film's most powerful and most disturbing strategies. These comparisons, I want to conclude by stressing, do *not* serve to minimize the horrors of the Holocaust but, on the contrary, to keep them relevant. They signify the Holocaust, not as the unthinkable Other, but as one distinctly possible effect of the misogynistic signifying situations through which those of us who share this history and culture are ourselves articulated.

Notes

1. The superimposition of Jewish ghettos and red-light districts in Italian cities was described to me by Deanna Shemek in a conversation about her unpublished article "Circular Definitions: Disciplining Gender in Italian Renaissance Festival," which describes the stigmatization of "both Jews and prostitutes in Ferrara and other cities by laws forbidding them to touch foodstuffs in public markets and requiring them to wear distinguishing signs on their clothing" (24).

2. The actual screen time given to Max is certainly longer (and differently framed) than that of a typical reaction shot. But since the shots of him with the camera or the spotlight are relatively "simple" with regard to the time it takes to "read" them, they do not have to be literally as long as, say, a shot of Bert dancing, in order to carry the same affective weight. A long-shot customarily takes longer to read than a close-up and is therefore left on screen longer in "real time" if a sense of equivalence in the "film time" is desired.

3. Cavani's "feminization" and "masculinization" of Max and Lucia differ from the gendering that occurs in the Hollywood film language analyzed by Mulvey and Doane, though, in not conflating the camera's gaze with the gaze of either character. The audience is not, in other words, rhetorically induced to identify with either character,

with the result that the gendering of the characters on screen is that much more denaturalized.

4. My argument about sexuality and gender in *The Night Porter* thus differs in one crucial respect from that of Kaja Silverman in her book *The Acoustic Mirror*. She would read Max as a psychological character, a mimetic subject, who can then be said to take or not take actions, and whose "male" subjectivity she sees as "impaired" rather than as fluid, unstable, and performative from the start. She also discusses Max in isolation from Lucia, as if his behavior were autonomous and rooted in a single psyche. By characterizing Max as an individual Freudian subject, I would argue, this reading does too little with the film's destabilization of the *categories* of gender and sexuality that produce the *appearance* of phallic or nonphallic males. In other words, it essentializes, in a subtle way, the sexuality of the characters (or rather that of Max), while I would emphasize the sexualities in this film as relational and performative. Whichever position one takes as a spectator, I would call attention to the enormous difference that position makes to one's reading of the film and to one's relationship to the two figures. There are virtually two different stories here, and a completely different relationship to the cinematic image, depending upon where one finds oneself.

In an earlier discussion of the film in her article, "Masochism and Subjectivity," Silverman presents a compelling argument about the gap between "the fiction of the active male subject" and male identification with "negation, passivity, and loss" (8). Here she does take into consideration the interaction between Max and Lucia. Though she structures her case around the categories "male" and "female," much of what she says hints at the possibility of their nonessential ontological status (6).

5. An interesting variation on Hollywood's struggle to eliminate ambiguity and conceptual movement from its constructions of subjects is described by Amelia Jones in her fine article on *Presumed Innocent*, " 'She Was Bad News': Male Paranoia and the Contemporary New Woman," in which she argues that several recent Hollywood films interestingly fail to contain a "phallic uncertainty," which they blame on the "new" career woman's expansion of "feminine identity" across traditional gender lines. Jones sees the failure of such films to contain the "new woman" as a moderately positive sign culturally. One could also draw more negative conclusions from this (lucrative) scapegoating of career women for the fundamental instability of the phallic male subject.

6. Mirto Golo Stone cites herself and Teresa de Lauretis, among others, as spectators who find the film unbearable. Both commentators construe Lucia as a conventional, psychological subject, similarly to the way Silverman construes Max. De Lauretis in 1976 wrote of the presentation of Lucia, "It is a harsh, unadorned, cruel view of the depth of one's self" (38). My point is that the film destabilizes the position of the spectator in ways that make such certainty about what one is seeing impossible.

7. For her eye-opening discussion of the power relations involved in the reading as well as the making of photographic images, I am indebted here to Martha Rosler's essay "In, Around, and Afterthoughts (on Documentary Photography)" in Richard Bolton's edited volume *The Context of Meaning: Critical Histories of Photography*.

8. For a brilliant, multifaceted discussion of the collusion between the binary thinking of gender and sexuality and "knowledge" as it has been constructed and construed in the West, see Eve Sedgwick's *The Epistemology of the Closet*. Sedgwick touches on the relation between fascism and the assumption of historically stable, internally coherent sexual identities on pages 154–55.

9. Laura Pietropaolo gives an excellent verbal transcription of this sequence in her article "Sexuality as Exorcism in Liliana Cavani's *Night Porter*" in the context of her

persuasive argument for the importance of seeing the flashback, the opera, and the film itself as versions of ritual, which she defines as "a formalized re-enactment with a cathartic purpose" (75–76). Her sense of ritual and my sense of performance are, I think, closely related. She describes the scene as follows:

> As the text of the duet is tenderly expressing that "the gentle love of man and woman shows that humans are a race apart" (Schikander 82) and the melody fills the theatre ever more rapturously, the camera moves back to the audience to close upon Lucia's profile. She turns full face feeling that someone is watching her. Next, for several seconds we focus on the magnetic stare on Max's face, then again on Lucia's tense profile. At this moment we have a flashback to the lager. As the duet spills into a cold, dingy dormitory, the camera again pans slowly, this time not over the composed, attentive members of Viennese society sitting in the theatre hall, but over a group of prisoners all sitting huddled together on rows of metal beds, all staring out with empty eyes. Then the camera lingers for several long seconds on one of the dormitory beds where an SS officer is sodomizing a male prisoner while in the background Papageno and Pamina are joyfully reiterating: "While love is ours, we'll freely give. . . . It's love that sweetens every sorrow. . . . With love we need not fear tomorrow, we feel its universal power" (Schikander 82). The camera then closes up on Lucia resting on a mattress. Max comes in and drags her away (74).

10. For a provocative, polemical feminist reading of the opera from which I have borrowed here, see Catherine Clément's rueful commentary on it in *Opera, or the Undoing of Women* (70–77).

11. Teresa de Lauretis particularly emphasizes this aspect of the film in her important 1976 *Film Quarterly* review: "Cavani's love story is not only the story of the relation between two individuals, but of the world around them, of the culture and history in which they exist, of the values, conflicts, and inner contradictions of a society which is, whether we want to see it or not, our own" (36).

12. Here Cavani's film seems to anticipate Craig Owen's excellent discussion of the "crossing of the feminist critique of patriarchy and the postmodernist critique of representation" in his well-known aricle "The Discourse of Others: Feminists and Postmodernism" (59).

Works Cited

Bettelheim, Bruno. "Reflections: Surviving." *The New Yorker* (August 2, 1976): 31–52.

Bulkin, Elly, Minnie Bruce Pratt, and Barbara Smith. *Yours in Struggle: Three Feminist Perspectives on Anti-Semitism and Racism.* Brooklyn: Long Haul Press, 1984.

Butler, Judith. *Gender Trouble: Feminism and the Subversion of Identity.* New York: Routledge, 1990.

Clément, Catherine. *Opera, or the Undoing of Women.* Foreword by Susan McClary. Trans. Betsy Wing. Minneapolis: University of Minnesota Press, 1988.

de Lauretis, Teresa. "Cavani's *Night Porter*: A Woman's Film?" *Film Quarterly* 30 (1976–77): 35–38.

Doane, Mary Ann. "Film and the Masquerade: Theorizing the Female Spectator." *Femmes Fatales: Feminism, Film Theory, Psychoanalysis*. New York: Routledge, 1991. 17–32.

Griffin, Susan. *Pornography and Silence: Culture's Revenge against Nature*. New York: Harper and Row, 1981.

Jones, Amelia. " 'She Was Bad News': Male Paranoia and the Contemporary New Woman." *Camera Obscura: A Journal of Feminism and Film Theory* 25/26 (1991): 297–320.

Levi, Primo. *The Drowned and the Saved*. Trans. Raymond Rosenthal. New York: Summit Books, 1988.

Mulvey, Laura. "Visual Pleasure and Narrative Cinema." *Visual and Other Pleasures*. Bloomington: Indiana University Press, 1989. 14–26.

Owens, Craig. "The Discourse of Others: Feminists and Postmodernism." *The Anti-Aesthetic: Essays on Postmodern Culture*. Ed. Hal Foster. Seattle: Bay Press, 1983.

Pietropaolo, Laura. "Sexuality as Exorcism in Liliana Cavani's *Night Porter*." *Donna: Women in Italian Culture*. Ed. Ada Testaferri. University of Toronto Italian Studies 7. Ottawa, Canada. Dovehouse Editions, 1989.

Rosler, Martha. "In, Around, and Afterthoughts (on Documentary Photography)." *The Context of Meaning: Critical Histories of Photography*. Ed. Richard Bolton. Cambridge MA: MIT, 1989. 303–40.

Sedgwick, Eve Kosofsky. *Epistemology of the Closet*. Berkeley: University of California Press, 1990.

Shemek, Deanna. "Circular Definitions: Disciplining Gender in Italian Renaissance Festival." Unpublished essay.

Silverman, Kaja. "Masochism and Subjectivity." *Framework* 12 (1980): 2–9.

———. *The Acoustic Mirror: The Female Voice in Psychoanalysis and Cinema*. Bloomington: Indiana University Press, 1988.

Stone, Mirto Golo. "The Feminist Critic and Salome: On Cavani's *The Night Porter*." *Romance Languages Annual 1989* (1990): 41–44.

Theweleit, Klaus. *Male Fantasies: Vol. 1, Women, Floods, Bodies, History*. Foreword by Barbara Ehrenreich. Trans. Stephen Conway et al. Minneapolis: University of Minnesota Press, 1987.

CONTRIBUTORS

Kay Armatage is Associate Professor of Cinema Studies and Women's Studies at the University of Toronto. She has published articles on Canadian and women's cinema and feminist film theory. Between 1977 and 1987 she directed seven films on feminist subjects, and for the past ten years she has been one of the senior curators for the Toronto International Film Festival. Current research is on women filmmakers of the silent era.

Giuliana Bruno, Associate Professor of Visual and Environmental Studies at Harvard University, is the author of *Streetwalking on a Ruined Map: Cultural Theory and City Films of Elvira Notari*, and coeditor of *Screen: Women and Film in Italy* and *Immagini allo schermo*.

Teresa de Lauretis is Professor of the History of Consciousness at the University of California, Santa Cruz. She is the author of *Alice Doesn't: Feminism, Semiotics, Cinema; Technologies of Gender: Essays on Theory, Film, and Fiction;* and *The Practice of Love: Lesbian Sexuality and Perverse Desire*. She is also editor of *Feminist Studies/Critical Studies* and *Queer Theory: Lesbian and Gay Sexualities*, a special issue of the journal differences.

Judith Mayne, Professor of French and Women's Studies at Ohio State University, is the author of *Cinema and Spectatorship, The Woman at the Keyhole, Kino and the Woman Question,* and *Private Novels, Public Films*.

Laura Mulvey has taught film in England and in the United States. She is the author of *Visual and Other Pleasures* and *Citizen Kane* and has codirected films with Peter Wollen, including *Riddle of the Sphinx* and *The Bed Sister*.

Midi Onodera is a Toronto-based independent filmmaker who has completed her first feature film, *Sadness of the Moon*. Her previous work includes *The Displaced View* and *Ten Cents A Dance (Parallax)*.

Laura Pietropaolo is Associate Lecturer at York University, where she teaches Italian language and literature. She is the author of articles on the cinema of Liliana Cavani and Ettore Scola and has translated the most recent work by Italian philosopher Ernesto Grassi.

B. Ruby Rich has written on issues of film, feminism, and sexuality for both the scholarly and the popular press. Currently a visiting professor at the University of California, Berkeley, she is a contributing writer to *Elle* magazine and the film/video editor of *GLO: A Journal of Lesbian and Gay Studies*.

Ada Testaferri is Associate Professor at York University. Her articles on the Italian Middle Ages, women poets of the Renaissance, and feminist theory have appeared in Canadian and Italian journals. She is the editor of *Donna: Women in Italian Culture*.

Monika Treut is an independent filmmaker who works in Hamburg and New York. Her films include *Seduction: The Cruel Woman*, *Virgin Machine*, *My Father Is Coming*, and *Female Misbehavior*.

Trinh T. Minh-ha is Chancellor's Distinguished Professor in Women's Studies at the University of California, Berkeley, and Associate Professor of Cinema at San Francisco State University. She is the author of *Woman, Native, Other* and most recently *When the Moon Waxes Red: Representation, Gender, and Cultural Politics*.

Marguerite R. Waller, Professor of English at the University of California, Riverside, teaches film, gender theory, and Renaissance literature. She is the author of *Petrarch's Poetics and Literary History* as well as articles on Dante, Petrarch, Wyatt, Surrey, Shakespeare, Fellini, Lina Wertmuller, Liliana Cavani, Maurizio Nichetti, George Lucas, and Hillary Clinton. She has received Fulbright grants to Italy, France, and Hungary.

Christine Welsh is a Métis from Saskatchewan. As a writer and filmmaker, she documents the historical and contemporary experience of aboriginal women in Canada in films such as *Last Buffalo Hunter*, *Our Children Are Our Future*, and *Women in the Shadows*. She is working on a book and film entitled *Keepers of the Fire*.

Patricia White is completing a manuscript on lesbian and classical cinema and is coediting an anthology entitled *Between and Beyond: Sexual and Cultural Identity in Women's Film and Video*.

INDEX